SOCIAL MOBILITY IN NINETEENTH- AND EARLY TWENTIETH-CENTURY ENGLAND

Also by Andrew Miles

BUILDING EUROPEAN SOCIETY
Occupational and Social Mobility in Europe, 1840–1940 (*editor with David Vincent*)

THE REMAKING OF THE BRITISH WORKING CLASS, 1840–1940 (*with Mike Savage*)

Social Mobility in Nineteenth- and Early Twentieth-Century England

Andrew Miles
Lecturer in Modern Social History
Department of Modern History
University of Birmingham

First published in Great Britain 1999 by
MACMILLAN PRESS LTD
Houndmills, Basingstoke, Hampshire RG21 6XS and London
Companies and representatives throughout the world

A catalogue record for this book is available from the British Library.

ISBN 0–333–62059–3

First published in the United States of America 1999 by
ST. MARTIN'S PRESS, INC.,
Scholarly and Reference Division,
175 Fifth Avenue, New York, N.Y. 10010

ISBN 0–312–22045–6

Library of Congress Cataloging-in-Publication Data
Miles, Andrew, 1961–
Social mobility in nineteenth- and early twentieth-century England
/ Andrew Miles.
   p.   cm.
Includes bibliographical references and index.
ISBN 0–312–22045–6 (cloth)
1. Social mobility—England—History—19th century.   2. Social
mobility—England—History—20th century.   3. Occupational mobility–
–England—History—19th century.   4. Occupational mobility—England–
–History—20th century.   5. England—Social conditions—19th
century.   6. England—Social conditions—20th century.   I. Title.
II. Title: Social mobility in 19th- and early 20th-century England.
HN398.E5M53   1999
305.5'13'0942—dc21   98–44283
                                                             CIP

This book is printed on paper suitable for recycling and made from fully managed and
sustained forest sources.

10   9   8   7   6   5   4   3   2   1
08   07   06   05   04   03   02   01   00   99

Printed and bound in Great Britain by
Antony Rowe Ltd, Chippenham, Wiltshire

For Finn and the future

Contents

List of Tables

List of Figures

Acknowledgements

This book has been a long time in the making. Its appearance will be greeted with sighs of relief in a number of places, not least on top of the Lickey Hills, where Julie and Finn have responded with love and tolerance to the unreasonable amount of disruption it has brought to their lives.

That it appears at all is due in no small part to the generosity of many people who have given up their time and ideas over the years since the original research project on which the book is based was begun. There is not space enough to mention them all here, but I thank them sincerely none the less.

I owe a particular debt of gratitude to those who have read, and in the process undoubtedly improved, parts of the text. They include Mark Smith and Julie Tait, who lent their considerable talents as style counsellors, Mike Savage, who offered valuable critical insight, and Ineke Maas, who also gave up far too much of her time trying to explain the intricacies of log-linear modelling to a reluctant mathematician. Clive Payne and Colin Mills have at various times been bothered by the same problem and they too have always responded with patience and kindness.

John Goldthorpe's intellectual influence inevitably loomed large in the writing of this book. However, his openness and encouragement since the early stages of the research have been no less important. Although the book has perhaps developed in ways which he didn't expect, David Vincent has remained a staunch supporter of this project, and a generous and perceptive adviser.

That process of development has been greatly assisted by the opportunity to present some of the evidence and arguments that appear in the book in various critical settings. These include research seminars at the Institute of Historical Research, the International Institute for Social History, and at Bristol, Edinburgh, Glasgow, Manchester Metropolitan and Oxford Universities, and also at conferences organised by the International Association for History and Computing, and by the American and European Social Science History Associations.

I am grateful to the ESRC for funding the initial research behind the book, and also to the School of Social Sciences at the University of

Birmingham for monies to help develop it. The British Academy has been generous in supporting my attendance at the conferences mentioned above, as has the School of Historical Studies at Birmingham.

Finally, I would like to thank a number of people who, often at very short notice, have put themselves out to assist me in checking and chasing up numerous loose ends during the process of production. They include Lisa Bates, Ed Button, Christine Campbell, David Coppock, Colin Clarkson, Adam Croton, Pat Grundy, Jacqui Home, David Horsefield, Roy Lowe, Morag Orrock and Eleanor Winyard. Here, too, I would like to express my gratitude to Aruna Vasudevan and Ruth Willats at Macmillan for their patience and efficiency.

Introduction

'What some men are, all without difficulty might be,' wrote Samuel Smiles in 1859. 'Great men of science, literature and art,' he continued, 'apostles of the great thoughts and lords of the great heart – have belonged to no particular class nor rank. They have come alike from colleges, workshops and farmhouses – from the huts of the poor and the mansions of the rich.'[1] This is probably the best-known contemporary statement about social mobility in nineteenth-century Britain, yet we know surprisingly little about its accuracy. Smiles was the most prominent contributor to the 'literature of success'; a series of tracts, pamphlets and books promulgating a 'gospel of advancement', organised around the myth of the self-made and self-dependent man. *Self Help*, from which these words are taken, and which was the most definitive exposition of the theme, depicted Victorian Britain as a land of boundless opportunity and marked the development of the genre into a full-blown mobility ideology.[2] This book is about what actually lay behind the Smilesean vision of the nineteenth century as an age of mobility.

Social mobility is the process by which individuals move between occupations and social groups, either between generations, or over the course of a lifetime. The concept is a familiar one to postwar Britons, 70 per cent of whom in 1972 were in a different social class from the one into which they were born,[3] and whose cultural icons have included such figures as the affluent worker, the grammar school boy and the yuppie. It is also one of longstanding fascination to British sociologists, whose surveys and studies of the topic are internationally renowned, and who have always appreciated the fundamental role that the process and pattern of mobility play in the structuring of society.

This stems from the recognition that social groups form and dissolve as the boundaries and relations between individuals, families and their social circles are redrawn over time, and particularly across generations. Smiles's claims notwithstanding, the popular assumption has always been that constraints on the free choice of careers, and also marriage partners, were much greater in the past than in the present, and that in the long run the twin processes of industrialisation and modernisation have been highly effective social solvents.

1

Today's putatively high rates of mobility have been recruited by those who argue that class is no longer a useful category of description and explanation in contemporary society.[4] And as the postmodern bandwagon has gained momentum, it has been joined by others doubting whether class identities were ever as important as a previous generations of labour and social historians claimed.[5] Yet the turn against class rests primarily on the issue of discourse and language and adopts a narrow, productionist view of the phenomenon it seeks to deny. Crucially, it includes no analysis of the structural dynamics and relations of class; in other words, of the processes by which social groups are made, unmade and remade through mobility.[6]

The debate about class is one central consideration of this book, and the findings presented here suggest that there is still something to recommend in traditional views of the significance and trajectory of class relations in Victorian and Edwardian Britain. Its other main focus concerns the broader, although not unconnected, issue of the relationship between modern capitalism and inequality. It is this question which is at the forefront of current sociological work on mobility, but which, given the temporal limitations of survey evidence, remains only partially within its grasp. The record of the past, on the other hand, suggests that present-day conceptions of this relationship are under-historicised, and, among other things, that the process of bureaucratisation played a key role in reconciling different 'eras' of mobility in modern society.

The relative neglect of historical social mobility in this country is a curious matter. As debates ranging from the origins of the English Civil War to the causes of Britain's economic decline show, the potential significance of mobility patterns for explaining continuity and change in British history is by no means unrecognised.[7] There is something of a source problem: finding and interpreting substantial evidence of mobility in the past is not entirely straightforward, and previous generations of scholars lacked the manipulative facilities offered by the advanced computer technologies of the present day. Yet, as Stephan Thernstrom demonstrated 30 years ago, in his pioneering studies of mobility in nineteenth-century America, this has not proved an insurmountable barrier elsewhere. Nor are the materials he used unknown or unavailable on this side of the Atlantic.[8]

A more plausible reason for the dearth of British historical engagement with mobility is possibly to be found in the relationship between the disciplines of history and sociology. As Mike Savage has recently suggested, historians' distrust of the sociological enterprise has dissuaded them from embracing the potentially useful tools of an ostensibly alien discipline.[9] Alongside matters of empirical substance, this necessarily makes any attempt to cast light on past patterns of mobility an issue of methodology. Accordingly, a central premise of this study is that no meaningful examination of historical social mobility can afford to dispense with the analytical frameworks developed by sociology, and one purpose of this book is to show how these can be applied in an historical context.

However, it seems equally clear that the disciplinary stand-off has disabled both sides. There is undoubtedly a degree of historical blindness in much sociological work on mobility, and this extends to John Goldthorpe's celebrated work on social mobility in contemporary Britain.[10] Extrapolating from his central finding, Goldthorpe invokes history, but then neglects to consult it. The evidence of the past which will be presented here suggests that this is a hazardous practice. Moreover, for all its achievements, there is clearly some truth to recent charges that the dominant sociological approach to social mobility risks narrowing down the research agenda to the point of prejudicing an understanding of what it seeks to explain.[11] It may be that historians, often forced into methodological pluralism and used to grappling with process and contingency, are best placed to resist this.

In trying to speak to different disciplinary constituencies simultaneously, the historian writing about social mobility faces the additional methodological problem of how to present his or her findings. The two dominant influences on the way in which this book is organised are the defining conceptual and technical role of contemporary survey-based research and the particular nature of the sources available to assess its conclusions in historical context. These two issues are taken up in chapter 1, which reviews in more detail the interests and arguments surrounding mobility, and discusses the evidence used in this study. Unlike researchers in the sociological tradition, who are able to generate data from sample surveys based on interviews or questionnaires, historians of mobility are forced to turn to material produced for rather different purposes. The main body of evidence employed here is generated from marriage certificates, and is a by-product of the early nineteenth-century state's growing interest in population statistics. This is used in combination with the personal life stories of nineteenth-century autobiographers.

The substantive analysis of the issues and debates discussed in chapter 1 begins in chapter 2, where the pattern of inter-generational social mobility is examined in terms of what it reveals about the process of 'demographic class formation'[12] in the nineteenth and early twentieth centuries. From here, the study proceeds by way of a series of refinements of this basic analysis, the purpose of this approach being to explain why the patterns of inter-generational change occurred, to test their representativeness against other dimensions of mobility, and to assess their bearing on the two main theses about the relationship between economic development and social mobility. Chapter 3 considers what the mobility flows between generations reveal about the underlying pattern of 'openness', or social fluidity, across the period. Chapter 4 explores the pattern of occupational movement beneath the social-class model employed in the previous chapters, in part to test the validity of that model, but also to reveal the more specific economic developments which underpin the relationship between industrialism, mobility and fluidity. Chapter 5 puts the marriage register sample itself into perspective, by investigating, with the help of autobiographical material, the changing dynamics of the nineteenth-century career, and to what extent the pattern of intra-generational change supports or undermines a snapshot view of mobility between the generations. In chapter 6, the assumptions and conclusions of the marriage analysis are subjected to further scrutiny in an evaluation of the mechanisms and experiences of mobility as revealed by some of the people behind the numbers. Chapter 7 breaks the silence on gender and mobility by examining how women's mobility in the marriage market complicates purely male perspectives on the questions of class formation and openness, and by using the autobiographical evidence once more to investigate the interaction of male and female careers. In conclusion, chapter 8 explores possible explanations, women's mobility among them, for the contrasting conclusions of this study and the major twentieth-century investigation of British mobility patterns.

1 Exploring the Land of 'Boundless Opportunity'

THE ISSUE OF MOBILITY

Concern about the implications of social mobility, or the lack of it, has a long pedigree in political and social theory. As Anthony Heath has written, the two enduring themes which have sponsored this interest are *order* and *efficiency*:[1] in other words, how does the pattern of mobility affect the way in which societies cohere and function? Most have argued that too little mobility can, by encouraging the formation of antagonistic groups or classes, lead to social upheaval, while *mobile* societies individualise success and failure, and weaken the bonds of group solidarity. Marx, for example, wrote famously in the third volume of *Capital* that, 'the more a ruling class is able to assimilate the foremost minds of a ruled class, the more stable and dangerous becomes its rule', and elsewhere pointed to the exceptional degree of social flux then popularly perceived to pertain in the New World as an explanation for the immaturity of the American labour movement.[2] However, some have argued that too much mobility can be just as dangerous as too little because it generates rootlessness, uncertainty and insecurity,[3] while others have shown that mobile societies can give rise to processes of group formation as well as disaggregation.[4]

In the twentieth century, social justice and economic performance have become central issues in the study of mobility. In rejecting the claims of apologists for classical liberalism such as Samuel Smiles, a positive commitment to a genuinely open society was, for example, at the heart of Tawney's ethical socialism and the defining feature of David Glass's pioneering postwar mobility survey at the London School of Economics.[5] From an economist's perspective, the importance of mobility is to be found in the way in which human capital resources are distributed. Those societies which are most successful at putting the right people in the right place, it is claimed, will themselves be better placed in the international market place, so that the more successful nations will tend to be the most meritocratic.[6]

All these issues converge in the principal contemporary debate about social mobility, emanating from American sociology, which

concerns the relationship between mobility and economic development. Standing in contradiction to orthodox Marxism's stress on
proletarianisation and revolution, but replacing Marxist determinism
with a teleology of its own, what has been called the 'liberal theory of
industrialism' constitutes the debate's central reference point.[7] At its
most ambitious, this theory claims both high and rising rates of
upward mobility and increasing equality of opportunity as characteristic of modern industrial societies. These developments, it is
argued, are functional requirements of the irreversible commitment
to technical and economic rationality in these societies. In turn,
mobility and openness serve to sponsor economic growth and to
legitimise liberal democracy.[8]

The major British contributor to this debate is John Goldthorpe,
whose position is aptly summarised in the title of his study,
The Constant Flux, which compares patterns of mobility found in
12 contemporary industrial societies. Echoing Pitrim Sorokin's 1920s
thesis, Goldthorpe and his co-author Robert Erikson refute the teleo-
logical claims of liberal theories of industrialism, arguing that *all*
industrial societies share common mobility regimes, remain marked
by significant class divisions and show no consistent tendency to
become more open over time.

The 'no trend' hypothesis supported by Erikson and Goldthorpe
essentially repeats the conclusion of the first cross-national mobility
survey conducted by Lipset and Zetterberg in the late 1950s, but from
a fundamentally different analytical perspective.[9] At issue here is the
crucial distinction between *absolute* and *relative* mobility, which
Goldthorpe, in particular, has done much to clarify. Absolute mobility
is the movement that can be seen occurring between economic or
social categories – the raw percentages of those rising, falling or staying
put. It is this measure which is relevant to the issue of class or group
formation, because it indicates the extent to which, in a basic 'demographic' sense, stable social collectivities are formed.[10] However,
because absolute rates of mobility are sensitive to a range of 'exogenous' structural influences, which vary according to time and place,
they are an unreliable guide to the 'openness' or 'fluidity' of social
structures, conceived in terms of the relative life chances of individuals
from different social backgrounds.

Lipset and Zetterberg's thesis of universally high but unchanging
levels of mobility across industrial societies was based on absolute or
de facto rates. Subjected to further and more refined testing, much
greater variation in these rates was subsequently found. However their

thesis was subsequently resurrected by Featherman, Jones and Hauser, who reformulated it in terms of relative mobility: net of structural effects, they argued, at the 'genotypical' level of mobility, there were good grounds for supposing a large degree of cross-national and temporal commonality.[11] In consequence, it is in terms of relative rates, and the 'endogenous' mobility regimes they reflect, that the debate about the generic pattern of mobility under industrialisation is now conducted.

In this context, Erikson and Goldthorpe's research provides strong support for the 'FJH-hypothesis'. Their conclusions are not entirely uncontested, however. On the basis of an earlier re-analysis of data from 35 countries, Ganzeboom, Luijkz and Treiman have argued – in terms much more favourable to the liberal thesis – for a slow but ultimately substantial increase in social fluidity over the course of the twentieth century.[12]

SOCIAL MOBILITY IN CONTEMPORARY BRITAIN

From its inception, British social mobility research has given a high profile to relative measures of mobility. Glass compared the degree of movement actually occurring with rates expected under conditions of 'perfect mobility'.[13] This allowed him to demonstrate that, in contrast to the egalitarian rhetoric of postwar social policy, the process of social selection to positions at the higher end of the stratification hierarchy in Britain worked to the marked disadvantage of those with working-class origins.

In his own work on Britain, begun in the early 1970s, Goldthorpe starts from a value position similar to Glass's – that is, a freely declared commitment to a genuinely open society.[14] The Nuffield survey showed that the middle decades of the twentieth century in Britain had been characterised by a marked increase in upward mobility. However, using the then novel technique of log-linear analysis, Goldthorpe was able to illustrate that, despite rising rates of movement by the sons of working-class men into the service class, there had been no shift towards greater equality of opportunity. The crucial variable here was the *expansion* of the service class, which allowed for greater upward mobility *without* altering the relative chances of men from different social backgrounds getting a service-class job. In other words, service-class sons benefited just as much from the increasing 'room at the top' as their working-class peers, ensuring the persistence of 'inequalities that are of a quite striking kind'.[15]

Any modification of this pattern, Goldthorpe went on, could only result from political intervention, the likelihood of which is, in turn, contingent on the dynamics of class relations. Hence, he turned to the question of absolute mobility, as an indicator of 'demographic class formation', and to the implications of *de facto* mobility for cultural identity and political action, in order to assess the prospects for change.

Despite rising rates of 'total' mobility, the Nuffield data illustrated two clear tendencies towards demographic class formation: the greater inter-generational stability of the expanding service class and the increasing homogeneity of the slowly contracting working class.[16] Qualitative evidence provided no indication that the mobility of those rising or falling was likely to destabilise the class into which they had been recruited. Nor, thanks to rising living standards, were there any signs of overt resentment among working-class men who had been left behind. However, such men were aware that they lacked opportunity in their working lives, and their commitment to collectivist solutions to social inequalities remained undiminished.[17] Writing in the 1970s, Goldthorpe stressed that the changing recruitment profile of the British working class in the postwar decades had helped to make it a more mature socio-political force, which could be seen pursuing its interests by trading its cooperation with the second 1974 Labour government for a 'social contract'.[18] However, in the conclusion to the second edition of *Social Mobility and Class Structure*, published ten years on, there is more stress on the conservative implications of the stabilisation of the service class.[19]

PERSPECTIVES ON THE BRITISH PAST

While Goldthorpe's own data are firmly located in the twentieth century, the degree of comparative support for his findings inclined him to the view that the pattern of constant social fluidity he had uncovered in contemporary Britain was more deeply rooted.[20] This is a position which contradicts the generally optimistic claims of Victorian commentators, but is one that has received some empirical support from Hope's reworking of Glass's data, which included men born in the 1880s, and from Penn's work on marital endogamy in Rochdale since the 1850s.[21] This may be an insubstantial basis from which to proceed to concrete conclusions about the nineteenth-century mobility regime, but it does, at least, possess the virtue of clarity.

Nothing quite as coherent has emerged from the work of British historians, who have tended to concentrate their energies in this sphere on studies of elite recruitment, and whose incidental approach to 'mass' mobility has produced only a patchy collection of data, dominated by evidence relating to the early nineteenth-century textile districts and the later phenomenon of a 'labour aristocracy'.[22] The account is limited further by the absence of work on relative mobility, and a tendency, in the face of this, to conflate mobility and fluidity. Nevertheless, knitting together the various empirical and interpretative strands, it is possible to discern a core argument: namely, that the relationship between industrialisation and upward social mobility across the period 1780–1914 was largely an antagonistic one.

Even from within the nineteenth-century liberal canon, Smiles's depiction of Victorian Britain as an open society did not go unchallenged. John Stuart Mill, for example, noted demarcations between different grades of labourers 'so strongly marked' as to be 'almost equivalent to an hereditary distinction of caste'.[23] Yet even Mill saw this as a temporary state of affairs. At least between neighbouring classes, he argued, the process of capitalist industrialisation was increasing competitive pressures, ensuring that, on an individual level, 'human beings are no longer born to their place in life'.[24]

Bagehot presented a similar picture, approvingly characterising Victorian society as a system of 'removable inequalities' to set beside the two less desirable alternatives: the equality of the United States and France, which was destructive of 'the instinctive emulation by which the dweller in the valley is stimulated to climb the hill', and the 'irremovable inequalities' of the eastern caste system, which retarded social improvement 'by restraining the wholesome competition between class and class'. By contrast, Britain was a society 'where many people are inferior to and worse off than others, but in which each may *in theory* hope to be on a level with the highest below the throne, and in which each may reasonably, and without sanguine impracticability, hope to gain one step in social elevation, to be at last on a level with those who at first were just above them'.[25]

Towards the end of the century, however, more pessimistic voices can be heard amongst economists concerned, in Arthur Marshall's words, with 'the obstacles which the conditions of any time and place oppose to the free mobility of labour'. Marshall noted the counteracting force of 'ethical, social and domestic habits' on economic forces which encouraged movement within rather than between classes. Mill, he says, had been vindicated, but the occupational grades which he identified still had to be thought of 'as resembling a long flight of steps of unequal length, some of them so broad as to act as landing stages'. More accurate still, he went on to suggest, was the metaphor of two separate flights of stairs, one representing manual, the other non-manual labour, 'because the vertical division between these two is in fact as broad and as clearly marked as the horizontal division between any two grades'.[26]

Just how pervasive was the Smilesean myth is difficult to gauge. Perkin writes that 'It was real myth in that it had a sufficient basis in fact ... to make it eminently plausible ... 'What some men are all without difficulty might be' was an argument which overwhelmed statistics and made the self-made man of the nineteenth century what the football pools winner is to the twentieth'.[27] Similarly, Harrison argues that a recognition that stations in life might be clearly marked off from each other was combined with an assumption of a sufficiently high degree of social mobility to make the idea widely attractive. Indeed, after 1848 the self-help ethos emerged, rather in the manner of a secular 'chiliasm of despair', he claims, to offer the working class a means of advance which Owenism, Chartism and trade unionism had failed to provide.[28]

Other studies suggest that the contradiction between rhetoric and reality was too great to sustain the myth. The immersion of the industrial proletariat of the manufacturing districts of Lancashire and the West Riding of Yorkshire in the social and cultural regime of the factory was so total, writes Patrick Joyce, that 'the middle-class gospel of improvement made few inroads into working-class life'.[29] Nor, according to Flora Thompson, did the mobility ideology find much purchase within village life and labour. Miss Shepherd, Lark Rise's new schoolmistress and embodiment of the 'changing spirit of the times', would read to her charges about Smiles's heroes and suggest that 'on the material plane people need not necessarily remain always upon one level'. But such experiences were, Thompson tells us, 'too far removed from those of her hearers to inspire the ambition she hoped to awaken'.[30]

What is not in doubt, however, is that there exists little hard evidence with which to test the substance of the myth. Perkin's claim that 'there is of course no doubt that there was a considerable amount of upward mobility in mid-Victorian England as in all periods of English history' has no empirical foundation, but rests on the application of 'Petty's

Law' – the tendency within economic development for movement from low- to higher-paid occupations as agricultural employment is supplanted by manufacturing, and then services. His secondary argument, that all the evidence points to 'a contraction of opportunities for social climbing during the mid-Victorian age', so that 'upward mobility for the working class was presumably at its nadir', is based on the decline of patronage and of free grammar school education for the poor since the eighteenth century, and Charlotte Erickson's finding that the numbers of Victorian steel and hosiery manufacturers recruited from humble origins were small and declining.[31]

The classic thesis of a golden age of mobility prior to, and in the earlier stages of, industrialisation finds less support in Erickson's work than Perkin suggests, but has remained common currency among British economic and social historians.[32] Three years after the publication of Perkin's *tour de force* it found more concrete empirical substantiation in the work of Michael Sanderson. His study of the impact of industrialisation on working-class upward mobility in late eighteenth- and early nineteenth-century Lancashire, based on the Lancaster Charity Register and a collection of marriage registers, represented the first direct attempt at a quantitatively based study of popular mobility.[33] As such, Sanderson's conclusion that the factory system closed off important channels of elevation for workers' sons, and that therefore industrialisation drastically reduced upward social mobility, has carried much weight. Nevertheless, Thomas Laqueur criticised Sanderson's data and approach, claiming that his focus on inter-generational mobility at marriage gave a misleading impression when there was 'every reason to believe that there was as much or more intra-generational as inter-generational mobility'.[34] This conviction was based on Anderson's work on the family in nineteenth-century Lancashire, which emphasises the volatility of the textile workforce. Yet Anderson also found that upward mobility was not the common experience of those on the move.[35]

Apart from the occasional appearance of figures to supplement studies of particular occupations, industries or towns,[36] the only other significant empirical engagement with mobility has occurred as a by-product of the influential debate about the nineteenth-century 'labour aristocracy'. As they sought to explain the absence of revolution in the world's first industrial society, Engels and Lenin drew attention to the role of an elite of skilled, unionised workers whose militancy, they argued, was bought off with the proceeds of Britain's exploitation of less developed economies.[37]

Eric Hobsbawm revived interest in the concept in a pioneering article in which he listed the distinguishing characteristics of this group. These included not only pay and conditions, but also 'relations with the social strata above and below' and 'prospects of future advance for themselves and their children'. 'Socially speaking', he argued, 'the best-paid stratum of the working class merged with what may loosely be called the "lower middle class"', but 'If the boundaries of the labour aristocracy were fluid on one side of its territory, they were precise on another.'[38] However, Hobsbawm's only evidence was some limited material on the social background of pupil teachers, and the attitude of nineteenth-century trade unions. Furthermore, in suggesting that the relationship between the labour aristocracy and 'higher strata' worsened at the end of the nineteenth century, he was willing to concede that, 'Here we are on badly surveyed territory, for little is known about such subjects as the prospects of promotion, of "rising out of the working class" and about similar subjects.'[39]

It was not until Hobsbawm's thesis was tested in a number of local studies that some statistics were collected on the scale of movement into and out of this sector. In his work on early and mid-Victorian Kentish London, Crossick provided some evidence of occupational and marital mobility which highlighted the degree of stability and cohesion at the top and bottom of the working class, and appeared to substantiate the claim that the labour aristocrats made more contacts upwards than with the sectors beneath them. His figures also suggested slightly rising rates of aristocrat upward mobility and increasing social distance between skilled and unskilled families over time.[40] Gray's work on Victorian Edinburgh also took in the crucial period at the end of the nineteenth century, but was restricted to marital mobility. His data suggested that here too the social relations of the mid-Victorian labour aristocracy were quite exclusive, but that they became less so over time, as fewer partners were taken from lower middle-class families and more from elsewhere within the working class.[41]

Facing challenges to its privileges in the workplace and to its status in the community, it is argued that the labour aristocracy found itself 'pressed into a common and apparently inescapable working-class universe'.[42] And for Hobsbawm, Gray and others, the broadening class organisation on both the industrial and political fronts in this period is a more or less natural corollary of these developments.[43] This model and trajectory of the labour aristocracy, together with its proposed political significance, has been rejected by Penn, but remains influential among historians.[44] Locating it within an overall framework of historical discourse on mobility, the notion of class separation which it contains not only echoes the contemporary concerns of Marshall, but points away in both directions: backwards to arguments about the adverse effects of industrialisation on a previously 'open' society; and forwards to the claims of economists and historians who have sought to account for Britain's subsequent economic decline by reference to the comparative rigidity of its social structure.[45]

HISTORICAL SOCIAL MOBILITY IN COMPARATIVE PERSPECTIVE

This would tend to place the British case in one of two quite distinctive camps within the much stronger empirical tradition of historical work on mobility which exists beyond these shores, and which is rooted in Thernstrom's influential studies of American cities in the 1960s. An attempt to produce an overall synthesis from the diverse range of studies within this tradition was made by Hartmut Kaelble in the mid-1980s. In his distillation of the long-tern pattern of historical change, Kaelble arrived at a modified version of the liberal industrialism, or 'modernisation', thesis.[46] The recent history of social mobility, he argued, can be divided into three distinct eras. The first of these – the transition from pre-industrial to industrial society – was not accompanied by a definite increase in mobility and fluidity because the impact of occupational change was minimal, rising life expectancy and population growth increased competition for jobs, and access to capital was vital for advancement. It was only in the post-1870 era of 'organised capitalism', characterised by the rise of large-scale enterprises and the emergence of the interventionist state, that there was discernible change. Mobility was encouraged principally by structural change, and particularly the growth of white-collar work. Kaelble is much less clear about whether this was accompanied by a shift in the balance of life chances, but implies that the changing economic, cultural and political climate made this a strong possibility.

His uncertainty reflects the fact that this was also a period affected by short-term events – the First World War and the Great Depression – which, he claims, had marked, and often adverse, effects on mobility and fluidity. He is in no doubt about the dynamic nature of the third era, however. Post-industrial society, which for Kaelble effectively encompasses the post-Second World War period, is characterised by a strong increase in the rate of absolute mobility due to the continuing expansion of the service sector and the rise of the professions, while the spread of meritocratic values, the establishment of welfare states and a political consensus in favour of positive social engineering has sponsored greater equality of opportunity.

Kaelble's conclusions have since been qualified by research from a project he has directed with Jürgen Kocka. This is confined to a group of cities and towns in the western part of Germany since 1825, but is one of the few studies to generate a long-term perspective on rates of mobility under industrialism. Its findings, as reported by Reinhard Schüren, suggest an increase in mobility between the working and middle/upper class during industrial development, which then declines with the transition to organised capitalism. If more social groups are delineated, then there is support for the argument that mobility rates rose in the transition to organised capitalism, but they did so between groups within the two basic classes, therefore contributing further to a process of demographic class formation on either side of the major class divide.[47]

The 'social class formation' thesis contradicts the idea of a trend towards increasing social integration which is implicit in Kaelble's synthesis. Although existing British evidence provides no perspective on social mobility via the labour market in the later nineteenth century, it is this position which corresponds more closely with the class separation arguments of the labour aristocracy theorists, and is, moreover, one that receives a degree of support in work carried out across the continent, including Eastern Europe.[48] It is, though, a conclusion which speaks only to the pattern of absolute or *de facto* mobility. Only a small number of advanced analyses of social fluidity in historical context have been carried out, and these offer contrasting conclusions. Evidence from nineteenth-century America and a re-analysis of the Berlin sample from the Kaelble/Kocka dataset suggest that there was a trend towards greater openness with the process of industrialism. On the other hand, recent studies of Quebec, the Netherlands and France in the same period have each found that there was no equalisation of mobility chances.[49]

THE RELICS OF MOBILITY

There are, as mentioned, two principal dimensions to social mobility: inter-generational and intra-generational. The former refers to transitions between parents and children, the latter to movements during an individual career. Sociological research generates its evidence for both through means of the sample survey, conducted on the basis of a taped interview or a questionnaire. Certain of a disappointing response to such approaches, the historian of the non-recent past must turn instead to evidence often collected for quite different purposes.

In common with the majority of European historical investigations, evidence of inter-generational mobility for this study has been generated from marriage records. As is the case with contemporary research, most attention will be devoted to this aspect of mobility, although this is partly because substantial and standardised material detailing career mobility is much harder to come by. However, this dimension is addressed directly in the second half of the book, when evidence of life-course movement and the experience of mobility, taken from autobiographical material, is brought to bear on the findings of the marriage register analysis.

The marriage sample, originally collected by David Vincent for a study of literacy,[50] stems from the requirement of the 1836 *Registration of Births, Deaths and Marriages Act* that church registers should record the occupations of the partners and their parents.[51] Each wedding thus provided a snapshot of occupational movement between the generations. A sample of at least 1,000 randomly recorded marriages from each of ten Registration Districts was taken at five-year intervals for the period 1839–1914. This yielded a total sample of 10,835 marriages.[52] The ten districts selected for their contrasting economic and social characteristics, were: the metal-working districts of Dudley, in the West Midlands, and Sheffield; the silk manufacturing area of Macclesfield to the south-east of Manchester; Stoke-on-Trent, famous for its near-monopoly of the British pottery industry; the more traditional urban districts of Lichfield in south-east Staffordshire, and Bethnal Green in East London; the mixed urban/rural areas of Wokingham and Nuneaton, situated close to the larger centres of Reading and Coventry respectively; and two predominantly rural, village communities in Cleobury Mortimer on the Shropshire/Worcestershire border to the west of Kidderminster, and Samford, sandwiched between the estuaries of the rivers Stour and Orwell, in south-east Suffolk.

As is well known, marriage registers are not without their limitations as a source. First, they necessarily exclude the experience of the non-marrying population. Over the period this amounted to a more or less constant 10 per cent of males at age 45, while among females of the same age the proportion was slightly higher, and rose from the

1880s to reach 14 per cent by 1901.[53] Second, although occupational information appears in the records of individual parishes before the 1836 Act, effective coverage in this country only begins at a point when industrialisation was underway, thus preventing comparison with 'pre-' or 'proto-' industrial society.[54] Third, there are the difficulties created by state control of access to records. In Britain, the Registrar-General's continuing refusal to allow general access to the complete registers in his possession restricts an inquiry to the records of Anglican marriages, and thereby prevents sampling across the whole population of marriage partners.[55] This matters little for the early years of the new system, as few partners chose to marry outside the parish church, but by 1914 over 40 per cent of marriages in England and Wales took place before the secular authority, or in Catholic, Nonconformist, Quaker or Jewish institutions.[56] Throughout the period, though, there was extensive variation across the country in the incidence of non-Anglican ceremonies, and in an attempt to reduce the dangers of drawing an increasingly unrepresentative sample, districts where the proportion of Anglican ceremonies remained particularly high were chosen.[57]

The remaining objections to the use of the registers concern the nature of the information carried by the marriage certificates themselves. There is, first, the problem of generalised occupational description, which is discussed further below.[58] Second, while there is space for its inclusion, the occupation of the bride was rarely recorded, although, as will be discussed in a later chapter, the limitation this imposes for perspectives on women's mobility may be more apparent than real.[59] However, the material's principal shortcoming stems from its 'snapshot' nature. To what extent does the occupation of the groom's father and of the groom entered in the register at the particular moment of the latter's marriage represent, respectively, his 'origin' and his 'destination'?

For some, the difficulty of determining the beginning and end of the process is a problem inherent in, and ultimately destructive of, the whole notion of 'inter-generational' mobility.[60] Modern enquiries approach this question by imposing standard starting and finishing points on the individual career, using information about age; in the Nuffield study, for example, class of origin was taken to be that of the father when the respondent was aged 14, his destination the position reached by age 35, after which significant changes were deemed to be unlikely.[61] Although some information is available where the grooms are concerned, the registers do not give the ages of the father, nor even any indication of whether he was still alive when the ceremony took place. It is, therefore, not possible to determine whether the occupation entered was his current or last position, or, if different, the role in which he had been/was employed for the greater part of his life. In the case of an older groom, or the youngest son of a large family, a father entered in the register as unskilled may have been a man with a more illustrious past; one of Mckenna's train drivers, perhaps, who, when their eyesight began to fail, 'could plummet overnight from express engineman to washer-out of sinks and toilet pans'.[62] On the other hand, there are reasonable *prima facie* grounds to suppose that in such circumstances the title entered will often refer to the individual's principal lifetime activity. The relevant space on the marriage certificate asks not simply for the participants' job but their *Rank or Profession*. Self-descriptions were, as already noted, invariably generalised, and it seems reasonable to assume that priestly mediation in the process of identification at such an event would tend to favour the option of a description based on longer-term standing in the community.

As to the matter of destination, most grooms married in their later twenties, at an average age some eight years short of 'occupational maturity' in Goldthorpe's terms.[63] This raises the possibility that the registers distort the 'true' pattern of mobility because they fail to account for career mobility after marriage. On the other hand, the people represented in the registers were, as Sewell has argued, a broad and important sector of the population,[64] while the potential loss of employment status brought on by physical failings in later life raises the question of just how far contemporary models of career development are applicable to nineteenth-century working lives. The fact that the registers do, in approximately 60 per cent of cases, give the ages of the grooms, means that some perspective on these problems can be gained from an analysis of a sub-population of older men.[65] This perspective and its implications for the findings of the rest of the study are discussed in chapter 5.

In their defence, the marriage registers remain one of only two sources of long-run quantifiable data on inter-generational mobility available to historians. Their great strength is the combination of numerical density and temporal scope which they offer. The alternative – census-tracking – is a more common procedure in the United States, and can generate information on both inter- and intra-generational mobility.[66] This, however, is a process which is susceptible to serious problems of sample reduction, as individuals disappear between re-numerations, and to the inherent uncertainties of the linkage process.[67]

The autobiographical evidence, used here to supplement and to contextualise the marriage records, is also an imperfect source. Testimonies are unstandardised and not always easy to verify. Their authors are self-selected, subjective in their judgements, distanced from many of the events they are attempting to recall and unrepresentative of the general population.[68] On the other hand, their accounts represent a rich source of uninterrupted work and life histories for the nineteenth century. Reconstruction via the census, even when the painstaking process of linkage is successful,[69] offers only ten-year snapshots of the life course. By contrast, the better autobiographies provide complete, self-contained records of careers, supplemented by important evidence of the subjective perception of mobility.

A surprisingly large number of nineteenth-century texts exist, many having been recovered quite recently by Burnett *et al.* for their annotated bibliography *The Autobiography of the Working Class*. This study draws on the texts listed in the first volume of the collection, covering the period 1790–1900. These are virtually comprehensive in their geographical coverage of Britain and, while there is a slight bias towards those engaged in the occupations of letters and speech, they are equally wide-ranging in their representation of different occupational groups.[70] Although an anthology of 'working-class' writing, the editors' criterion for inclusion – 'those who for *some period* of their lives could be described as working class, whether defined in terms of their relationship to the means of production, their educational experience and cultural ties, by self-ascription, or by any combination of these factors'[71] – means that a large proportion spent part of their lives in a different class.

For the purposes of this study, data were collected on two levels. From the 804 autobiographical abstracts in the collection, 479 of the more complete life-story outlines, concerning men born between 1723 and 1895, were selected in order to elicit information about the changing shape of career patterns, and the timing and outcome of work-life transitions. In addition, 100 of the texts were studied in more detail for complementary evidence relating to the mechanics, experience and meanings of mobility.

CODING THE PAST

The concept of mobility presupposes the existence of categories between which movement can take place. Yet the monitoring of transitions between the thousands of job titles thrown up by the marriage registers can have only limited meaning without some further, broader categorisation of occupational information which in turn takes account of the specific social and economic context under consideration. If Sorokin's assertion that 'Any organised social group is always a stratified social body' is accepted, it follows that the organisation of 'social space'[72] is crucial to the study of social and occupational mobility. How this is done will determine not only what is meant by 'mobility' but also how much of it there can be.

Sociological studies embrace an extensive variety of approaches to the categorisation and classification of occupations. Nevertheless, most approaches can be seen to gravitate towards one of two distinct positions, each reflective of a particular world-view: on the one hand, investigators working within the liberal tradition, where society is seen in terms of an occupational continuum along which there are essentially no sharp breaks, employ ranking systems based on notions of occupational 'status' or 'prestige'. By contrast, those adopting a *neo-Weberian* framework, which presupposes the division of society into antagonistic classes, group occupations into discrete categories based on their distinct 'class position'. Although variable in detail, the broad outlines of most classifications generated from these respective positions are, in practice, fairly similar. Moreover, in some cases there is even a tendency to conflate one type of categorisation with an analytical approach and terminology more appropriate to the other.[73]

Goldthorpe and his associates adopted a sevenfold class scheme which they claimed to be distinctive in so far as the categories employed were designed to provide a high degree of differentiation in terms of both occupational function and employment status.[74] This system is attractive, and could be applied in the case of the most detailed auto-biographies, but it is impractical for occupational descriptions as laconic as those entered in the marriage registers. The Nuffield researchers were able to elicit precise information concerning the market situation of their respondents. But the reader of a marriage certificate is more typically presented, in the case of skilled craftsmen for example, with rather more basic occupational identities – cabinet-maker, mason, cordwainer, tailor, and so on. While the autobio-graphical evidence suggests, in fact, that employer/employee distinc-tions can easily be exaggerated, only very rarely can it be determined whether such men were journeymen or small masters, or indeed whether, having been reduced to the ranks of casual, sweated outwork, they had moved out to the margins of the artisan category.[75]

As no general scheme of classification sensitive to the bewildering array of nineteenth-century occupations exists, one is faced with the choice of constructing a new system from scratch, or searching further, beyond the refined frameworks of modern investigations, for alternative, simplified twentieth-century schemata which can be adapted for the task to hand. The first option is only feasible when dealing with a local economy with a limited range of employment, so it was decided that the most satisfactory solution to the weight and coverage of the information generated by the registers was to be found in the Registrar-General's occupational and social classification scheme for the 1951 census.[76] In this, many thousands of occupational titles are subsumed into 981 occupational groups which are further divided into 28 occupational orders. Most importantly, each occupational group is additionally coded for one of five broad-based social classes.

Based on the 'general standing' of an occupation in the community, this is effectively a status or prestige scheme. Nevertheless, while the criteria of allocation may differ, the distinctions drawn bear more than a passing resemblance to the major class divisions identified by the Nuffield researchers. Because of its essentially descriptive nature, and the interests and assumptions behind its evolution, the Registrar-General's scheme has attracted its fair share of criticism from historians and modern investigators alike.[77] Yet it remains a flexible tool, which can be adapted to provide more theoretical purpose and which has an established track record in historical research.[78] The fit between the 1951 and nineteenth-century occupational worlds was not perfect, but there were surprisingly few anomalies.[79] Following a thorough interrogation of each code and entry, adjustments to the scheme were made on the basis of a comparison with the 1911 and 1921 classifications,[80] together with information gleaned from histories of the relevant localities and particular industries. The resulting contents and defining characteristics of the five classes are summarised in Appendix 1.

2 Social Mobility and Class Formation

Although the impression of social flux peddled in the work of Samuel Smiles implies that Victorian society was open and potentially class-less, his collection of success stories hardly qualifies as a statistically representative sample, nor indeed was its real purpose.[1] Ironically, however, Smiles was writing in a period characterised by the genesis and development of systematic, state-inspired information-gathering, a by-product of which – the marriage register evidence – allows his vision to be tested.[2]

The issue of openness is bound up, in an analytical sense, with the need to move beyond appearances: the observable mobility flows between generations are an unreliable guide to the question of *fluidity* because of their susceptibility to structural influences, in particular those exerted by economic change on the social division of labour. As others have recognised, however, what drives and conditions move-ment in the somewhat abstract terms of structural forces and relative mobility chances is unlikely to be of great visibility, and therefore concern, to the particular individuals and families who experience it. It is the outcome rather than the motor of change which matters.[3]

Here, the assumption of much thinking on the social significance of mobility is that not enough of it of the right kind, or too much of it in the wrong direction, is potentially disruptive, because those who are prevented from fulfilling their ambition will tend to make common cause with others who share their frustration. This, then, refers us back to the second of the images conjured by the Smilesean vision. Drawing on Gidden's notion of 'structuration' and Parkin's concept of 'social closure', Goldthorpe has argued that mobility is integral to the process of class formation.[4] It is the rate of mobility which deter-mines the demographic identity of social collectivities and the salience of the boundaries between them. Demographic class formation is, in turn, a necessary, if not sufficient, condition of socio-cultural identity and collective action.

In these terms, the marriage register evidence lays bare the Smilesean myth. There was change across the generations in nine-teenth-century society, but the mobility that took place was restricted in both volume and direction. Marshall's observations on the division between the manual and non-manual worlds, and the greater likelihood of movement within classes, are more apposite. Over time, the total volume of movement increased, providing support for Mill's early rendition of the theory of industrialism, but it did so in ways which most affected the internal relations of the working class, a development which bears out a central element in both the labour aristocracy and social class formation theses. The refinement provided by analysis of local context qualifies the assumption, explicit in the industrialism thesis, that modern economies are more socially dynamic than others, but also suggests that the specific claims of the social class formation theory cannot be reconciled with the data.

ORIGINS AND DESTINATIONS, 1839–1914

'Thus I began and ended my life as a Handloom weaver. And in this sense my work was done,' wrote Yorkshireman William Hanson in his autobiography, published in 1883. In between, he had dabbled in an ill-fated cloth-selling concern and assisted in the running of his crippled son's grocery business. But for most of his life he was a 'skilled' textile worker like his handloom weaver father before him. Henry Burstow, born in Horsham in 1826, did not follow in his pipe-making parents' footsteps, but became, and remained for 40 years, a shoemaker.[6] Although one of these men was occupationally stable in relation to his father and the other mobile, both had in common a lack of more broadly defined class movement.

Table 2.1, an outflow matrix describing the distribution of men by class background across the entire sample, suggests that in most nineteenth-century families, and especially those connected with skilled occupations like Hanson's and Burstow's, such continuity between the generations was the norm. Indeed, the clustering of figures along the diagonal cells of this table, which show the percentage of men from each class who followed in their fathers' footsteps, highlights the essential stability of English society in this period. Throughout the sample population six out of every ten men experienced no change in terms of their immediate social background, with those from the skilled and unskilled sectors of the working class – classes III and V – appearing particularly immobile. Yet if the predominant impression is one of relative constancy, the analysis also shows that Victorian and Edwardian society was far from stagnant. While fewer than three in ten

Table 2.1   *Class distribution of grooms by class of father, 1839–1914*
(percentage by row)

			Son's Class				
Father's Class	I	II	III	IV	V	n	%
I	42.8	33.2	15.9	4.3	3.8	208	(2.0)
II	2.7	50.2	25.8	12.2	9.1	1782	(17.5)
III	0.3	6.8	72.8	10.3	9.8	4277	(41.9)
IV	0.4	7.4	33.2	45.6	13.3	1186	(11.6)
V	0.0	2.9	21.3	14.1	61.7	2757	(27.0)
n	156	1421	4588	1595	2450	10210	
%	(1.5)	(13.9)	(44.9)	(15.6)	(24.0)		

of Hanson and Burstow's peers could expect to experience mobility in class terms, half or more of those from the semi-skilled working class, or from either of the two non-manual classes, were likely to do so.

In Robert Roberts's opinion, 'the real social divide', in the turn-of-the-century Salford community in which he was brought up, 'existed between those who, in earning their daily bread, dirtied hands and face and those who did not'. Table 2.1 suggests that in this sense Salford was a microcosm of the nation, confirming that for those born below it the line running between the predominantly manual working class and the largely non-manual middle/upper class represented a fundamental cleavage in nineteenth-century society.[7] The extent of upward movement across this line was universally limited, regardless of origin. Moreover, if a worker's son was lucky enough to be among the one in 20 of his generation crossing this social barrier, the overwhelming likelihood was that his achievement would extend no further than the corner shop or the clerk's stool. Typical in this regard were men like Edward Davis, who, coming from a family reduced to the 'poor class of society' by parental intemperance, started his working life in a button factory in 1834 aged six, but, having turned a supplementary cake-making sideline into a full-time business in his twenties, finished as a retail confectioner; or Ernest Ambrose, who in 1890 became an invoice clerk in the same Suffolk mat factory in which his father had been a foreman.[8]

Placed in their proper statistical context, Smiles's collection of notables take on the appearance of an isolated and highly unrepresentative minority. Rather, the figures would appear to confirm Perkin's 'football pools winner' analogy;[9] the myth of the self-made man, dragging himself up from rags to riches, was just that. Fewer than one in a 1,000 sons of the labouring poor made the transition from the bottom of the social spectrum to class I, which, in the Registrar General's scheme, is not a classic elite, but a broader category rooted in the entrepreneurial and professional middle class.

Yet, if working men were united in their broader class prospects, within their own ranks they were deeply divided. The figures for father–son continuity in classes III and V reiterate the fundamental importance of the skill axis in working-class stratification. While those from semi-skilled backgrounds displayed a certain degree of cosmo-politanism in relation to the rest of their class, at either end of the working-class spectrum men's horizons were overwhelmingly those of the status group into which they were born.

But, although the gulf between the families of the skilled and unskilled was wide it was not fixed. Internal exchange was far more likely than a journey beyond the boundaries of the working class as a whole. Only 5 per cent of labouring men shared the experience of James Bowd, juvenile plough-driver turned farm manager,[10] and escaped from their class, but one in three was mobile elsewhere within it. Downward mobility from the skilled ranks was unlikely, but it was hardly rare. And like Thomas Jordan, whose gassing in the First World War prevented him from returning to the Durham coalfield, and eventually confined him to work as a lollipop man, 50 per cent of those making the drop were reduced to unskilled employment.[11] At the same time, opportunities for internal advancement were not inconsiderable. A third of men with semi-skilled backgrounds were in skilled occupations by the time they came to take a bride, and this group outnumbered those moving from class IV to class V by almost three to one. Similarly, the sons of unskilled men were 12 times more likely to be upwardly mobile within the working class than to leave it, and much more likely to move into skilled rather than semi-skilled positions as they did so.

For opposite reasons, the view from the other side of the barrier dividing members of the working class from their social superiors was, especially for those close up against it, almost equally unpropitious. Rates of downward mobility among the sons of middle-class and elite men were surprisingly high, but the consequences were particularly serious for those from lower-middle-class backgrounds.[12] Most of those relegated from the elite were spared the indignity of manual employment, and those who were not were at least highly likely to retain the relative respectability of a skilled position.

In sharp contrast, class II was strongly associated with the world of manual labour, its sons displaying a degree of insecurity well documented in studies of the European lower middle class.[13] Just three in 100 men born into this class were in elite positions at the time of their marriage, confirming that the process of upward mobility in the nineteenth century was subject to multiple-barrier effect.[14] Like James Ashley and Thomas James, however, almost half of men originating in class II were found in manual employment on their wedding day. For Ashley the transition may not have seemed too dramatic. The son of self-employed bakers, he became a hat finisher, then a shaper, for Christy's of Bond Street. James's decline, on the other hand, was more fundamental, his woollen manufacturer father's death condemning him to manual work within the trade, which, although alleviated by periods in business, was the situation to which he returned in his fifties. Ashley was in the majority as far as downwardly mobile lower middle-class men were concerned, but James's remained the experience of a large minority, amounting to more than one in five class II men altogether, and 40 per cent of all who became workers.[15]

The distribution of men by origin provides only one perspective on the relationship between fathers and sons as it relates to the process of class formation. There is also the question of inflow mobility, or how movement away from the previous generation worked itself out in the composition of the next (Table 2.2). The pattern of recruitment reveals the homogeneity, or otherwise, of classes. It also provides one measure, when applied to the composition of elite or higher-level groups, of social 'closure'.

Table 2.2 *Class composition of grooms by class of father, 1839–1914 (percentage by column)*

Father's Class	Son's Class					n	%
	I	II	III	IV	V		
I	57.1	4.9	0.7	0.6	0.3	208	(2.0)
II	30.8	62.9	10.0	13.6	6.7	1782	(17.5)
III	8.3	20.5	67.9	27.5	17.1	4277	(41.9)
IV	3.2	6.2	8.6	33.9	6.4	1186	(11.6)
V	0.6	5.6	12.8	24.4	69.6	2757	(27.0)
n	156	1421	4588	1595	2450	10210	
%	(1.5)	(13.9)	(44.9)	(15.6)	(24.0)		

In these terms, there is evidence of considerable upper- and lower-middle-class cohesion in nineteenth-century England. More than 50 per cent of those holding class I or class II positions were second-generation men. On the other hand, given that more than two out every five men in these classes had been recruited externally, neither can be considered inaccessible to outsiders. Clearly, however, we must also distinguish between types of outsider. Repeating the basic divergence which was evident in their outflow profiles, the external component of the elite was overwhelmingly middle-class by origin, while the great majority of new entrants to the lower middle class were workers' sons.

The relative sizes of the classes was central to the structuring of their recruitment. For example, both class I and class II drew more heavily from the much larger manual constituency than the low rates of upward mobility among workers' sons would seem to allow. Of the 8,220 sons of working-class fathers sampled, just 19 managed to achieve class I status. Yet, in doing so, they took up one in eight of all available elite positions. Similarly, as many as one in three class II men had working-class origins, and even though the upward mobility chances of skilled men's sons were no better than those of men hailing from class IV, the size of the skilled sector meant that it was the former who predominated in this group.

Within the working class, the high levels of inheritance in classes III and V translated into equally impressive rates of self-recruitment. Sons following in their fathers' footsteps worked predominantly alongside men with similar social backgrounds, strengthening the divide between the skilled and the unskilled. What still bound the working class as a whole together, however, was the limited impact of incursions from above, and the fact that internal recruitment was – comparatively speaking – much more important.

Once more, differentials in class size mitigated the effects of what was, in proportional terms, a substantial downward flow of individuals from the higher reaches of society. Fewer than one in 100 working-class men had grown up in an upper middle-class family, and only the anomalously heterogeneous class IV recruited more than 10 per cent of its personnel from the lower middle class. Even so, 80 per cent of first-generation men in semi-skilled positions had fathers who were, or had been, in manual employment, and even at the two heavily self-recruiting poles, the great majority of outsiders were other working-class men.

In sum, the patterns of inter-generational realignment displayed in Tables 2.1 and 2.2 highlight the limited nature of working-class interaction with a non-manual world whose upper echelons were all but out of reach. The barrier between the classes was high, and below it was to be found a body of men whose horizons were predominantly confined to the sphere of manual labour. In these terms, the nineteenth-century English working class was a phenomenally well-defined demographic entity; structurally at least, Perry Anderson's depiction of workers in Victorian England inhabiting an isolated, hermetically sealed enclave would seem largely justified.[16] The impression of working-class homogeneity is qualified, however, by the complex system of movement and cohesion which characterised its internal relations. On the one hand, workers were sharply divided by 'skill': Robert Robert's assertion that 'No view of the English working class ... would be accurate if that class were shown merely as an amalgam of artisan and labouring groups united by a common aim and culture' is no less applicable in terms of its members' mobility and recruitment.[17] On the other hand, while not as considerable as some would have it,[18] there was a sufficient degree of movement between working-class strata to influence perceived career horizons.

At this level, parents could still entertain real hopes, and serious fears, for their sons. The son of a skilled man, for example, could grow up in the knowledge that he was fairly safe from demotion, but if he did follow in his father's footsteps he would see one in five of his contemporaries lose their status. Likewise, a labourer's son could certainly expect to follow his father into unskilled work, but from the amount of movement around him would know that this was not inevitable. In between, for men born into the semi-skilled sector, to move was more normal than to stay put. This degree of inter-generational redistribution meant that those who did follow in their fathers' footsteps experienced more than occasional contact with outsiders from elsewhere within the working class. This was spectacularly so in the case of the semi-skilled sector, but even the overwhelmingly second-generation skilled and unskilled sectors witnessed significant incursions of first generation men, enough to dispel the image of the skilled sector as a closed shop, or of the unskilled sector as a self-perpetuating proletarian rump.

As a whole, the bourgeoisie was much better acquainted with the working class than vice versa. However, the spectre of the manual world loomed largest in the pasts and futures of lower- middle-class families. The position of men born into such families verged on the precarious: their chances of avoiding demotion rated only slightly better than even, while the class as a whole contained a substantial minority of interlopers who had travelled up from the manual ranks below. In the other direction, the elite remained as distant a horizon as the non-manual world as a whole did to the sons of working-class men. Yet this barrier, like the one beneath it, was semi-permeable. Viewed from the perspective of the elite, intra-class relationships may, in fact, have been highly significant, for the lower middle class seems to have played a crucial role in absorbing descending elite sons.

TRENDS IN CLASS MOBILITY

In marked contrast to the Smilesean vision, John Stuart Mill's initial account of the dynamics of the Victorian social system stressed its class-based nature:

> each employment being chiefly recruited from the children of those already employed in it, or in employments of the same rank with it in social estimation ...[19]

This certainly accords more closely with the patterns of movement observed across the marriage register sample, but is not an accurate summary of those patterns because it overplays the degree of restriction in operation. Later in the same passage, however, Mill goes on to claim that, under the impact of industrialism, this system was beginning to break down.

> The changes ... now so rapidly taking place in usages and ideas are undermining all these distinctions; the habits or disabilities which chained people to their hereditary condition are fast wearing away, and every class is exposed to increased and increasing competition from at least the class immediately below it.[20]

Figure 2.1, which provides a simplified measure of the changing pattern of movement across the period, would seem to lend weight to Mill's general argument. It shows a very clear, and accelerating, trend towards greater mobility over time. By the turn of the century the ratio of change to continuity increased to nearly one in two from only one in three at the beginning of the period. Yet this table also re-emphasises the tensions between mobility and stability. At no point did those on the move outnumber those staying put.

This is a strong pattern but the terms of reference are vague. There is no indication of where the principal foci of activity were, nor

Figure 2.1   *Total mobility rate by marriage cohort*

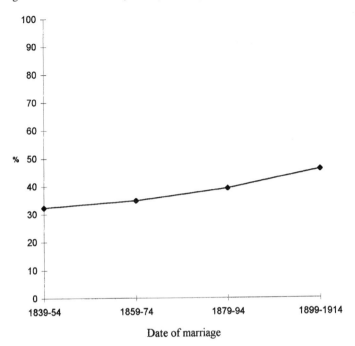

whether change was relatively localised or more expansive. The full detail of inter- and intra-class change is presented in Tables 2.3 and 2.4. Looked at, in the first instance, from the perspective of the relationship between the two major class groups in nineteenth-century society, these analyses tend to confirm Marshall's impression that, in the midst of increasing social flux, the barriers between manual and non-manual labour were only partially affected.

While the argument that industrialisation *adversely* affected the rate of upward mobility from the working class appears to be contradicted by these figures, there were certainly no substantial gains for working-class families holding middle-class aspirations for their sons. Although upward mobility increased extensively in proportional terms, this was from a very low base. Throughout the period the quantity of movement out of the class never rose above a modest trickle, and journeys into the established middle class remained

Social Mobility in England

Table 2.3   *Class distribution of grooms by marriage cohort (percentage by row)*

Father's class	I	II	III	IV	V	n	%
			Son's Class				
I							
1839–54	36.7	43.3	15.0	5.0	0.0	60	(2.1)
1859–74	53.5	30.2	7.0	4.7	4.7	43	(1.7)
1879–94	46.6	25.9	20.7	5.2	1.7	58	(2.5)
1899–1914	36.2	31.9	19.1	2.1	10.6	47	(1.9)
II							
1839–54	2.9	44.9	29.9	10.9	11.5	488	(17.1)
1859–74	3.6	52.8	23.1	10.6	9.9	415	(16.7)
1879–94	1.8	52.1	25.2	13.8	7.1	436	(18.5)
1899–1914	2.5	51.7	24.4	13.5	7.9	443	(17.6)
III							
1839–54	0.1	5.0	80.7	5.2	9.0	1134	(39.8)
1859–74	0.4	6.3	75.4	8.1	9.8	1034	(41.6)
1879–94	0.2	7.5	71.9	11.1	9.3	968	(41.2)
1899–1914	0.5	8.4	63.4	16.6	11.1	1141	(45.2)
IV							
1839–54	0.4	6.4	30.5	47.8	14.9	249	(8.7)
1859–74	0.4	5.2	33.0	46.7	14.8	270	(10.9)
1879–94	0.7	8.9	33.9	45.4	11.1	280	(11.9)
1899–1914	0.3	8.5	34.6	43.7	12.9	387	(15.3)
V							
1839–54	0.0	2.4	18.1	8.4	71.1	918	(32.2)
1859–74	0.0	2.8	19.9	12.2	65.2	724	(29.1)
1879–94	0.0	3.1	21.5	17.7	57.7	610	(25.9)
1899–1914	0.2	3.6	28.9	23.0	44.4	505	(20.0)
n							
1839–54	38	340	1312	311	848	2849	
1859–74	43	331	1112	344	656	2486	
1879–94	39	359	1044	405	505	2352	
1899–1914	36	391	1120	535	441	2523	
%							
1839–54	(1.3)	(11.9)	(46.1)	(10.9)	(29.8)		
1859–74	(1.7)	(13.3)	(44.7)	(13.8)	(26.4)		
1879–94	(1.7)	(15.3)	(44.4)	(17.2)	(21.5)		
1899–1914	(1.4)	(15.5)	(44.4)	(21.2)	(17.5)		

Table 2.4   *Class composition of grooms by marriage cohort*
(percentage by column)

Father's class	Son's Class						
	I	II	III	IV	V	n	%
I							
1839–54	57.9	7.6	0.7	1.0	0.0	60	(2.1)
1859–74	53.5	3.9	0.3	0.6	0.3	43	(1.7)
1879–94	69.2	4.2	1.1	0.7	0.2	58	(2.5)
1899–1914	47.2	3.8	0.8	0.2	1.1	47	(1.9)
II							
1839–54	36.8	64.4	11.1	17.0	6.6	488	(17.1)
1859–74	34.9	66.2	8.6	12.8	6.3	415	(16.7)
1879–94	20.5	63.2	10.5	14.8	6.1	436	(18.5)
1899–1914	30.6	58.6	9.6	11.2	7.9	443	(17.6)
III							
1839–54	2.6	16.8	69.7	19.0	12.0	1134	(39.8)
1859–74	9.3	19.6	70.1	24.4	15.4	1034	(41.6)
1879–94	5.1	20.3	66.7	26.4	17.8	968	(41.2)
1899–1914	16.7	24.6	64.6	35.3	28.8	1141	(45.2)
IV							
1839–54	2.6	4.7	5.8	38.3	4.4	249	(8.7)
1859–74	2.3	4.2	8.0	36.6	6.1	270	(10.9)
1879–94	5.1	7.0	9.1	31.4	6.1	280	(11.9)
1899–1914	2.8	8.4	12.0	31.6	11.3	387	(15.3)
V							
1839–54	0.0	6.5	12.7	24.8	77.0	918	(32.2)
1859–74	0.0	6.0	12.9	25.6	72.0	724	(29.1)
1879–94	0.0	5.3	12.5	26.7	69.7	610	(25.9)
1899–1914	2.8	4.6	13.0	21.7	50.8	505	(20.0)
n							
1839–54	38	340	1312	311	848	2849	
1859–74	43	331	1112	344	656	2486	
1879–94	39	359	1044	405	505	2352	
1899–1914	36	391	1120	535	441	2523	
%							
1839–54	(1.3)	(11.9)	(46.1)	(10.9)	(29.8)		
1859–74	(1.7)	(13.3)	(44.7)	(13.8)	(26.4)		
1879–94	(1.7)	(15.3)	(44.4)	(17.2)	(21.5)		
1899–1914	(1.4)	(15.5)	(44.4)	(21.2)	(17.5)		

virtually unknown: the one and only individual sampled who could recount a truly Smilesean tale of rags-to-riches achievement was the son of porter who became an Anglican clergyman and was married in Lichfield in the year that the Great War broke out. In that same year the sons of working-class men were twice as likely to have left the class than they would have been 75 years earlier, but more than nine out ten were, nevertheless, still destined to walk up the aisle as workers themselves.

The arrival of this small but expanding contingent of upwardly mobile men had a much more marked effect on the composition of the middle class than their leaving did on working-class stability. Altogether, the proportion of non-manual positions held by workers' sons rose from a quarter in the 1840s to more than a third by the turn of the century. The rising influx of workers' sons was encouraged by the changing shape and composition of the social division of labour, in particular the rapid growth of white-collar employment in the later nineteenth century. This accounts for the fact that, while the middle class became more heterogeneous in terms of its origins, there was no decline in the ability of most bourgeois families to pass on status and advantage to their own offspring.

The exception here was the elite, or, most likely, that part of it whose fortunes were tied up in land, which clearly began to experience difficulties as mid-Victorian 'equipoise' gave way to agricultural depression in the 1870s.[21] According to social class formation theory, we might expect this crisis to have been offset by closer relations between the upper and lower middle classes, but, if anything, rates of intra-class mobility and recruitment seem to have declined. Instead, an increasing number of upper-middle-class sons – one in three by 1900 – were consigned to spend at least part of their careers in manual employment. Despite this trend, however, and the fact that both sectors of the bourgeoisie consistently lost more sons to the working class than vice versa, middle-class downward mobility continued to make no more than a limited impact on the integrity of the working class.

Thus, the changing pattern of exchange between the two main classes made some impression above the line which divided them, but precious little below it, where both the stability and coherence of the Victorian and Edwardian working class remained virtually undisturbed. As with the pattern of movement across the whole sample population, however, the principal effects of change were felt not so

Figure 2.2   *Direction of working-class mobility by period*

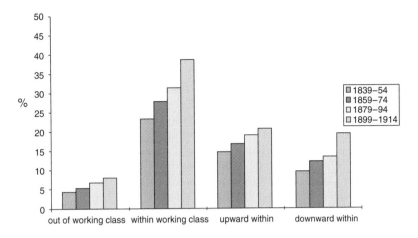

much between as within classes, and between status groups inside the working class in particular (Figure 2.2).

In all, over 80 per cent of the transitions involving the sons of working-class men took place among the manual grades, which meant that intra-class mobility was never insignificant. Between 1839 and 1914, however, the chances of moving in this way almost doubled, from one in five to nearly 40 per cent. The forces of attrition affected exit and entry barriers equally. Those making no move in each generation worked among an increasingly diverse peer group, suggesting a substantial process of homogenisation.

The semi-skilled sector was at the core of this process. From both skilled and unskilled backgrounds, the flow of men into this sector trebled across the period. Long-range movement also increased substantially, although predominantly from the bottom up rather than the top down. By the beginning of twentieth century the experience of a man like Henry Herbert, the son of a Gloucestershire farm labourer who became a shoemaker, was shared by almost a third of those whose fathers were in unskilled employment.[22]

For most of the period, in fact, and in partial compensation for the derisory chances of movement out of the class, there was an excess of upward over downward traffic. The gap narrowed slowly throughout the nineteenth century until a sharp acceleration in the overall demotion rate after 1900 brought the numbers rising and falling into roughly equal proportion. The main reason for this is the rise in the number of men from skilled backgrounds who were unable to follow in their father's footsteps. On the one hand, skill remained, in these terms at least, impressively resilient and well-defended right through to end of the period. However, the pressures visited on this sector by economic downturn and reorganisation in the 1880s and 1890s are clearly visible in the more uncertain prospects of skilled men's sons 20 or 30 years later.

The effects of the homogenisation process were felt most dramatically towards the bottom of the social scale, where the horizons of men born into class V, mobile or not, were transformed. In the period 1839–54, three-quarters of unskilled workers were second generation men, and 70 per cent of their sons were themselves destined to become so. However, by the early 1900s more were leaving for better paid and higher status working-class positions than were staying put, and two out every five unskilled jobs were filled by men – including a hefty contingent of skilled workers's sons – who had come from other working-class backgrounds.

In summary, broadening out the perspective to incorporate the changing profiles of all five classes would seem only to confirm further the prescience of Mill's observation. But while the evidence certainly sustains the image of an increasingly dynamic society, a number of qualifications must be made. In the first place, industrial capitalism was not, or at least had not yet become, the universal social solvent Mill implied. Some chains were more substantial than others and, in consequence, rates of wear varied. At most the process of attrition was responsible for a substantial blurring of distinctions, but it was never so extensive that it rendered them obsolete. Second, and relatedly as far as the significance of changing mobility rates is concerned, it is the quality as much as the quantity of movement which is important. More movement does not simply equate to social disaggregation, for while the rise in mobility would, on the face of it, seem to have weakened the potential for solidarity above the manual/non-manual divide, the indications are that it was strengthened below; looser chains, in Mill's terms, only revealing the wider parameters of a prisoner's incarceration. Finally, change accelerated throughout the period, but Mill exaggerated its impact and rapidity in his own period. Rather, the most significant shifts occurred from the 1890s onwards, as the catalytic compound of economic, social and political changes associated with the last quarter of the nineteenth century began to work itself out.

MOBILITY IN CONTEXT

In contrast to the comparative, case-study basis of, for example, Foster's work, the issue of local or regional context is not the central concern of this study.[23] However, in view of the distinctiveness of nineteenth-century communities, and the variable speed and complexity of urban and economic development in this period, we cannot simply assume that the averaging process produced a nationally representative outcome.[24] Comparing patterns in context also offers a rather more subtle assessment of the relationship between economic development and mobility.

Petty's Law assumes 'the movement of labour with economic growth from agriculture to industry and services'.[25] Given that the spread of industrialisation in nineteenth-century Britain was never all-embracing, the application of this model to the examination of mobility patterns by district-type should reveal that regions closer in their economic characteristics to the 'primary' end of the evolutionary spectrum were less dynamic than those in which the secondary and tertiary sectors held a relatively high profile. Opposing Petty's Law, and the analogous assumptions of the thesis of industrialism, is the argument that the development and consolidation of modern industrial capitalism inhibited mobility between, while encouraging movement within, classes; so that the most dynamic social formations in these terms should be those in the earlier stages of industrial development, the more 'advanced' locations having begun to solidify along class lines.

Breaking down the sample for the purpose of interrogating these arguments is not a straightforward procedure. In the first place there are the dangers associated with reduced sample sizes, while the number of separate registration districts presents problems of manageability.[26] Each of these limitations can be overcome, to some extent, by collapsing the districts into categories which possess wider substantive meaning in economic and social terms. Yet the administrative origin of the registration district system militates against this. The geographical coverage of the individual districts varied, and as result they often encompassed a range of peripheral settlements and local economies. With the exception of Bethnal Green, none of the districts in the sample can be considered pristinely 'urban' or 'rural', 'industrial' or 'agricultural'.[27] Re-classification therefore proceeds, as follows, on the basis of each district's *predominant* economic characteristics.[28]

Industrial

This category combines Stoke, Dudley, Sheffield and Macclesfield on
the basis that, by comparison with the remainder of the sample, it was
in these districts that large-scale or factory-based production was most
advanced, or where the potential for its development was greatest. The
manufacture of pottery, which dominated the economy of Stoke-on-
Trent, was largely dependent on hand technology, but was, nevertheless, a mass-production industry, organised on a planned factory basis
from the end of the eighteenth century.[29] The scale and organisation of
the north Staffordshire coalfield which served the potteries was transformed in the wake of rising demand for iron in the district between
1840 and 1875. In 1860 Earl Granville's Shelton works were producing
50,000 tons of pig iron annually, and four years later was employing
1,500 people.[30] The south Staffordshire coalfield was characterised by
'small, shallow, ill-equipped' pits worked with a minimum of capital'[31]
and Dudley's wrought nail trade was almost entirely carried out on a
non-factory basis. However, pig iron and, later, steel production was
carried out on a larger scale, and the area was also known for the
heavier industrial production of ships' chains, cables and anchors.
When the nailing industry declined in the 1870s, new factory-based
engineering and clothing industries took its place.[32] Like Dudley, 'the
primary industrial city' of Sheffield was a centre of metal and metal
goods manufacture.[33] Here, employment in the 'heavy' – factory-based
– trades increased by 300 per cent between 1850 and 1914, which was
six times the growth rate in the largely subcontracted 'light' trades.
Meanwhile, Sheffield's miners, who made up the second largest
occupational grouping in the district, worked in the expanding and
heavily capitalised south Yorkshire field, where, in the 1860s, the
average pit workforce was twice as large as in the west of the county.[34]
Macclesfield was one of the first towns to introduce the water-powered
silk-throwing mill. In its heyday the silk industry employed up to 14,000
operatives, and by 1850 domestic silk weavers were in a similar state to
their counterparts in cotton. When free trade brought crisis in the
1860s many of the alternatives to silk – such as cotton manufacture and
rope making – were also factory-based.[35]

Urban

Just as the industrial category includes areas that were substantially
'urban', the districts in this category were, in fact, no less concerned

with manufacturing. But in combining Bethnal Green and Lichfield under this heading the intention is to provide a counterpoint to the newer expressions of urban development and industrial organisation encompassed by the first category. The urban category is characterised by economies which were longer-standing and generally more diversified, and whose forms of industrial organisation were more traditional, or, at least, smaller in scale. Bethnal Green, which formed part of the capital's 'traditional industrial perimeter', was full of work-shops making furniture, toys and silk products.[36] In Lichfield, tradi-tional crafts, such as leather goods manufacture, retained their importance in this period, and heavier industry was inhibited by the demand for labour made by an important market gardening sector. New, larger-scale industries concerned with metal working and light engineering developed in the later nineteenth century, from which point the brewery industry was in the ascendant.[37]

Urban–Rural

This category is also distinguished by its mixed economic charac-teristics, but here a substantial agricultural ingredient was present. It includes two districts based on small market and manufacturing towns – Wokingham and Nuneaton – serving local villages and hamlets located in wider rural hinterlands. Both experienced demographic and economic developments which resulted in closer relationships between town and country, and both were influenced by the nearby centres of Reading and Coventry respectively. The Wokingham district's economy was dominated by a mixed, but predominantly arable, agriculture, while the town itself provided a range of trades, with leather goods making and building particularly influential. Although connected to Reading and the south of England by the South Eastern Railway in 1849, Wokingham was largely bypassed by the process of industrialisation. However, developments in agri-cultural technology and the town's role as a local service centre ensured it growth and prosperity, the more so 'as village self-sufficiency eventually gave way to a rural-urban interdependence'.[38] Noted, early in the nineteenth century, as 'a very improving market town', Nuneaton's staple industry up to the 1860s was ribbon weaving. This was supplemented by coal mining in the east Warwickshire field which underwent rapid development after the coming of the railway to the town in 1849. Coal helped to sustain the local economy when depression hit the silk trade after the commercial treaty with France in 1860, and remained the 'backbone of town development' during the period of rapid population growth, urban expansion and industrial diversification between 1875 and 1914. These processes helped to break down the isolation of surrounding villages, the 'complex interaction of town effect upon country and vice versa' resulting in 'an intricate state of mutual interdependence'.[39]

Rural

The districts of Cleobury Mortimer and Samford were dominated by agriculture. Together, they encompassed a wide range of farming activity: Samford, a highly fertile landscape characterised by large, highly capitalised farms devoted to arable cultivation; Cleobury Mortimer, a mixed-farming area combining permanent upland pasture, stock-keeping, some grain crops, dairying, hops and orchards. Just as the countryside continued to leave its mark on the urban centres of nineteenth-century England, so no area of the size of the registration districts was entirely cut off from urban and/or industrial development. Cleobury Mortimer includes men who worked in the stone quarrying and mining industries of the Clee Hills, together with coal miners from the Wyre forest, and, despite the poor communications which tended to isolate communities within the district, there was also contact with the carpet-making centre of Kidderminster immediately to the east. The north-western sector of the Samford district was close to Ipswich, a traditional port, which underwent rapid commercial and industrial development in the second half of the nineteenth century.[40] Nevertheless, these were areas which were more, and for longer, isolated from the process of modern industrial development than any in the remainder of the sample.

Together with Hodge-like stereotypes of the rural labourer, assumptions about the extreme social inertia of the society in which he lived have long characterised much writing on the agricultural history of the nineteenth century.[41] Some confirmation of this image is presented in Table 2.5 which compares the total mobility rate in each district category over time. The most notable feature of this table, however, is the absence of any striking difference in the total mobility rates; the differential between the most and least mobile category is covered by less than 10 percentage points, and between the most and least mobile districts, Bethnal Green and Cleobury Mortimer, by just 13. Across the whole period the general prospects of men born into the quiet backwaters of rural Suffolk and Shropshire were not hugely

Table 2.5 *Total mobility rate by marriage cohort and district category*

Percentage of grooms in:		1839–54	1859–74	1879–94	1899–1914	All	n
					Date of Marriage		
Same class as	(a)	66.5	64.2	62.7	54.5	(62.2)	2445
father	(b)	62.8	62.5	55.3	49.6	(57.7)	1129
	(c)	66.5	66.3	58.0	54.1	(61.4)	1385
	(d)	76.0	68.3	65.2	57.1	(66.9)	1380
Different class	(a)	33.5	35.9	37.3	45.5	(37.8)	1487
from father	(b)	37.2	37.5	44.7	50.4	(42.3)	829
	(c)	33.5	33.7	42.0	46.0	(38.6)	872
	(d)	24.0	31.7	34.7	42.9	(33.1)	683
Upwardly mobile	(a)	16.0	17.6	17.1	20.3	(17.7)	696
	(b)	15.6	18.0	23.2	21.3	(19.4)	380
	(c)	16.0	17.6	22.5	26.3	(20.4)	461
	(d)	11.8	17.7	18.2	22.2	(17.4)	358
Downwardly	(a)	17.5	18.1	20.2	25.2	(20.1)	791
mobile	(b)	21.6	19.5	21.5	29.1	(22.9)	449
	(c)	17.5	16.2	19.5	19.7	(18.2)	411
	(d)	12.2	14.0	16.5	20.8	(15.8)	325

Key: a = industrial b = urban c = urban/rural d = rural

different from those in districts providing part of the prime motive force behind the workshop of the world.[42] Second, it follows from this that men from all regions alike were relatively *immobile*. The underlying stability of Victorian society was all-pervasive. Only in Bethnal Green and Sheffield, and then only at beginning of the twentieth century, did the mobile ever outnumber the stationary.

Nevertheless, in sample-wide terms, and giving some substantiation to Petty's Law, rural society *was* the least tractable. Overall, over two-thirds of those based in the countryside made no movement away from the class of their fathers compared to 58 per cent of all grooms marrying in the urban districts. On the other hand, the unspectacular mobility rate found in the industrial districts would seem to indicate that there was no straightforward relationship between mobility and economic development.

In all categories of district the total mobility rate rose over time, suggesting that, whatever the particular admixture of structural ingre-
dients, the process of economic growth and the long-term development
of an industrial society in the wider sense favoured more movement.
Yet the process was most dramatic where there was most scope for
change. Before the 1860s, only one in five men in the rural community
of Samford were found in a different class to their fathers, a rate of
movement lower by 9 percentage points than anywhere else. However,
the contraction of agricultural employment in the 1880s and 1890s
transformed the situation, and by 1914, with almost half the population
on the move between generations, Samford had achieved near parity
with the other districts.

Purveyors of pessimistic prognoses about the relationship between
factories and mobility will find the evidence in the bottom half of Table
2.5, which indicates the basic character of the expanding mobility
opportunities in each district category, equivocal. Overall, the general
prospects of some kind of advance were among the least favourable
within the industrial sector. However, the traditional urban environment, where, according to this line of argument, the prospects should
have been much brighter, was the context which generated the highest
risks of demotion.

Over time the picture is more supportive of the pessimists' position.
In the rural sector the overall increase in mobility was responsible for
as many advances as it was declines. But within the industrial category
the ratio between successes and disappointments became increasingly
unfavourable from the mid-Victorian era onwards. Only the urban–
rural communities, where strongly rising chances of 'getting on' were
not cancelled out by a substantially enhanced risk of falling, can be
firmly designated 'improving' societies in these terms. Here the ratio
of upward to downward moves increased from 0.91 to 1.33 over the
sample period.[43]

In the case of both Nuneaton and Wokingham much of this would
appear to be explained by the development of these market towns as
centres of local commerce, industry and bureaucracy, and their attraction to those pushed out of contracting agricultural economies. As
Waller writes, 'From field-hand to urban-domestic was elevation of a
kind for the country girl. So was the wage promotion and prospects
which urban employment held out to her country brothers.'[44] The
nearby and rapid expansion of Coventry and 'biscuitopolis' Reading
respectively can only have enhanced this effect.[45] Flora Thompson
provides us with an insight into the forces and tensions underlying this

process in Laura's parallel journey from 'Lark Rise' to 'Candleford', in the shadow of Oxford, and with it her elevation into the world of the urban lower middle class.[46]

It has already been established that Laura's mobility was of a kind all too rare within working-class communities, and Figure 2.3 confirms that where one lived made little difference in this sense. In each type of district the chances of advancing across class lines were slim, although in each case there was also some improvement over time. It is on this particular point that the arguments of Perkin and Sanderson rest, and while the differences are very slight, the established, differentiated economies of the urban districts *were* the most receptive to the aspirant worker's child. It was also only in this context that any members of the sample reached the elite. Nevertheless, the industrial category was the next most promising context, and by 1914 rates of working-class upward mobility in all but the rural districts had caught up with, and passed, those in the urban realm.

The revelation that industrial workers' sons' prospects became marginally brighter over time raises a questionmark against the Schüren/Kocka thesis. On the other hand, the fact that change was again strongest in the urban–rural category lends it some support. None of Smiles's heroes was to be found here, confirming Snell's suspicion of artistic licence in Hardy's elevation of ex-hay trusser Michael Henchard to mayoral office in Casterbridge.[47] But in Wokingham the chances of crossing over at least part way into the

Figure 2.3   *Working-class upward mobility by district and period*

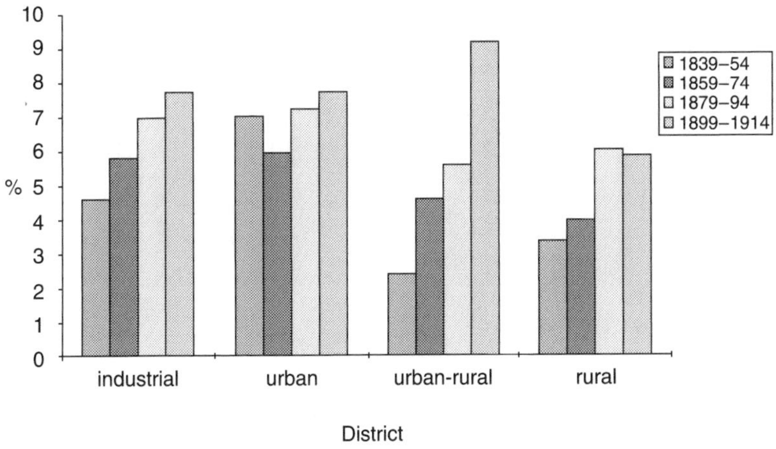

middle class did, nevertheless, increase sixfold between the middle and the end of the nineteenth century.[48]

By contrast, men born into Samford's predominantly agricultural labour force experienced little change in their basic class prospects, and it is in these terms that the image of nineteenth-century rural social inertia remains most appropriate.[49] Although not unchanging, the relationship between workers and bourgeoisie continued, in almost every respect, to be most distant in the Victorian and Edwardian countryside. The demographic cohesion of the nineteenth-century rural middle class remained formidable, and its sons were also considerably more secure than their urban or industrial peers. Downward mobility did increase in the wake of agricultural depression in the 1870s, and rather more so in the eastern arable economy of Samford than in the mixed-farming district of Cleobury Mortimer, yet the middle class as a whole in these districts remained relatively stable (Figure 2.4).[50]

Elsewhere, the general expansion of upward movement from the working class translated, from a middle-class perspective, into a process of dilution from below which was both continuous and, by the end of the period, quite marked. On the other hand, the pattern of middle-class *prospects* varied quite extensively from district to district.

Figure 2.4   *Middle-class recruitment and mobility by district and period*

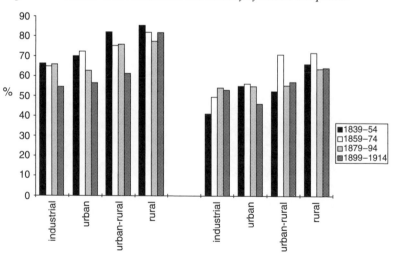

The sons of the urban-rural bourgeoisie, while never quite as safe, shared the experience of their rural cousins in remaining more or less as secure at the end of the period as at the beginning. However, the urban middle class appeared to lose its grip on the transmission of status at the end of the period. In the East End of London this was in any case never very strong, and as early as the 1870s and 1880s three-quarters of a relatively small middle class were finding themselves downwardly mobile by the time they came to take a bride. Part of the explanation for this lies in the changing character of Bethnal Green and its economy as it absorbed those displaced by demolition in the centre of the city. According to Stedman Jones, this process forced many of the more substantial bourgeoisie out, and the shrinking numbers who remained had less prospect of passing on their position to sons in an increasingly manual economy.[51] In Lichfield things were less volatile, but here too there were grounds for concern, as the prospects for middle-class sons worsened quite dramatically at the beginning of the twentieth century.

The pattern of change in the industrial districts moved in completely the opposite direction. In this case, the least stable bourgeoisie of all appears to have undergone a process of maturation, finding it easier to hand on status and advantage to its offspring as the century progressed. From three in five in the 1840s, the chances of men born into the industrial middle class experiencing a decline in their class fortunes were reduced to less than 50 per cent by the turn of the century. From the other side of the manual/non-manual divide, this process resulted in a gradually contracting industrial working class becoming ever more cohesive, so that by 1914 the chances of a wage worker finding himself toiling alongside the sons of middle-class men were the same as they had been in the countryside 75 years earlier.

Viewed from this combination of perspectives the contextual comparison provides its strongest support to date for the pessimists' case. In two important respects the classes were growing further apart in the industrially most advanced environment. Yet the class formation argument extends beyond what was happening between classes to what was happening within. The national picture revealed a clear process of working-class homogenisation, but suggested no such process above the manual/non-manual divide. For the pessimists' case to be well founded the former development would have to be reflected solely, or at least most dramatically, in the industrial environment, and the growing divide between the two bourgeois classes only, or most clearly, in the 'non-industrial' areas.

In these terms, Table 2.6 suggests that the 'class formation' thesis should be rejected. In the first place, total rates of intra-class mobility, both above and below the class divide, were similar right across the contextual canvas. The internal polarities of the working class exercised most influence in rural society. But it is in the industrial category, thanks to the stability and cohesion of its large skilled manual workforce, that the next lowest rate of intra-class transition is to be found. At the same time the degree of interchange between the two non-manual classes, likewise measured in terms of the percentage of all middle-class sons moving elsewhere within the class, was highest in the urban and urban-rural environments and least impressive amongst the industrial bourgeoisie.

Table 2.6 also confirms that the process of working-class homogenisation was not confined to the more 'advanced' areas but had a clear, consistent and marked effect in all districts. The figures offer some encouragement to the class formation theorists, in so far as the rate of change was noticeably faster in the industrial context than in the urban–rural. However, the biggest transformation to the internal relations of the class was experienced in rural society, where the proportion of men on the move more than doubled.

Here change was felt at all levels as the agrarian economy was transformed in the latter part of the nineteenth century. Elsewhere it was more focused. In all non-rural districts the primary focus of the homogenisation process was the unskilled sector, skill remaining

Table 2.6   *Intra-class mobility by marriage cohort and district category*

		1839–54	1859–74	1879–94	1899–1914	All	n
				Date of Marriage			
Percentage of middle-	(a)	5.2	4.0	4.4	3.6	(4.3)	30
class sons moving	(b)	9.8	5.9	7.2	6.8	(7.6)	30
elsewhere within	(c)	9.0	8.6	7.7	5.2	(7.5)	32
their class	(d)	6.6	8.0	0.0	6.1	(5.2)	25
Percentage of working-	(a)	22.2	25.8	27.0	36.9	(27.8)	900
class sons moving within	(b)	24.8	28.0	35.7	40.3	(32.2)	503
their class elsewhere	(c)	26.3	28.4	33.2	36.2	(30.8)	564
within their class	(d)	16.0	26.7	28.2	37.3	(26.5)	420

Key: a = industrial b = urban c = urban/rural d = rural

almost as well defended at the end of the period as at the beginning. But mobility – as opposed to recruitment – patterns varied, change occurring principally from the bottom up in the urban and urban rural districts, and from the top down in the industrial context. By 1914, labourers' sons in the former were as mobile as their industrial cousins, whose prospects of some kind of advancement had, in any case, always been relatively good. On the other hand, the sample-wide downturn in skilled men's sons' prospects at the end of the period was mainly a product of change in the industrial context, although members of 1899–1914 marriage cohort here were still twice as likely as not to become skilled men themselves.

The overall pattern of change inside the bourgeoisie is difficult to interpret because of the small numbers involved at the top of society. However, the indications are equally damning for the class formation theory in its full and specific version. None of the lower-middle-class groups showed a sustained tendency towards closer involvement with their respective elites. As the overall analysis suggested, the only detectable trend is in the opposite direction. This is certainly the main impression in the crucial industrial context, where both elite movement into and recruitment from the class II went into quite dramatic decline.

Drawing the main strands of this analysis together, the most striking result of the contextual breakdown is not the contrasts it identifies, but the marked degree of similarity it reveals in the pattern and trend of movement across different economic environments inside nineteenth-century English society. The relationship between districts largely substantiates the claim that we are dealing with a national framework of change.

On the face of it, the analysis would seem to confirm the 'evolutionary' model implicit in Petty's Law. Rural structures were notable for their greater rigidity, and while being some way from 'the mobile society', it was in the urban context, where one might expect tertiary development to be much more advanced, that rates of flux were highest. Beyond this, however, the strict application of simplistic morphogenetic metaphors becomes more difficult.

The most 'advanced' category – the industrial – performed less spectacularly than expected. In the broad context of modern economic development, there followed the predicted increase in mobility, as predominantly rural communities were exposed to the forces of urban and industrial change. But industrial localities themselves were not the most dynamic. There was change here, but this was overshadowed by a strong tendency for the rates of mobility in different environments to converge.

The assumption of modernisation theory, that industrial development will generate more movement, which will, in turn, promote greater social integration, must now be qualified further. Not only did the pattern of integration work in ways that favoured demographic class formation, but it was in only the industrial context that there were clear signs of the classes growing further apart. In this development there is *prima facie* evidence to support the claims of the social class formation theorists. But at the same time relationships inside the bourgeoisie did not become more intimate, the flow of movement out of the working class did not dry up, and the process of working-class homogenisation was found to be characteristic of English society as a whole.

CONCLUSION

Nowhere and at no point was nineteenth- and early twentieth-century English society a land of 'boundless opportunity'. Later, in *Principles*, Mill moved somewhat closer to Smiles, asserting that even if the prospects for the working class as a whole had not substantially improved, 'human beings are no longer born to their place in life'. But the evidence here suggests that even half a century after these words were written the opposite was still the experience of more than half of the population.

From within the Victorian and Edwardian working class the occupational horizons of most families were confined to their own skill sectors, and beyond it the status and advantages of a middle-class existence remained out of reach to all but an isolated few. An equivalent structuring of recruitment consolidated the demographic identity of this class, but at the same time reinforced its internal polarities. By contrast, many within the ranks of the nineteenth-century bourgeoisie enjoyed only a tenuous hold on their status, although its more solid citizens could usually limit the damage when a more appropriate place could not be found. Likewise the latter, as a class, was largely insulated from the unsavoury degree of incursion from below suffered by the lower middle class.

John Stuart Mill correctly identified the general direction of change within this developing industrial society. Over time an increasing number of journeys was undertaken, and as a result distinctions amongst the manual grades, in particular, began to blur. Here, perhaps, in what was a distinctive process of homogenisation, we can talk in more concrete terms than hitherto of the 'making' of the English working class. Yet there was nothing 'fast wearing' about the more fundamental social divisions. Looking up from below, there were only marginal changes in the relationship between classes in the broader sense. Looking down from on high, the legacy of urban and industrial development was more mixed. In the areas most isolated from the forces of industrialism the bourgeoisie largely retained its stability and identity, while in those communities most exposed to these forces the period witnessed a middle class, growing in social strength, increasingly distance itself from the toiling mass beneath.

3 Industrialisation and Social Fluidity

Historians and sociologists alike have argued that the processes of industrialism and social mobility are inextricably linked. 'Just as the industrial system tries to combine non-human factors of production efficiently', wrote David Landes in *The Unbound Prometheus*, 'so it will seek to maximise its return from wages and salaries by putting the right man in the right place.' The 'logical concomitant of this "universalistic" standard of selection,' he continued, 'is mobility: otherwise, how make the choice effective? A competitive industrial system ... will increase social mobility, raising the gifted, ambitious, and lucky, and lowering the inept, lazy, ill-fortuned ... Industrialization is, in short, a universal social solvent ...'[1]

According to this formulation, the mobility generated by industrial development is of a particular quality. Premised upon a rational assessment of merit – 'putting the right man in the right place' – industrial societies are also 'open', or 'fluid', societies. There will be *more* mobility because the mechanisms of industrialism require, and reinforce, greater *equality of opportunity*. Referring back to the triple concerns of those interested in mobility, noted at the outset, open societies are considered to be more economically efficient and socially just, and therefore more likely to be politically stable.

It is this rational-functional model which informs arguments about the relationship between mobility and the 'rise and decline' of nations within the world economic system. These include the thesis that it was the exceptional fluidity of American society that laid the foundations of that country's rapid economic advance from the end of the nineteenth century, but also the parallel notion that Britain's relative economic decline, which began in the same period, reflected a creeping social sclerosis. A comparatively open social structure, which authors such as Landes identify as the crucial catalyst facilitating Britain's early industrial revolution, had given way a hundred years later, it is claimed, to a much more rigid, class-based system.

We now know that there was, in fact, a steady and unequivocal increase in the rate of social mobility in Victorian and Edwardian England. In one sense, therefore, English society was, quite obviously, *more* disaggregated on the eve of the First World War than at any time in the previous 70 years. On the other hand, the process of dis-aggregation was focused in such a way as to suggest that, in other respects, the social system was indeed becoming more rather than less stratified over time. However, neither a rising mobility rate nor a process of class formation need imply anything about the pattern of *relative* mobility chances. As Goldthorpe found, a more mobile society is not necessarily a more equal one, and, by the same token, a process of class formation need not lead to a reduction in fluidity. Accordingly, this chapter begins the examination of *why* the changes in the observ-able pattern of mobility between generations in the period 1839–1914 occurred. There was more mobility, but did this in fact reflect a more *open* society?

Mid-Victorian commentators were in no doubt that English society was open, or at least was becoming so as the consolidation of industrial society continued. For Samuel Smiles, failure to make one's way in the world reflected not class-based constraints, but the moral shortcomings of the individual. In a more subtle vein, Bagehot argued for the greater viability of British society because, unlike America and France, it embodied a distinctly hierarchical system of unequal con-dition and reward, but, unlike Asian society, one that was traversable. The implication of Mill's comments about greater competition between classes, the demise of ascription and this being reflective of changing habits and attitudes, is that industrialism generates not only more mobility but greater fluidity.[2]

Empirically speaking, however, there is even less to go on than before. Goldthorpe's work confirms Glass's emphasis on the degree of restriction operating at the top of the social structure, and he rejects the claims of those who, like Landes, argue that greater equality of opportunity is a necessary concomitant of industrialisation.[3] But Goldthorpe's data are from the middle of the twentieth century, and it is only the similarities in the pattern of social fluidity which have been found across a range of other, present-day societies with different levels of industrial development that forms the basis of his expectation that there has been no significant trend in the degree of openness in British society for longer than the specific period of the Nuffield study. Hope's reworking of Glass's figures gives some support to this expecta-tion, but this stretches the analysis back only to a late nineteenth-century birth cohort. Penn's data are also supportive, and begin in the mid-nineteenth century, but his focus is solely on marital endogamy from a restricted sample of marriage records in one Lancashire town.[4]

Even in places where there is a stronger tradition of research into past patterns of social mobility systematic engagement with the issue of social fluidity in historical context is a very recent development. In part the product of longstanding conceptual confusion, the issue is also technical one, historians having been slow to adopt the multiplicative modelling techniques standardly applied to mobility data by sociologists. Where such models have been applied to historical data the results have varied according to context. When applied here, they reveal that the distribution of opportunities in Victorian and Edwardian society was dramatically unequal. However, they also cast doubt on the prevailing assumption that there have been no trends in fluidity since the onset of mature industrialisation in Britain.

A LAND OF BOUNDLESS OPPORTUNITY?

Applying Glass's standard of 'perfect mobility' to the marriage data suggests that the degree of inequality of opportunity in Victorian and Edwardian society was profound. The Registrar-General's elite was 57 per cent self-recruiting across the period, which means that the sons of class I men were 30 times better represented in class I than they should have been on the basis of their relative weight in the general population.[5] The sons of unskilled men, on the other hand, were present in only 2 per cent of their due proportion.

Another simple indication of the degree of restriction in operation can be obtained from 'disparity ratios', which compare outflow figures to express the relative chances of men from differing backgrounds gaining, or risking, entry to the same destination.[6] In these terms, 43 per cent of elite sons followed in their fathers' class footsteps, but only 0.04 per cent of unskilled workers' sons achieved a class I position: a disparity of more than 1,000:1.

Considered over time, disparity ratios, by indicating 'whether or not changes in the structure of objective mobility opportunities are being equally reflected in the mobility experience of individuals alike',[7] do provide a measure of mobility which allows for structural context. Their use for this purpose is not entirely unproblematic, however, and most sociologists now approach the problem of characterising the associations between origins and destinations independently of the structural effects reflected in the marginal distributions of the mobility table by means of 'odds ratios'.[8]

Following Goldthorpe, an odds ratio can be thought of as representing the outcome of a competition 'between men of different class origins to achieve – or avoid – one rather than another location within the class structure'.[9] A resultant value of 1 would reflect an equal competition: that there was effectively no association between the respective origin and destination classes involved. When the relative chances of men from the top and the bottom of Victorian and Edwardian society being found in class I rather than class V positions are compared, however, it turns out that those with elite backgrounds held an advantage in excess of 70,000 to 1 over those brought up in the families of the labouring poor.

STRUCTURAL CHANGE AND THE PATTERN OF MOBILITY

As Goldthorpe showed, a trend in the pattern of mobility occurring between generations – even one leading to a more mobile society – may be accounted for entirely by 'exogenous' structural forces, leaving the underlying mobility regime, or pattern of fluidity, undisturbed. In such a case, no consistent variation in a complete set of odds ratios – one for every pair of origin classes in relation to every possible pair of destination classes – would be detectable. The marriage register data are analysed and discussed in these terms in the following sections. But first it is necessary to identify how structural change might have influenced the pattern of mobility in nineteenth-century society.

The principal structural pressure on mobility rates is the process of occupational expansion and contraction within the division of labour caused by economic change. In these terms, the main sectoral shifts brought about by the development of the nineteenth-century British economy were, in fact, highly conducive to the mobility flows which can be observed in the mobility tables of the previous chapter.

The first two decades of the period under scrutiny saw the consolidation of industrial capitalism, with railway building, and the expansion of the metal-making and coal extraction industries which supported it, ushering in a period of relative stability and prosperity during the 1850s and 1860s.[10] Britain's world economic hegemony was subsequently challenged from the 1870s onwards, and throughout Europe competitive pressures gave rise to an era of 'organised' capitalism, characterised by concentration in industry, collective organisation in the labour market, the rise of bureaucratic employment structures and an expansion in the role of the state. Lash and Urry argue that in the transition from what was, much more literally than is often recognised, the 'workshop' of the world under liberal capitalism to the world's *Makler*, or 'middleman', economy, Britain reflected these developments to a much more limited extent than the German ideal-type.[11] Nevertheless, the growing concentration on commerce and services in this country only underlined the main structural shift experienced by all developed economies in this period – the rapid expansion of the tertiary sector.[12]

This is clearly evident in a comparison of census data showing the distribution of the economically active population between 1851 and 1911 (Table 3.1). The profile of agricultural employment declined dramatically, and there was a corresponding rise in the relative importance of commercial, service and transport occupations, the former almost quadrupling in size over the 60-year period.[13] The transformation was such that on the eve of the First World War there

Table 3.1   *Distribution of the economically active population by occupational sector, 1851–1911 (per cent)*

	1851	1881	1911
Agriculture	27.3	17.1	11.1
Mining, Quarrying	5.9	6.8	9.3
Manufacture	35.0	32.8	34.9
(Textiles	10.1	6.3	4.1
Metals	8.2	11.0	13.9
Clothing	8.4	4.3	3.3
Food, Drink, Tobacco	5.3	5.6	6.2
Wood	2.3	2.1	2.2
Bricks, Glass, Pottery	1.1	1.3	1.1
Paper, Printing	0.9	1.5	2.0
Chemicals, Oil, etc.)	0.6	0.8	1.2
Building and Construction	7.6	9.9	8.8
Domestic and Personal Service	2.9	2.7	3.5
Armed Services	1.0	1.5	1.7
Public Administration	1.0	1.2	2.1
Professional and subordinate services	2.5	2.9	3.2
Commerce and Finance	1.4	4.0	5.7
Transport and Communications	6.6	9.8	12.2
Total Occupied (thousands)	6,545	8,852	12,927

Source: B.R. Mitchell and P. Deane, *Abstract of British Historical Statistics*, Cambridge, 1962, p. 60.

Table 3.2 *Distribution of grooms by class and occupational category by period (per cent)*

	1839–54	1859–74	1879–94	1899–1914
I	**1.3**	**1.7**	**1.7**	**1.4**
Independent	0.9	0.9	0.7	0.3
Professional	0.4	0.8	1.0	1.1
II	**11.9**	**13.3**	**15.3**	**15.5**
Business	5.0	6.5	6.6	5.9
White-collar	2.2	2.6	4.7	5.7
Farming	4.7	4.2	4.0	3.8
III	**46.1**	**44.7**	**44.4**	**44.4**
Workshop	21.8	17.6	15.6	14.1
Capitalist	6.5	3.8	2.7	1.1
Factory	9.6	11.2	13.6	12.1
Mining	7.3	10.3	9.1	13.2
Service I	0.8	1.9	3.4	3.9
IV	**10.9**	**13.8**	**17.2**	**21.2**
Industrial	4.1	5.0	5.4	6.1
Agricultural	0.6	0.5	0.4	0.6
Service II	6.2	8.3	11.4	14.5
V	**29.8**	**26.4**	**21.5**	**17.5**

Note: For discussion of the occupational categories used in this table see chapter 4, pp. 69–70 below.

were more men employed in transport than on the land. Manufacturing's share remained constant, but within it textiles and clothing declined and those associated with some of the products of a more modern industrial, literate and consuming society expanded. Elsewhere the fuelling of such a society required that mining's share of the division of labour virtually doubled.[14]

These developments are not directly traceable in class terms from the census because, as noted previously, a social classification of occupational information was not attempted until 1911. They are, nevertheless, clearly reflected in the marginal distribution of grooms by class (Table 3.2), which shows that classes II and IV – the main destinations of those on the move between generations – expanded across the sample period, and that they did so at the expense of class V.

By no means all the labourers in the sample were agricultural workers, but the contraction of class V is principally reflective of the accelerating exodus from the countryside after the rise of foreign competition in an increasingly open market from the 1870s. Behind the expansion of class II is the growth of white-collar employment, a development which, the marriage register data suggest, was at its most rapid in the last quarter of the nineteenth century.[15] The doubling of the proportion of men found in semi-skilled employment by 1914 highlights the mixture of modern and traditional forces which underpinned the emergence of the modern economy. The most dynamic sector in class IV was the transport industry, but its most representative figure remained the driver of a horse-drawn vehicle.[16]

The other main force with the potential to cause structural mobility is demographic change. The complex interaction of factors involved in this sphere make firm conclusions difficult, but here too there is evidence of some correspondence with the changing pattern of mobility. In contrast to the demand effects of economic development, demographic behaviour – although itself inextricably bound up with economic change in this period – is principally a supply-side pressure on mobility. Recent work on fertility and class by Szreter and others has cast serious doubt on the utility of the classic social diffusion model of family size limitation.[17] Nevertheless, it seems that the basic outline of the picture painted by this model remains intact.[18] Broadly speaking, middle-class families became smaller in size in the second half of the nineteenth century than working-class families. The resulting reduction in transmission pressure for middle class jobs from within the middle-class would therefore have tended to encourage working-class upward mobility to fill the gaps, although this tendency may have been offset in part by a widening of the gap in mortality rates between different occupational groups over the same period.[19]

TRENDS IN SOCIAL FLUIDITY

Was the rising rate of mobility in Victorian and Edwardian England merely a reflection of such structural forces, or were social barriers genuinely falling? The large number of odds ratios to be considered before a conclusion can be reached – 100 in the case of a five-class framework – makes it virtually impossible to interpret the overall pattern of social fluidity with the naked eye. Log-linear modelling, a technique that has transformed the study of mobility by allowing the issue of fluidity to be subjected to rigorous analysis, offers a solution to this problem.[20]

Log-linear models provide a way of testing statistically whether a complete set of odds ratios is consistent with hypotheses about the association between origin and destination class, and whether this association changes over time. The full procedure involves moving through a hierarchy of models, beginning with the simplest possible then building up in terms of complexity by adding associations and interactions. Each new model is tested against the cell values actually observed to determine 'goodness of fit', the aim being to identify the most 'parsimonious' configuration that will satisfactorily account for the existing frequencies.[21]

Given prevailing assumptions about the long-term pattern of fluidity in modern societies, however, it is the performance of what is termed the 'constant social fluidity' (CnSF) model that is of primary interest. This is the model that specifies that the set of odds ratios characterising the association between origin and destination remains identical across cohorts.[22] Effectively, therefore, this corresponds to a situation – as in postwar Britain – in which all the changes in the pattern of mobility that we can actually see occurring are accounted for by structural developments rather than any alteration to the balance of opportunities between individuals with different class origins.

Table 3.3 shows that the CnSF model achieves a very substantial reduction in the deviation (G^2) when compared with the conditional independence model – introduced here as a baseline only, as it posits the highly unlikely scenario of there being no association at all between origin and destination class. However, according to model testing conventions, a deviation of 147.6 with 48 degrees of freedom does not represent a particularly good fit.

This establishes that corresponding odds ratios are not identical between marriage cohorts, and that the underlying mobility regime therefore differs over time. Yet this result does not infer anything about *how* it changes. The variation could be random and inconsistent rather than reflective of a trend. To test for trends we can apply the uniform difference, or 'unidiff', model introduced by Erikson and Goldthorpe in *The Constant Flux*. As its name implies, this model stipulates that the odds ratios for the four different marriage cohorts 'differ uniformly (though not by a constant amount) in moving together either towards or away from independence'.[23]

Table 3.3 *Results of fitting the conditional independence, constant social fluidity, and uniform difference models to intergenerational mobility tables over four marriage cohorts, and parameter estimates for the model of uniform change in association between class origins and destinations*

Model	G^2	BIC	df	p	Δ
Con. Ind.	6113.0	5523.0	64	0.00	32.9
CnSF	147.6	−295.5	48	0.00	4.1
Unidiff	71.9	−343.5	45	0.01	2.5

β Parameter estimates of the model of uniform change by cohort*	2	3	4
	−0.06	−0.14	−0.31

Note:
* Parameters for cohort 1 (the earliest) are set at zero.

When applied to the data, the outcome is a highly significant improvement in fit over the CnSF model. Moreover the size and direction of the movement in the Beta parameter values under the model demonstrate that the trend confirmed by the model is in fact indicative of a strong uniform change towards greater fluidity. What this means is that, at the same time as it was responsible for more mobility, the consolidation and development of industrial capitalism in England were generating a more open society into the bargain.

FLUIDITY IN CONTEXT

Again, however, the possibility remains that this result is not fully representative, that significant contextual variation might be obscured. It may be that one or two districts display the observed global tendency towards increasingly fluidity so strongly that, in the averaging process, stagnation, undulation, or even a weak trend in the opposite direction elsewhere are being masked. What light, then, does a disaggregation of the pattern of fluidity by district-type throw on this matter, and on the various theories of mobility and economic change?

When the same modelling procedures are applied to each district-type separately, the results provide an unequivocal answer to the first part of this question (Table 3.4). The trend towards a more open

Table 3.4   *Improvement in fit (ΔG^2) over the constant social fluidity model and parameter estimates for the model of uniform change in association between class origins and destinations by marriage cohort in four district-types*

District		β Parameter estimates for cohort		
	ΔG^2	2	3	4
Industrial	14.8	–0.06	–0.08	–0.28
Urban	15.6	–0.02	–0.18	–0.33
Urban-rural	12.3	–0.00	–0.13	–0.25
Rural	18.2	–0.16	–0.19	–0.34

Note:
Given that the uniform difference model takes up 3 degrees of freedom over the CnSF model, the improvement in each case is significant at the 5% level.

society was indeed universal. In each case the unidiff model both fits significantly better than the model for constant social fluidity and reveals a strong and consistent trend towards greater social fluidity.

In order to answer the second part of the question, the analysis must be extended to consider how the mobility regimes of the different districts stood in relation to each other, and whether there were changes in their ranking over time. To look at their comparative standing across the period as a whole, we can again employ the unidiff model, but in this case to determine whether it can detect a change in the odds ratios from district to district, rather than between marriage cohorts. The result, shown in Table 3.5, is striking. Starting from the assumption that the rural context is likely to have been the most rigid, and that this should therefore be the baseline district, we find that there is indeed a very clear and consistent trend in the pattern of fluidity between districts. As the Beta parameters under the model show, the urban-rural context was more open than the rural, the urban more than the urban rural, and most fluid of all was industrial environment.

This evolutionary framework is one that would seem to lend considerable weight to the thesis of industrialism. Yet there remains the issue of whether this particular hierarchy of openness prevailed right across the sample period.[24] In order to explore this question, we can adopt an approach which combines the analysis of changes in time and space. Table 3.6 shows the outcome of a series of models, adapted from the unidiff model, which consider the pattern of association

Table 3.5 *Results of fitting the conditional independence, common social
fluidity, and uniform difference models to intergenerational class mobility tables
in four district types, and parameter estimates for the model of uniform change in
association between class origins and destinations*

Model	G^2	BIC	df	p	Δ
Con. Ind.	5456.0	4865.0	64	0.00	29.8
CmSF	113.4	−329.7	48	0.00	3.3
Unidiff	71.6	−343.8	45	0.01	2.4

β Parameter estimates of the model of uniform change by district*	2	3	4
	−0.11	−0.19	−0.24

Note:
* Parameters for district 1 (rural) are set at zero.

between origins and destinations by district-type and marriage cohort
simultaneously.[25]

The best fitting model in this series is clearly model 5, which
describes a common trend in all four districts and stable differences
between districts over time.[26] In other words, this model suggests
that the cross-sample hierarchy of fluidity by context illustrated in
Table 3.5 prevailed throughout the period. It compares favourably
with model 3, which posits variation in the pattern of association
between districts but not over time, model 4, which indicates change
over time but does not permit the pattern of association to vary

Table 3.6 *Results of fitting different models of social fluidity to
inter-generational class mobility by district type and marriage cohort*

Model	G^2	df	BIC
1. Conditional independence	5637.8	256	3275
2. Constant and common social fludity	408.3	240	−1807
3. Uniform difference between districts	371.4	237	−1816
4. Uniform change over time	353.6	237	−1834
5. Uniform change over time and between districts	313.2	234	−1847
6. Uniform difference between all tables	308.5	225	−1769

between districts in each period, and also model 6, which allows for different trends in each district.

An examination of the parameter estimates of this last model (see Table 3.7) confirms that the patterns of development in each of the four districts ran very much in parallel. They show both rising fluidity in each district and a more or less consistent ranking of the districts across the period. Within this overall framework, however, it can be seen that there was still a small degree of fluctuation in the relationship between the districts. First, the rural and then the urban and urban-rural districts made gains on industrial society as change here slowed down in the 1880s and 1890s. From this point on, the urban and industrial environments display almost identical levels of fluidity, although the industrial context does manage to reassert itself in relation to the other two district-types during the surge in fluidity which was experienced in all contexts at the beginning of the twentieth century.

STRUCTURE AND FLUIDITY

With the finding of a 'national' trend towards greater openness to the fore we can speculate about what the pattern of *de facto* movement between classes might have looked like had there been no change in the underlying pattern of fluidity across the period. In other words, how much, and what kinds of, mobility would there have been if the only forces acting on the relationship between classes were structural ones? This is a similar question to the one posed by Goldthorpe in *Social Mobility and Class Structure in Modern Britain* about the mobility regimes of different nations, but one which instead compares the effects of change over time.[27]

Table 3.7 *Parameter estimates for the model of uniform change in fluidity between all district types and marriage cohorts (model 6 in Table 3.6), using cohort 1 in the rural district type as the reference category*

District type	Cohort			
	1	2	3	4
Rural	X	–0.18	–0.20	–0.34
Urban-Rural	–0.20	–0.19	–0.33	–0.45
Urban	–0.27	–0.26	–0.42	–0.59
Industrial	–0.32	–0.38	–0.40	–0.59

Such 'counterfactual' propositions are a familiar, although because of the *ceteris paribus* assumption involved, far from uncontroversial device of economic historians, who have applied them to issues ranging from the impact of railways on the economic development on nineteenth-century America to cost/benefit analysis of the British Empire.[28] Goldthorpe's pragmatic defence of their use in this type of case is that the question 'is relatively well-defined and delimited and that it appears *not* to be of a highly "context-dependent" kind'.[29]

Table 3.8 shows, in comparison to the values actually observed, the cell percentages which result when the pattern of social fluidity which characterised the 1839–54 mobility regime is built into the structural framework of the 1899–1914 mobility table. This is done using the iterative scaling procedures applied by Mosteller, by which the earlier table is transformed into one with the marginals of the later, while maintaining the odds ratios which characterise the original table.[30]

The significance of the trend towards greater fluidity in bringing about a more mobile society is very clear from this analysis. In the case of four out of the five classes, controlling for shifts in mobility chances produces differences in the outflow distributions in excess of

Table 3.8   *Class distribution of grooms by class of father. Observed rates for 1899–1914, compared with the rates which would have resulted (fitted) in 1899–1914 under the mobility regime (pattern of fluidity) prevailing in 1839–54*

Father's Class		Son's Class					
		I	II	III	IV	V	Δ
I	Observed 1899–1914	36.2	31.9	19.1	2.1	10.6	
	Fitted 1899–1914	38.3	45.6	9.4	6.7	0.0	20.4
II	Observed 1899–1914	2.5	51.7	24.4	13.5	7.9	
	Fitted 1899–1914	3.3	52.7	21.0	16.2	6.7	5.6
III	Observed 1899–1914	0.5	8.4	63.4	16.6	11.1	
	Fitted 1899–1914	0.1	7.8	74.9	10.3	6.9	11.0
IV	Observed 1899–1914	0.3	8.5	34.6	43.7	12.9	
	Fitted 1899–1914	0.4	6.9	19.6	65.2	7.9	21.6
V	Observed 1899–1914	0.2	3.6	28.9	23.0	44.4	
	Fitted 1899–1914	0.0	4.0	18.3	18.0	59.7	15.8

Note:
Δ is the dissimilarity index. This shows, in percentage terms, how much reallocation of cases would be required in order to make the distributions identical.

10 per cent, and in two cases of 20 per cent or more. Overall, it can be calculated that, under the influence of structural change alone, the total mobility rate would have only risen from 32 per cent to 34 per cent, compared to the increase to 46 per cent that actually occurred.

Among classes I and II, the changes in fluidity affected the distribution of the mobile much more than the amount of mobility *per se*. In each case the overall degree of 'opening up' was fairly marginal. The impact on the total volume of movement taking place among the working class was much greater. In the case of the semi-skilled the proportion of sons on the move at the end of the period was more than one and a half times greater than it would have been had structural influences alone been at play. For both these men and their peers from unskilled backgrounds this greater than expected amount of mobility was expressed principally in movement up into the skilled working class; the former were 75 per cent more mobile into class III than they would otherwise have been, and the latter 60 per cent.

There was somewhat less difference between 'expected' and observed rates of upward class mobility in the wider manual/non-manual sense. In part this is a function of the smaller percentages involved, and there were some quite large proportional changes in the rates of movement into class I. However, the differences in movement into the lower middle class were much less spectacular, and where the unskilled were concerned the observed rate of elevation into class II would seem to be entirely explicable in terms of structural change. Altogether then, this analysis creates the strong impression that it was within the working class that the process of declining inequality was most profound.

FACILITATORS OF FLUIDITY

What could account for a trend towards a more open society? As Kaelble suggests, the search for causal factors affecting the pattern of social fluidity must range across a number of areas.[31] Political intervention in favour of greater equality of opportunity is the main variable cited by Goldthorpe when explaining the small differences in fluidity between contemporary industrial nations which can be detected within an overall pattern of commonality.[32] However, unlike the situation in, for example, the Grand Duchy of Poznań, the nineteenth-century British state was both small and largely unobtrusive.[33] The first surge of British welfarist legislation – which Kaelble sees as reducing the

differentials in the ability of classes to deal with 'critical life situations' –
occurred during the period of the Liberal Administration which came
to power in 1906. A limited series of measures in any case, it came too
late to have affected men marrying before 1914.[34] Legislation such as
the 1894 reform of local government franchise, which saw working
people elected to local councils and the Boards of Poor Law Guardians,
brought individuals into positions of influence. But it is unclear how far
this, or the late nineteenth-century appearance of working-class factory
inspectors, magistrates and School Board members, benefited the
prospects of the class as a whole.[35] The developments traced in later
chapters suggest that the effects of meritocratic reform of the Civil
Service after 1870, as gradual and limited as this was, might have been
rather more important.[36]

Forster's 1870 Education Act is unlikely to have harmed the relative
position of working-class children. Universal provision of elementary
schooling did not, for some time, mean universal attendance, and, as
Vincent observes, the literacy rate 'had passed 60 per cent before the
State spent a farthing on education [in 1833], and had reached almost
90 per cent before it entered the field in its own right'.[37] Nevertheless,
as chapter 4 shows, much of the general rise in literacy, however generated, was concentrated in the working class, and, taken in conjunction with developments in the sphere of occupational recruitment,
seems to have been of some significance.

Neither the 1870 nor 1902 Education Act was designed to sponsor
the development of what Kaelble calls 'meritocratic mentalities'
among the predominantly working-class consumers of elementary
education. However, an initially hostile response to the new state-
sponsored education system gradually gave way to an awareness that
formal credentials were becoming more economically relevant.[38] This,
in turn, sponsored developments in school structures and curricula
which were, in fact, quite at odds with the intentions of the original
legislators.[39] In chapter 6, a further indication of this shift can be seen
in the growing sense of ambition shown by autobiographers born in
the last third of the nineteenth century.

As explained earlier, demographic developments – which Kaelble
includes in his list – are more relevant to questions of structural
mobility than fluidity. Declining family size can be a significant factor
in reducing inequalities in critical life situations, but for the large
majority this process only began towards the end of the sample
period, and in any case still left the average middle-class family with
fewer mouths to feed. Improvements in housing and health probably

did lead to declining social differentials in this sense, as did the marked rise in working-class real incomes between 1850 and 1914.[40] However, while there is good evidence of income convergence between occupational and skill groups within the working class from 1870 onwards, there is no clear indication of a similar convergence taking place between working-class and middle-class living standards.[41]

The amount of geographical mobility experienced in the nineteenth century was substantial, and workers moved more often than members of other social groups.[42] Migration, as the autobiographers demonstrate, was not always enforced or detrimental to an individual's prospects, nor did immobility necessarily indicate greater security. Nevertheless, enforced migration was, despite structures of kin and neighbourhood support, generally disruptive.[43] There are contradictory indicators as far as changes in the rate of internal migration over time are concerned. Urban working-class communities clearly became more settled and began to mature from the 1880s onwards. On the other hand, economic pressures visited on agriculture in the 1870s created a new exodus from the countryside, the railways, which became more affordable in this period, made geographical mobility easier, and turnover rates among the poorest members of the urban community remained high.[44]

As already suggested, there is, in the process of urbanisation itself, a potential, though perhaps temporary and confined to periods of rapid growth, for greater fluidity. In Waller's assessment, 'the urban social stratification is more intricate and fluid ... the heterogeneity of the citizens is more marked in origins, opinions and behaviour'.[45] Certainly, the concentration and flow of both people and information in towns – broadening horizons, increasing expectations, offering a greater range of more diverse occupations – contrasted strongly with the more hidebound structures and traditions of the countryside.

The urban/industrial environment was also the base for a range of developments in the occupational sphere, which must be counted among the most fruitful sources of the trend towards greater fluidity revealed in the preceding analysis. Crucially, the occupational composition of classes, and the character of the occupations within them, changed over the course of this period in ways that encouraged more open recruitment across class and status barriers. It is on this particular point that the evidence used in this study can offer something more than generalised observation, and a more extensive discussion of these developments forms the basis of the next chapter.

CONCLUSION

The analyses presented in this chapter have confirmed that the increasing rates of interchange between classes in the period 1839–1914 cannot be attributed to changes in the structure of objective mobility opportunities alone. Underlying the shifting pattern of *de facto* mobility was a regular and generalised process of equalisation in the life-chances of men from different social origins. Breaking the sample down according to economic and cultural context strongly confirms the national character of this trend.

If economic efficiency is partly a product of the rational distribution of factors of production, human as well as material, then these findings seem to suggest that there are more fruitful avenues to go down in search of explanations for Britain's economic decline. Despite the fact that those in critical positions within the economy cannot be singled out, the pattern of rising fluidity should have assisted rather than hindered the position.

On the other hand, there is likely to be a threshold effect involved in such a relationship, for what has been established here is a trend *towards* greater fluidity. While inequalities of opportunity underwent a marked reduction in scale over the 75-five year period under scrutiny, the final outcome was by no means an open society. Thus, even in 1914 the sons of elite men were still 1,000 times better placed than men from unskilled working-class backgrounds in the competition to achieve class I status and avoid a position in class V; on either side of the major class divide the sons of class II men were still 16 times more likely to gain access to the lower middle class, while avoiding class III, than the sons of skilled manual workers; and between those from the top and bottom of the working class, the sons of skilled men remained six times better placed when in competition with the sons of unskilled men for skilled rather than unskilled futures.

Nevertheless, the findings presented here are, on the face of it, sharply at odds with the results of Goldthorpe's work on contemporary Britain, and his suggestion that the constant pattern of social fluidity he uncovered in the twentieth century was a phenomenon of longer standing. The thesis of a commonality in mobility regimes across time and place in industrial society does allow for episodic variation, but the smooth rhythms of change in the marriage data suggest something more akin to consistent flux than a sudden tremor.[46] On the other hand, the results clearly do lend credence to the claims of the modernisation theorists, although it could be argued that the detailed topography of change is not entirely consonant with their expectations: industrial society was the most open of all across the period as a whole, but came under pressure in the last quarter of nineteenth century when the urban context mounted a serious challenge for this title.

This would suggest that both the main theories about the relationship between economic development and mobility ought to consider history more seriously. By doing so, it becomes possible to appreciate that each contains essential truths, and indeed how, in the specific case of modern Britain, the results of the Nuffield survey might, after all, be reconciled with this study's findings. This though is the theme of the final chapter of this book. In the meantime, the reasons behind the trend towards a more open society before 1914 require further exploration.

4 Occupations, Classes and Mobility

Occupational titles form the basic raw material of this study. Extrapolation from the job descriptions recorded in the marriage registers and autobiographies to analyses of 'class' mobility, can be justified on the grounds that 'occupations are at once the most obvious and the most effective predictor of differential location within the structure of social inequality'.[1] Most of the major twentieth-century mobility surveys start from a similar premise. However, the assumption that occupation and class are interchangeable is by no means uncontentious. A target of the recent revision of traditional approaches to class analysis within both history and sociology,[2] it has also drawn objections from within the more specific field of mobility studies. According to one critic of Goldthorpe's work, for example, a neglect of the occupational processes underlying patterns of class movement has led him to underestimate the 'true' degree of social flux operating in contemporary British society.[3]

There is a certain amount of mispresentation involved in this particular criticism, and, more generally, it is important to recognise that the 'processes which condition occupation' may after all be *class* processes.[4] Nevertheless, it remains the case that the occupational components of classes, and of class mobility, need to be taken seriously. Closer attention to the world of work, as the major defining framework of the 'social' in this case, will provide a clearer picture of the relationship between industrialisation and mobility.

Accordingly, this chapter seeks to address two general questions. First, from the perspective of class formation, what are the implications of an occupational focus for earlier conclusions about the identities of, and relationships between, social groups? Does the averaging process hide a far more complex range of experiences which might imply greater flux, or, as suggested by Kocka, and by critics of the labour aristocracy thesis, more pervasive, potentially fragmentary, affiliations centred on 'vertical' associations of craft or industry?[5] Second, having established that the process of industrialisation in its broadest, long-term meaning is associated with a general loosening of social bonds, both in terms of *de facto* mobility *and* fluidity, what is it about this relationship which is operational?

The history of work has hitherto been constrained to the extent that it has been largely able to offer only static, cross-sectional studies of particular industries, companies and institutions. A major dynamic of economic change – the movement of the working population itself between sectors of employment – has been missing. What does such a perspective reveal about where the 'chains binding men to their hereditary condition' began to break, and why this was a process which reflected not just a redistribution in the number of jobs in different classes, but also in the relative life chances of their incumbents' families?

OCCUPATIONAL IDENTITY

Occupations and classes

For men like Thomas McLauchlan, born the son of a miner in Ryhope, County Durham in 1888, following his father down the pit was just part of life's 'normal progression'.[6] When, in 1824, the death of his fisherman father left a family of six without a breadwinner, the 11-year-old James Scott was himself 'sent to the fishing' on the Moray Firth, 'a crew taking me for pity's sake to begin seafaring life as a calling'.[7] In the late 1830s, George Mitchell, the son of a master mason in Somerset, was refused an apprenticeship by his father because his work as a farm labourer allowed the family to benefit from a truck system by which his mother could obtain produce on the strength of his wages. Despite this setback, however, Mitchell succeeded in entering the trade – one without the community associations of a mining or fishing village – before his twentieth birthday.[8]

On the face of it, a significant amount of occupational reproduction within nineteenth-century families is to be expected. This was a period in which many forms of economic activity were locally specific, and in which formal educational credentials played a minor role in recruitment outside of the professions and a small number of bureaucratised occupations.[9] Nevertheless, when put to the test, the scale of replication at this basic level is startling. Applying the Registrar-General's framework, the marriage register sample contains 438 separate occupational unit groups. Although some groups are more heavily represented than others, this, in theory, allows for a possible 191,844 different origin and destination combinations. Yet across the whole sample the same occupation was handed down from one generation to the next in over 40 per cent of families (Figure 4.1) and, while the practice was in decline throughout the period, not until the first decade of the twentieth century did the proportions fall below this figure. A comparison with rates of class stability would suggest that social identities were, to a considerable extent, built on more specific occupational identities, although it also seems clear that the former became relatively more important over time as a result of a faster rate of disaggregation at the occupational level. With some predictable variation – for example, occupational continuities were generally stronger in the countryside than in the towns – this was a process common to all classes in all districts.[10]

There is, however, one aspect of this analysis which suggests that the estimate of overall occupational stability is probably exaggerated. This concerns the degree of occupational differentiation in the data. The often amorphous, single-term professional titles given in the registers may well be better indicators of occupational identity than more refined descriptions,[11] but in some instances it is clear that they

Figure 4.1   *Total mobility rate (occupational and class) by period*

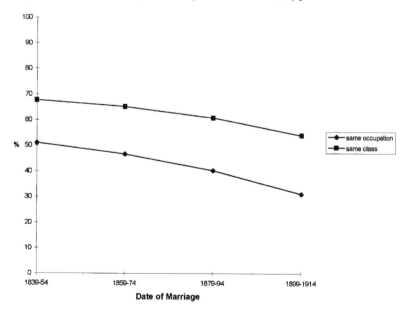

might give a misleading impression of solidarities at this level. This is particularly the case with the all-encompassing term 'labourer', which not only dominates class V, but whose weight in the sample as a whole tends to magnify the overall impression of occupational inertia.

Occupational Categories

How best to make sense of the volume of information carried by those data at the occupational level is not entirely clear. To proceed on the basis of over 400 occupational groups is clearly impractical. The Registrar-General's system of occupational orders could be employed, but this would complicate matters because it is cross-class in character, and because some groups cannot reliably be allocated according to industry.

The questions raised at the beginning of the chapter require that the framework adopted should illuminate the processes associated with the development of an industrial society. Classically, in terms of the changing division of labour, this is seen to involve the basic sectoral transformation loosely applied in the discussion of context in the previous chapter: the decline of 'primary', agricultural occupations and the rise of manufacturing and services. Beyond this, traditional views of industrialisation as a revolutionary process have stressed the transformation of the work process through mechanisation and the division of labour, and the movement of production into the increasingly bureaucratised and scientifically managed factory.[12]

Since the mid-1970s, however, a new orthodoxy has emerged, which stresses the complex reality of 'combined and uneven development' that lies behind such a model.[13] It has been shown that in almost every sphere of production old forms and practices co-existed with the novel, and that large numbers of people continued to be employed in more traditional industries.[14] Within manufacturing, 'handicraft' production often survived where the machine could not supplant the initiative, experience and dexterity of men and women, where it remained more profitable to continue employing workers in their own homes, and where mechanisation in one part of the production process could not be extended to another. The factory destroyed skills, but it also created them. Some contained machine minders who were able to act like craftsmen, while others employed workers whose skills were indispensable, and could still therefore be counted as genuine artisans.[15]

In an attempt to accommodate both these models, the discussion throughout the remainder of this chapter will draw on an analysis of mobility extending from a division of the five classes into 14 occupational categories. Class I is therefore divided into those who were financially *independent* and those in established *professional* or higher salaried positions. Class II has been split into a *business* sector comprising the classic petty bourgeoisie, *white-collar* employees, and a separate category of *farmers*. Within the large class of skilled manual occupations five distinctive groups have been identified according to the characteristic form of industrial process or mode of organisation involved: a *workshop* or 'craft' category, where production was typically small-scale and unmechanised, and based on the handicraft skill of artisans; a *capitalist* sector, where work was mostly carried out in small unmechanised units, or domestically, but as part of a subdivided process of production dependent on a localised structure of merchant capital; *factory*, where a subdivided, mostly mechanised, production process was carried out in larger, integrated units; *mining*, a category dominated by face-workers in coal mines; and a 'new' *service* sector, a group composed in the main of the 'uniformed working class' who operated the new transport, policing and communications bureaucracies. The smaller semi-skilled sector is divided into an *industrial* category made up of factory, mill and mine workers; an *agricultural* sector composed of farm specialists; and a more traditional 'old' *service* sector dominated by horse-drawn transport workers and gardeners, but including groups such as soldiers and domestic servants. Due to the overwhelming predominance of the anonymous 'labourer', no attempt has been made to differentiate between the unskilled.

This scheme is put into operation in Tables 4.1 and 4.2, while the mobility profiles of some of the main, single-occupation groups they contain are shown in Appendix 2. The importance of occupation to class stability and coherence is again plain to see. But only in a minority of cases was the relative importance of lateral mobility – movement into or from another occupational group within a class – negligible. As others have suggested, the extremely high rates of self-recruitment among farmers made them something of an 'hereditary caste', cutting them off from the rest of the middle class,[16] and it seems clear that semi-skilled occupational groups maintained far stronger relations with other classes than their own. Yet, at the same time, a third of those taking up clerical work from other occupational backgrounds, 40 per cent of all 'outsiders' in shopkeeping, and 50 per cent of first-generation manufacturers, came from elsewhere within class II. Sixty

Table 4.1 Occupational sector distribution of grooms by occupational sector of fathers (percentage by row)

Father's sector	Son's sector														n	%
	inde	pro	bus	whc	farm	work	cap	fact	mine	serv I	indu	agri	serv II	lab		
Independent	27.8	13.0	12.0	22.2	2.8	8.3	0.9	4.6	0.9	0.0	1.9	0.0	2.8	2.8	108	(1.1)
Professional	11.0	34.0	11.0	16.0	2.0	5.0	0.0	9.0	0.0	3.0	1.0	0.0	3.0	5.0	100	(1.0)
Business	1.1	2.3	35.7	9.5	2.6	18.1	1.6	7.0	2.4	2.6	3.0	0.1	7.2	6.7	697	(6.8)
White-collar	1.1	3.0	9.6	29.3	2.2	17.4	0.7	10.7	2.6	3.0	4.1	0.0	9.6	6.7	270	(2.6)
Farming	1.0	0.6	11.2	3.1	41.0	9.0	1.0	2.7	3.2	2.1	2.8	0.9	9.6	12.0	815	(8.0)
Workshop	0.3	0.2	4.4	3.0	1.3	50.1	1.7	10.5	3.6	1.8	4.9	0.2	7.2	11.1	1926	(18.9)
Capitalist	0.0	0.0	2.3	1.1	0.2	6.1	56.6	5.9	6.8	1.4	4.8	0.2	3.4	11.1	440	(4.3)
Factory	0.2	0.1	3.2	4.2	0.2	10.0	1.4	54.8	6.2	1.5	5.7	0.0	5.4	7.1	959	(9.4)
Mining	0.1	0.0	1.4	1.0	0.1	5.1	0.8	7.7	69.6	1.4	2.4	0.0	2.3	8.0	784	(7.7)
Service I	0.0	0.6	3.6	4.8	0.6	16.7	0.6	11.9	6.0	26.8	3.6	0.6	8.3	16.1	168	(1.6)
Industrial	0.2	0.0	2.2	3.5	0.2	13.2	1.1	12.8	7.9	2.6	32.5	0.2	10.4	13.0	453	(4.4)
Agricultural	0.0	0.0	3.8	2.9	3.8	9.6	0.0	4.8	2.9	0.0	2.9	26.0	21.2	22.1	104	(1.0)
Service II	0.6	0.0	3.7	3.2	1.1	14.1	1.4	8.1	4.1	4.8	3.7	0.3	42.8	12.1	629	(6.2)
Labouring	0.0	0.0	1.4	0.6	0.8	7.5	1.2	4.2	6.5	1.8	3.5	0.4	10.2	61.7	2757	(27.0)
n	73	83	608	385	428	1782	370	1177	1010	249	523	54	1018	2450	10210	
%	(0.7)	(0.8)	(6.0)	(3.8)	(4.2)	(17.5)	(3.6)	(11.5)	(9.9)	(2.4)	(5.1)	(0.5)	(10.0)	(24.0)		

Table 4.2   Occupational sector composition of grooms by occupational sector of fathers (percentage by column)

Father's sector	inde	pro	bus	whc	farm	work	cap	fact	mine	serv I	indu	agri	serv II	lab	n	%
Independent	41.1	16.9	2.1	6.2	0.7	0.5	0.3	0.4	0.1	0.0	0.4	0.0	0.3	0.1	108	(1.1)
Professional	15.1	41.0	1.8	4.2	0.5	0.3	0.0	0.8	0.0	1.2	0.2	0.0	0.3	0.2	100	(1.0)
Business	11.0	19.3	41.0	17.1	4.2	7.1	3.0	4.2	1.7	7.2	4.0	1.9	4.9	1.9	697	(6.8)
White-collar	4.1	9.6	4.3	20.5	1.4	2.6	0.5	2.5	0.7	3.2	2.1	0.0	2.6	0.7	270	(2.6)
Farming	11.0	6.0	15.0	6.5	78.0	4.1	2.2	1.9	2.6	6.8	4.4	13.0	7.7	4.0	815	(8.0)
Workshop	6.8	3.6	13.8	15.1	5.8	54.1	8.6	17.2	6.8	13.7	18.0	7.4	13.7	8.7	1926	(18.9)
Capitalist	0.0	0.0	1.6	1.3	0.2	1.5	67.3	2.2	3.0	2.4	4.0	1.9	1.5	2.0	440	(4.3)
Factory	2.7	1.2	5.1	10.4	0.5	5.4	3.5	44.7	5.8	5.6	10.5	0.0	5.1	2.8	959	(9.4)
Mining	1.4	0.0	1.8	2.1	0.2	2.2	1.6	5.1	54.1	4.4	3.6	0.0	1.8	2.6	784	(7.7)
Service I	0.0	1.2	1.0	2.1	0.2	1.6	0.3	1.7	1.0	18.1	1.1	1.9	1.4	1.1	168	(1.6)
Industrial	1.4	0.0	1.6	4.2	0.2	3.4	1.4	4.9	3.6	4.8	28.1	1.9	4.6	2.4	453	(4.4)
Agricultural	0.0	0.0	0.7	0.8	0.9	0.6	0.0	0.4	0.3	0.0	0.6	50.0	2.2	0.9	104	(1.0)
Service II	5.5	0.0	3.8	5.2	1.6	5.0	2.4	4.3	2.6	12.0	4.4	3.7	26.4	3.1	629	(6.2)
Labouring	0.0	1.2	6.4	4.4	5.4	11.7	8.9	9.8	17.8	20.5	18.5	18.5	27.7	69.4	2757	(27.0)
n	73	83	608	385	428	1782	370	1177	1010	249	523	54	1018	2450	10210	
%	(0.7)	(0.8)	(6.0)	(3.8)	(4.2)	(17.5)	(3.6)	(11.5)	(9.9)	(2.4)	(5.1)	(0.5)	(10.0)	(24.0)		

per cent of those not taking up their fathers' occupation in handicraft moved into another job in class III, and while only 20 per cent with fathers in service employment in this class were likely to be occupationally stable, two-thirds could expect to find a position of equivalent status. Even at the other end of the spectrum, among the formidably immobile miners and potters, there was at least as much horizontal as downward mobility.

Nor is there anything in these figures to disturb fundamentally the general conclusions reached earlier about class identities in the wider sense. In all categories the chance of exchanging a working-class past for a middle-class future was slim. At the level of more specific occupational groups, there is, inevitably, more variation. Printers', policemen's and soldiers' sons, for example, left the working class in proportions ranging from 18 to 29 per cent. Even so, the elite still remained a far-off vista for all men with working-class backgrounds. Several working-class groups recruited middle-class sons at rates in excess of 20 per cent. Within grain milling, brewing and also printing, this probably reflects the fact, undetectable in the data, that a proportion of the people declaring these general occupational titles would have been businessmen rather than employees. In most cases, however, downwardly mobile sons from non-manual backgrounds accounted for no more than 15 per cent of the workforce.

Although several occupations in class II do show signs of a broader-based middle-class identity, in almost every case this has to be considered alongside the fact that a sizeable proportion of sons were lost to the working class. Generally speaking, men with fathers in white-collar occupations had the least favourable prospects, although the sons of schoolteachers, for example, were rather more secure than the sons of men in clerical employment. With the exception of publicans – a somewhat marginal group on this evidence[17] – the business sector was generally more stable, as well as significantly better insulated from the pressures below. The sons of shopkeepers, merchants and manufacturers had a better than even chance of being in a middle-class job at the time of marriage, while those who managed to follow in their fathers' footsteps formed part of a peer group which was predominantly middle-class by origin.

The two upper-middle-class categories of propertied and professional men shared broadly similar outflow and inflow profiles. The sons of the former were more likely to be downwardly mobile, but the chances of their *déclassement* being temporary were presumably higher. Wealth was also apparently more accessible, or rather less closed, to the upwardly mobile sons of workers than the culture and credentials of the professions, which took 93 per cent of their recruits from the middle class.

An Aristocracy of Labour?

First impressions, then, would seem to confirm Kocka in his contention that occupational solidarities could threaten class allegiances. In each of the five classes rates of occupational immobility clearly exceeded those for class immobility. Apart from the possibility that the data exaggerate occupational stability, however, it also shows the relative importance of extra-occupational movement to have been substantial. Discounting the problematic class V, mobility rates inside classes ranged between 62 and 81 per cent of the numbers remaining occupationally immobile. In no case did those on the move in this sense constitute less than one quarter of all those who became occupationally mobile. And if social affiliations in the broader sense are considered, class identities were considerably stronger: men from middle-class backgrounds who were occupationally mobile inside classes I and II outnumbered their immobile colleagues by two to one, and even if class V is included, the mobile sons of working-class men remaining in manual employment were in a clear majority over those taking up their fathers' occupation. But the argument about the primacy of occupation would itself seem to rest on a somewhat dubious premise. An antagonistic relationship between occupational and class identity cannot simply be assumed. As Hobsbawm has argued, 'the existence of vertical divisions within the working class does not prove that they are more significant than horizontal ones'. The sectional demarcation struggles in the shipyards about which Reid writes were, he contends, 'disputes for monopoly rights, i.e. for artisans defending their status or those with a chance of acquiring it, for recognition as members of a superior stratum'.[18]

The evidence does provide some support, most especially perhaps in the rate of exchange between handicraft occupations, for the notion of a wider skilled identity implicit in the labour aristocracy theory. As to the relationship between this group and other strata and classes, however, the analysis in chapter 2 suggest no clear pattern of better prospects, or reduced exposure to risk, among skilled men.

This, though, was evidence from a very much more broadly defined group than would normally pass for an aristocracy of labour. Yet even with greater occupational definition there are limits to the extent to which this elite and its behaviour can be addressed. In the first place, the question of membership rests on a number of further defining characteristics – including wage rates, conditions of work and wider cultural associations – which is simply not available for the 8,000 or so skilled individuals in the marriage sample. Secondly, there is the technical problem of identifying small masters within the data, leading to a possible underestimation of class mobility, although this issue is, in any case, clouded by the conceptual uncertainties of the labour aristocracy theory's own proponents as to what, precisely, should count as upward mobility.

With these qualifications to the fore, the best that can be done is to examine those particular occupational groups which are the most likely candidates for inclusion. If, for example, the membership of Hobsbawm's 'super aristocracy' between the 1840s and the First World War is considered,[19] some degree of differentiation is revealed. Figure 4.2 shows that those with fathers in these occupations were 50 per cent more likely to move into class II than other skilled workers' sons, and 100 per cent more likely than men from the working class as a whole. In terms of numbers, however, this still meant fewer than one in eight labour-aristocrat children made such a journey. Similarly, members of this composite group and their sons were also better protected than others against dilution or loss of status by association with unskilled labour, but in neither sense can it be argued that they were insulated from the rest of the working class.

Figure 4.2 *Labour aristocrat mobility and recruitment*

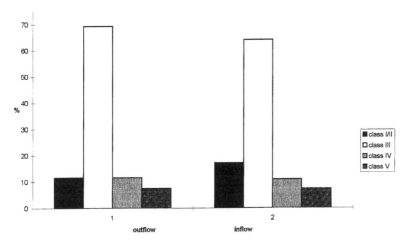

OCCUPATIONAL SUCCESSION

The construction of a career is a complex affair involving the interaction of individual choice with cultural pressure and structural constraint. The private and subjective aspects of this process are explored in a later chapter. Here the focus is on the more impersonal forces shaping movement and stability, beginning with an examination of why the tendency for sons to follow fathers was stronger in some occupational groups than in others. According to Hout, 'there is no one comprehensive reason for high (or low) immobility in an occupation', but much, he suggests, will hinge on its desirability, whether opportunities for sons are plentiful, and how far it possesses 'structural attributes favourable to inheritance'.[20]

Employment Structures and Kinship Recruitment

The analysis of the autobiographers' careers in chapter 6 confirms that fathers continued to play a central role in negotiating their sons' entry into the labour market throughout the period. In poorly paid, unstable or low-status occupations sons might have been better off searching out their own opportunities,[21] but otherwise, for a father to make provision for a son to follow in his own occupational footsteps was at once the most obvious and direct solution to the problem of finding employment with good prospects. In the first instance, then, we might expect the mobility profiles of particular occupations to reflect their tractability in terms of the ability of incumbents to regulate access in favour of kin, and that this would vary according to the labour processes, patterns of employment relations and forms of business organisation involved.

On this basis, we might also expect to find a particularly favourable basis for inter-generational succession in handicraft occupations where, inherent in the possession of genuine skill, was a degree of power over its transmission; where the characteristically small scale of workshop production and the interpersonal nature of working relationships helped facilitate family preference in the allocation of places; and where patrimonial policies were often negotiated with employers and institutionally enshrined in union rule books. 'Every Sheffield craftsman would feel it an intolerable grievance not to be able to bring his own son into his trade,' the Webbs noted in 1911; while the masons 'push their sons forward as rapidly as possible' and 'have been known to bring as many as six or seven sons to the trade'.[22]

The statistics certainly bear out the Webbs in the case of these two particular examples. The sons of Sheffield cutlers and edge tool makers took up their fathers' occupation in almost 60 per cent of cases, and a similar proportion of all masons in the sample reported having the same occupation as their father. However, while still substantial, rates of occupational continuity across the handicraft sector as a whole were much lower than this, averaging out at one in three, and although 50 per cent of craftsmen's sons did end up following a trade of some kind,[23] to follow the same occupation as one's father was more common in the domestic trades, mining and even factory employment.

A similar disparity between immobility rates in the trades and in skilled factory work was found by Anderson in his work on mid-nineteenth-century Lancashire, and by Chapman and Abbot who surveyed the same county in 1913.[24] The relatively high wages of the cotton mills were clearly an important factor here, as they also seem to have been in the Sheffield and Black Country heavy trades, and among skilled workers in the pottery industry.[25]

However, systems of kinship recruitment were also a feature of many factory-based occupations. Contemporary views of the emerging factory system may have stressed that 'for large-scale production on modern lines, a free circulation of labour was required',[26] but as late as 1915 a Board of Trade enquiry into apprenticeship and industrial training reported that most engineering firms gave preference to their employees' sons.[27] As Joyce has shown, family employment was used by employers in the northern textile mills as an important means of integrating their workforces.[28] 'Permitting workers to treat the workplace as an extension of the family', writes Vincent, 'reinforced the paternalism which employers were trying to foster.' Allowing employees some discretion over recruitment sponsored loyalty and discipline and helped stabilise industrial relations. It also ensured employers got the type of worker they wanted at minimum cost.[29]

The clearest cases of a link between low rates of inter-generational continuity and an inability to regulate access from within are to be found in service sector employment. In class III this category is mainly represented by men working in the new bureaucracies created by the railway companies, the Post Office and the police force. Taking the armed services as their cue, these were large, impersonal organisations which, while offering the unique prospect of a job for life, and perks ranging from clothing to pensions, subjected their uniformed workforces to military-style discipline.[30] By the 1850s policemen and postmen were recruited, at least partly, by way of open examination.[31] The tendency towards formal credentialism was less marked on the railways where, although *de facto* literacy and numeracy were required in order to understand timetables and rule books, systems of director patronage still held sway.[32] But by whichever method, selection was firmly at the discretion of the employer. Having gained entry, workers were entitled to embark on elaborate systems of promotion, but once more the decision as to how far and how fast they travelled lay with their superiors.[33] The experience of David Barr indicates that kinship networks could still operate in such contexts,[34] but the fact that only 13 per cent of railway men, 5 per cent of postmen and 7 per cent of policemen were sons of the same would suggest they were of limited scope.

Occupational identities were weakest of all among the growing numbers of administrative, managerial and professional workers in middle-class service employment. Only one in ten of the nation's male white-collar workforce shared the same occupational title as his father, and the chances that his own son would do the same were no greater. Clerks, who formed the bulk of this workforce, were recruited by a mixture of patronage and the more openly competitive devices of the employment agencies, the 'situations vacant' columns of news-papers, and examinations.[35] In the more informal environment of the counting house, or in the security-conscious world of banking and insurance, family connections may have been more important. In London, for example, Booth found that commercial firms often gave preference to the sons of their employees, and Anderson confirms that some Liverpool houses also maintained a tradition of family employment.[36] However, the sample figures show that only one in six clerks' sons took up a similar career to that of their fathers, while almost 95 per cent of men in clerical positions were outsiders.

Self-recruitment and succession rates in management were lower still. These are partly explained by the late emergence of a significant managerial stratum in British industry, which is reflected by the small numbers of managers in the sample, but would also seem to support Savage *et al.*'s assessment of the inherent weaknesses of this group in Britain.[37] Owing to the characteristic development of the firm in the nineteenth century and the colonisation of the educational system by professionals, they argue, British managers remained subordinate to their employers and dependent on unstoreable 'organisation assets'. The other side of this argument – that the professions developed a more distinctive and cohesive presence through their manipulation of cultural capital and their links with the state[38] – is also borne out by the data. With the exception of Anglican clergy, rates of direct occupational succession among the established professions were not especially high. But as a group, two-fifths of those in higher professional positions were themselves sons of professional men.

Career Stage

Alongside craftsmen, another apparent anomaly in these figures concerns the surprisingly uncertain prospects of men whose fathers were in business, or had property and capital. It is here, 'for reasons related to legal inheritance and to socialisation'[39] that we might expect to find the firmest basis of all for the maintenance of security and status between generations. Yet just one in four grooms whose fathers were independently wealthy could report the same of themselves. And while there was, as Bechhofer and Elliot suggest,[40] a substantial self-reproduced core at the heart of the petty bourgeoisie, direct succession rates in business were similarly unspectacular. Only in farming did they exceed 40 per cent.

The exact status of those who have been included in these categories remains uncertain, of course, and this may be part of the explanation, but one obvious key to the shortfall is the context in which an occupational title was being recorded. A marriage certificate not only captures individuals momentarily, but provides a comparison between men at different stages in their working lives. In some cases, therefore, the amount of direct occupational succession may be underestimated – giving a misleading impression of instability – because a group of relatively youthful grooms will not have had time to attain the status of their fathers.

It is this disjunction which, at least in part, explains the disparity between self-recruitment and stability in the case of most proprietorial groups. To take one example, the number of men who had become farmers 15 or so years into their working lives was only slightly more than half the total population of men with farming backgrounds. Those among the latter who were able to declare the same occupation as their father on their marriage certificate are therefore bound to be almost twice as prominent within the group of younger farmers as they were among their original peer group. If the snapshot were to be taken later in the groom's career, allowing sons time to take over the business or come into their inheritance, we might expect to see the proportions even out.

The question of how age and career mobility affect the overall pattern of social mobility generated by the marriage register data is taken up more fully in the next chapter. Here, it is worth noting that relatively low rates of occupational succession among businessmen and property owners may also reflect particular problems of inheritance in parts of this sector. A craftsman could arrange to pass on the mystery of his trade to one or all of his sons while still retaining it himself. The capitalist's assets, on the other hand, were ordinarily more finite.[41] This was particularly the case on the land, where, in consequence, primo-geniture was normally practised, and hence only one son could inherit. Capital freed from land was more liquid, and the middle class generally favoured partible inheritance. But, unless the benefactor was very rich, this could only be a partial solution to the dilemma of ensuring enough resources to effect continuity of status for each of several children. If he was not, the splitting up of a going concern might be no more feasible than the division of an estate.

It is also important to recognise that work-life effects were not confined solely to property-related occupational groups. In arduous occupations such as mining, younger men predominated. This is one reason why there are more mining grooms than fathers in the sample, and why, in contrast to the typical profile in business, rates of occupational succession are higher than those for self-recruitment. Other occupational groups affected by an age factor are those in which internal advancement was based on adherence to 'seniority rules'.[42] The most celebrated example of this process is to be found in cotton spinning, but in the data it would seem to be particularly apparent among specialist workers on the land. Here the familiar disparity between succession and recruitment is especially marked. In part, this reflects the declining importance of these occupations across the period. But it also reflects the fact that, in the districts sampled, animal keeping tended to be a prerogative of older men.[43] As with property, this would have reduced the likelihood of occupational continuity among those of marrying age while ensuring that, among the smaller group of younger men who did attain such positions relatively early in life, opportunities fell disproportionately the way of insiders.

In the new bureaucracies it took some time before the advocates of merit prevailed over those who, like Anthony Trollope, saw promotion according seniority as a fairer and more efficient system.[44] Consequently, while kinship recruitment was undoubtedly difficult to achieve, the structure of promotion between grades might mean that here also a certain amount of continuity within families has been missed by the data. While Thomas Arthur Westwater, a cleaner in his father's box at 13, had become a fully-fledged signalman himself by 21, and 'Driver Barron' took just seven years to qualify, the journey between rungs, let alone ladders, could often take a lifetime.[45]

Another setting in which advancement was regulated according to seniority, and therefore where the transition from semi-skilled to skilled status was underpinned by age as well as ability, was in process work such as metal manufacture or paper making.[46] Here, however, the problem of underestimating the degree of succession barely arises because those entering their trades in the register tended not to differentiate, using the generic term 'furnaceman' or 'vatman' to identify themselves. In a few cases grooms were described as hammermen or strikers, an intermediate, semi-skilled position from which it was possible to graduate to the fully skilled status of the smith. But this was one case where promotion was not guaranteed.[47]

Divisions of Labour

The structural availability of an occupation is conditioned by the division of labour in three senses: by age, by time and by geography. The effect of historical time on occupational stability has already been suggested in the case of certain groups, and will be considered more fully below. Following on from the discussion of context in the chapter 2, the third of these variables concerns the interaction between 'density' and 'place'. In other words, the likelihood of occupational continuities within families, together with opportunities for mobility, will, in large part, depend on the industrial structure of the local economy and the place of a particular occupational group within it.

This can be illustrated by returning to the apparently anomalous hierarchy of occupational stability and cohesion among skilled workers. While it may still have been the case that potters, metal makers and factory weavers – the principal groups of factory workers in the sample – could exercise some degree of selective restriction on those entering their workplaces, a key factor in the propensity for sons to follow their fathers into these occupations seems to have been their physical concentration.

Each was strongly associated with a particular district where they provided most of the available skilled employment and were highly prominent in the overall division of labour. The pottery industry, in which almost two-thirds of skilled workers were themselves the sons of potters, provides perhaps the best example. Ninety-five per cent of all

potters found in the sample came from the registration district of
Stoke-on-Trent, where they comprised nearly half the skilled workforce and more than a quarter of the total working population.[48]
In Burslem only one in ten residents throughout the nineteenth
century was *not* employed in connection with the pottery industry.[49]
Finding that there was 12 times more employment in cotton in
Oldham in 1861 than the national average, John Foster claimed that it
was a one-industry town. By comparison, the people of the six towns
were, in the same year, *156* times more likely to be working in pottery
manufacture than the rest of the country.[50]

Not only did the sheer weight of these occupations in the local
economy favour inter-generational continuities, but the wider
industrial character of the districts in which they were concentrated
imposed a particular framework of limitations and possibilities where
alternative destinations, and the recruitment of outsiders, were
concerned. For example, the industrial districts' economies were
generally dominated by skilled work. In Stoke, for example, class III
accounted for 60 per cent of all jobs and class V for just 13 per cent,
while in rural Samford these proportions were almost reversed.
Herein lies a large part of the explanation why factory workers' connections with the unskilled sector were relatively, and perhaps
surprisingly, weak.

By the same token, it is the decentralisation of the craft sector
which helps to account both for the higher rates of occupational
mobility among its sons, and their higher chances of downward
mobility. Notwithstanding a certain urban-industrial bias, the individual components of the workshop economy were distributed right
across the villages, towns and cities of nineteenth-century England.[51]
In this case, the fact of dispersal served to limit the number of opportunities available in a given trade in any one location. Individual crafts
only exceptionally accounted for more than 2 per cent of the division
of labour in any one of the ten registration districts sampled, and
succession rates were similar in each.[52] The nature of the competition
for places and the range of alternatives for sons unable or unwilling to
follow in their fathers' footsteps again depended on the character of
the particular local labour market in question. However, because
craftsmen were almost as common in rural as in industrial economies,
and mobility into class V was as high as one in seven in the former,
this is reflected in the profile of handicraft as a whole. On the other
hand, the craft sector's reputation is only partly rehabilitated by its
scattered distribution, for when the sons of craftsmen and factory

workers are compared on common ground it is still the trades which had the stronger contacts with the territory below.

In varying degrees the pressures exerted by their position in the division of labour are reflected in the profiles of all occupational categories, although the variation confirms that distribution and structure are not all-embracing explanations. The mobility profile of miners, for example, is partly a function of the industry's geography. But while in Stoke-on-Trent the pottery industry provided twice as many jobs as mining, the succession rates among miners and potters here were the same.

Culture and Community

While the weight of a particular occupation in the local economy affected the likelihood of sons following fathers, in none of the examples where levels of inter-generational occupational stability were high can the rate of succession be accounted for statistically – according to perfect mobility expectations – in these terms. In each case, in other words, the proportion of self-recruited men far outweighed the relative importance of the occupation in the division of labour as whole.

One possibility is that the immobility in such cases also reflects the formation of distinct occupational cultures. This is a notion associated particularly with studies of the 'traditional' working class in the 1950s and 1960s which suggested its rooting in isolated single-occupation communities whose introspection generated powerful cultural pressures in favour of occupational, and by extension social, solidarity.[53]

The concept of occupational community has most popularly been applied to mining. Dennis *et al.*'s famous study of Ashton in the 1950s reported that:

> The effect of a common set of persisting social relations, shared over a life-time by men working in the same industry and in the same collieries, is a very powerful one ... Solidarity ... is a very strongly developed characteristic ... [The boy brought up in a mining family] is typically destined to be a miner ... To take his place in the community ... a young man cannot for long stay out of mining.[54]

The testimony of men such as Thomas McLauchlan, mentioned above, and of Thomas Jordan, another son and grandson of Durham miners from the same period, tends to support this image of pit life and culture as a centripetal force, channelling expectations and fixing horizons in terms of the immediate community.[55]

On the other hand, more recent work has convincingly challenged the image of the typical nineteenth-century pit community as a self-contained industrial village. Benson writes that 'diversity is perhaps the outstanding characteristic of the nineteenth-century coal industry'.[56] The coalfields covered by the sample were not characterised by isolated settlements. In the Black Country and north Staffordshire miners were 'lost in a vast tide of sprawling urbanisation'.[57] In Sheffield, they made up a fairly small proportion of a diverse working population, while those in Cannock Chase and Shropshire were rooted in wider rural communities.[58]

There are plenty of less romantic reasons why the vast majority of miners' sons in these areas – nowhere less than 65 per cent, and up to 82 per cent in and around Nuneaton – continued to follow their fathers into the industry. Clearly, financial incentives were important. Although there were variations between and within fields, and fluctuations by year, at most times in most places miners' wages were relatively high.[59] Work underground could also offer more independence than other forms of employment.[60] Jobs were easy to come by in an expanding industry, and here also employers actively recruited from the families of their workers.[61]

However, the idea that cultural insularity played a part in the 'continuing tradition of internal hereditary recruitment'[62] in mining cannot be dismissed entirely. While some fathers tried to dissuade their sons from following them down the pit, Thomas Jordan's father took his young boy underground to keep him company at night, and later, despite an offer of alternative employment, insisted that he also became a miner.[63] Jordan's own assessment is that the demands, uncertainties and shared dangers of working underground made miners into a 'peculiar breed of humans', and Church notes that pit work 'contributed to a sense of immutability … and a status apart from society' which was strongest in single-industry villages but identifiable 'even among the miners who lived in large towns and cities.'[64]

Even though he never actually liked working underground, Jordan returned to it after the First World War when he was drawn back to the community by marriage. As explained in chapter seven, where they are explored in more detail, marriage patterns provide one test of wider community identities. Where occupational communities were strong, we might also expect to find high rates of occupational endogamy. Table 4.3 compares rates of occupational self-recruitment and endogamy among a number of occupational groups. Whether we consider occupational endogamy *per se* or the endogamy rates of second-generation men, the tendency towards intermarriage in mining was clearly strong. Only potters and weavers are comparable in these terms, and then, some way behind, nailers and second-generation seafarers. With the exception of printing, where, if a son followed in his father's footsteps, there was a reasonable expectation of marriage to a daughter of a man in the trade, most individual crafts and businesses display much lower rates of occupational endogamy, although, as with occupational mobility, marriage within the handicraft or business sector more broadly was considerably more likely. On the other hand, even in the coalfields two out of three wives were not from a mining family. The sons of miners were almost twice as likely to marry a miner's daughter as men who had no family tradition in the industry, but they too were more likely to marry a woman from outside.

PATHWAYS AND PROSPECTS

From the factors which promoted continuity across the generations we turn to the question of why, notwithstanding the structural pressures exerted by the division of labour, those unable, or choosing

Table 4.3   *Rates of occupational inheritance and endogamy in selected occupational groups (per cent)*

	Rates of self-recruitment	Rates of endogamy	Endogamy of 'outsiders'	Endogamy of 'insiders'
Shopkeepers	31.3	11.6	10.9	14.3
Clerks	5.8	3.9	3.2	10.0
Masons	59.1	12.1	15.4	10.8
Shoemakers	42.1	11.7	11.2	12.8
Printers	20.8	6.0	2.6	22.2
Spinners	25.0	0.0	0.0	0.0
Weavers	60.9	36.4	31.7	40.0
Nailers	53.3	26.2	22.4	29.6
Potters	60.6	41.2	36.7	44.7
Engineers	23.0	3.8	4.6	2.4
Seamen	22.8	10.5	4.5	30.0
Miners	54.1	33.7	24.8	40.7

not, to follow in their fathers' footsteps, took the paths they did, and why particular occupations recruited from one source rather than another. Unlike the autobiographies, the marriage data cannot reveal the individual decision-making processes involved in job choice, but they do suggest the existence of distinct channels and cultures of mobility linking particular origins and destinations, together with a number of factors that helped promote mobility.

Mobilising Influences

Mobility prospects seem to have been enhanced by three factors in particular: the social relations of an occupational group, geographical mobility and the possession of at least basic educational skills.

As Sewell noted in the case of nineteenth-century Marseilles, while artisans and labourers spent their work time predominantly with members of their own trade or class, service sector employment brought opportunities for a wider range of connections.[65] By the very nature of their jobs, those employed in transport and communications were exposed to more information about the variety of vacancies on offer in the local labour market. Salesmen, postmen and railway guards, for example, had direct dealings with the public, and Booth writes of the London cabmen's 'constant contact with all kinds of people'.[66] In addition, workers in this sector were mostly based in expanding urban communities, so increasing the number of options available to their offspring.

The registers cannot provide direct evidence of the process, but it seems clear that migration, particularly from the countryside to towns, produced occupational and often social mobility. One fifth of the autobiographers cited geographical mobility as a means of finding a new job, and while communities in the countryside, which in any case had never been entirely static, began to loosen up considerably towards the end of the century, an agricultural labourer's son's chances of substantial social advancement within rural society remained as negligible as they had been in Elmdon 50 years before, or in Dorset a further fifty years earlier.[67] Increasing numbers looked to the rapidly growing towns to improve their circumstances and, as Burnett notes, many were helped by the spread of village schools and the effects of educational reform.[68]

By revealing the relative proportions of partners able to sign their name, as opposed to having to represent it by means of a cross, the marriage registers can provide an indication of the relationship between mobility and basic educational credentials. Both Vincent and Mitch have recently demonstrated that mobility chances were strongly correlated with literacy.[69] Literate sons, as Table 4.4 shows, were considerably more upwardly mobile than those who could not read or write, and, by the same token, illiterate men were at much greater risk of losing their social status. The literate sons of craftsmen, for example, had a 1 in 10 chance of crossing into the middle class, but for their illiterate peers the probability was just 1 in 50. At the same time, the latter were three times more likely than the former to end up in a labouring job. As for the sons of labourers themselves, it is impossible to distinguish migrants from non-migrants, but, in total, almost half of those who could sign their names in the registers had improved on their father's position, compared to one in four of those who could not.

The other conclusion to be drawn from these figures, however, is that to be literate was neither a guarantee of success nor a prerequisite for it. Altogether, nearly a quarter of the men from handicraft backgrounds who could wield a pen failed, nevertheless, to acquire a skilled job, and, of course, for every one literate son of a labourer who

Table 4.4   *Mobility rates by literacy (literate grooms upper row figures,
illliterate grooms lower row figures)*

			Son's Class				
Father's class	I	II	III	IV	V	n	%
I	43.4	33.7	15.6	4.4	2.9	205	(98.6)
	0.0	0.0	33.3	0.0	66.7	3	(1.4)
II	2.9	52.3	25.7	12.0	7.1	1638	(92.0)
	0.7	26.6	26.6	14.7	31.5	143	(8.0)
III	0.4	8.2	71.4	11.7	8.3	3376	(78.9)
	0.0	1.7	78.0	4.9	15.4	901	(21.1)
Craftsmen	0.5	10.0	67.4	13.4	8.7	1618	(84.0)
	0.0	1.6	68.5	6.5	23.4	308	(16.0)
Factory workers	0.4	8.8	71.7	12.3	6.8	791	(82.5)
	0.0	1.8	83.9	6.0	8.3	168	(17.5)
Miners	0.2	3.1	83.4	5.7	7.6	519	(65.3)
	0.0	1.5	86.8	2.9	8.8	272	(34.7)
IV	0.4	8.4	34.9	45.0	11.3	986	(83.1)
	0.5	2.5	25.0	48.5	23.5	200	(16.9)
V	0.1	3.7	25.9	18.5	51.7	1662	(60.3)
	0.0	1.6	14.3	7.4	76.8	1094	(39.7)

managed to escape his father's fate there was another who did not. The vast majority – over 90 per cent – of those who achieved middle-class status having grown up in a working-class family were able to sign their name in the register, but while literacy was a skill which could be useful even when not strictly necessary, less than a third of those making this transition did so by entering employment in which the ability to read and write was a formal requirement.[70]

Channels and Routeways

Rather than credentials, the most likely means to success for the aspirant sons of nineteenth-century workers was the acquisition of property or capital (in the traditional sense) which would allow them to set up in business. For every clerk among the group of middle-class men from working-class homes, there were two shopkeepers or farmers. However, the emphasis on particular pathways into the middle class varied according to occupational origin, and did so in ways which were bound up with culture and location.

The sons of craftsmen, for example, were the second most literate working-class group, but among the least likely to be found in office jobs. Here, a strong sense of tradition and self-identity elevated 'the trade' itself to the pinnacle of ambition and produced contempt for 'puny and parasitic clerks'.[71] According to Hobsbawm, tradesmen fathers 'wanted nothing better for their sons ... a trade was at least as desirable or better than anything else on offer'.[72] As we have seen, the figures strongly support this argument, for while the rate of direct occupational succession was not especially high in most individual trades, half of all craftsmen's sons did indeed become members of the wider artisan community. On average, handicraft occupations recruited a fifth of their membership from other trades, which was at least three times the rate of recruitment from any other single occupational category.

The trades themselves could, of course, provide a passport to middle-class status for those who made the transition from journeyman or independent to employer. The data cannot reveal how often this took place, but the popularity of commercial and proprietorial destinations among those who travelled into the middle class by other routes ties in with the cultural associations of tradesmen, who not only tended to look down on the emerging white-collar workforce but are known to have spent much of their institutionalised leisure time rubbing shoulders with the local petty bourgeoisie.[73] Moreover, to the extent that the sample's craftsmen fathers were small master business-men this may have served to inculcate attitudes and aspirations favourable to capital accumulation among their sons.

On the other hand, several groups show a stronger affinity for white-collar pathways out of the working class than might be expected on the basis of the distribution of middle-class positions. The upwardly mobile sons of factory workers, for example, and of men employed in the new service industries, were twice as likely as trades-men's sons to take up white-collar employment. This would seem to reflect the distancing of these groups from the cultural orientation, contacts and expectations of tradesmen, but also, on a more practical level, the absence of any obvious basis for capital accumulation in this context. On the other hand, their predominantly urban location meant there were more jobs of this type to be had in the local economy, while both the new bureaucracies and the larger manufacturing concerns had administrative staffs of their own to recruit. The chances of gaining privileged access to the former may have been slim, but the experiences of Ernest Ambrose and James Cruickshank suggest that some factory workers' sons were able to take advantage of opportunities materialising on their own doorstep.[74]

One group which contradicted the typical pattern in handicraft were printers' sons, whose behaviour reveals the trade to have been, in these terms, somewhat schizophrenic. Of all those with trade back-grounds, printers' sons had the best chance of being in charge of their own business by the time they came to marry. But at the same time the number signing the registers as salaried employees was double that from any other craft. The obvious explanation for this is that literacy was, uniquely, a *sine qua non* of the trade, and their proximity to the written word almost certainly ensured that printing families were both more accommodating towards, and their sons better placed to take advantage of, clerical and administrative opportunities.

As noted above, literacy was also an important distinguishing char-acteristic of the uniformed working class, but in this case the prefer-ence for white-collar destinations inside the middle class is suggestive of a broader qualification culture, which linked credentially-oriented occupational milieux across class boundaries. Not only was clerking an important lower-middle-class destination, but men from this back-ground were also twice as likely as any other group to become a lower professional, and three time more likely to gain access to the more established professions.

There are further traces of this culture in the pattern of interchange inside the middle class. Although very few made the journey from class II to class I, men from white-collar backgrounds were more likely to gain access to the professions than those whose fathers were businessmen. Travelling in the opposite direction, the sons of pro-pertied men were actually more likely than those from professional families to move into a white-collar job. As suggested above, however, it is probable that a number of those from propertied backgrounds who took up administrative or sales positions in class II were merely fulfilling a temporary white-collar apprenticeship before they took over a family concern or came into an inheritance. And while such men were twice as likely to be found in this type of routine white-collar work as men from professional backgrounds, the latter were, in turn, twice as likely to take up a lower professional position.

Routes between different types of manual employment also show signs of demarcation. There was, for example, something of a barrier between traditional forms of production and heavy industry. Taking into account the relative sizes of the categories, miners' sons found it much easier to move into the factory than the workshop. By the same token craftsmen's sons were substantially under-represented among the ranks of pitmen. With the prominent exceptions of engineering and brewing, the futures of those on the move from factory back-grounds were also oriented more towards heavy industry than the trades. The chances of movement in the opposite direction were higher, but mostly amongst those trades with industrial connections, such as blacksmiths.

For those seeking to leave the land, traditional forms of service, rather than manufacture, were particularly prominent. Here there was a natural interface with occupations like gardening, but domestic service, the army and the sea were all well-established routes for those from rural backgrounds. The railway companies also looked to the countryside as a more promising source of malleable recruits than the more organised occupational cultures of the towns.[75] However, service-sector employment proved an important destination for the sons of the unskilled more generally. The cabman's trade, for example, was easily picked up, and in London, where licences were liberally distributed, 'one to which all sorts of men find their way'.[76]

The other particularly accommodating avenue of upward mobility for the sons of labourers, both agricultural and urban, was coal mining, where high wages could be obtained by those whose financial and educational means were limited.[77] Almost one in five miners hailed from labouring backgrounds, and in the more rural coalfields the rate of recruitment was almost a third. At the same time the colliery can be seen as the focus of a more specific industrial channel along which families like the Armstrongs of Nenthead, previously involved in slightly more marginal extractive industries like quarrying or tin, copper and lead mining, could easily transfer.[78]

NOVELTY AND OBSOLESCENCE

The changing patterns of occupational stability and exchange which underlie the cross-sample profiles are perhaps best interpreted as an expression of the shifting balance between old and new types of production, organisation, employment relations, location and attitudes.

In a general sense this is an obvious conclusion. The changing shape of an economy will cause the expansion of some sectors at the expense of others, and, mediated by the market mechanism – albeit restricted in various ways – this process will push and pull the human factor of production along in its wake. The occupational evidence provides the necessary definition with which to see precisely where these shifts were occurring, and reveals a remarkably regular pattern (Appendix 3). In line with expectations, the general pattern of occupational mobility within and between classes reflects the flow away from the primary sector, and the contracting modes of production within the secondary, into tertiary occupations, and towards larger-scale, if not always entirely modern, sectors within industry. The marked and continuous shift away from class V, in large part a reflection of the exodus from the countryside, has already been noted. The figures also clearly highlight the evacuation of the workshop and capitalist sectors, in favour of factory and mine, and the movement towards the services at all levels of the social structure.

However, they reflect not only change in the quantitative terms of expansion and contraction, but also in a qualitative sense. As some occupations declined, not only did they begin to shrink in importance, but they underwent a change of character. The occupations which replaced them were generally informed by a different set of organisational assumptions, and in particular by a different set of recruitment practices. Occupational change altered the composition of classes, and this affected the rates at which they were able to stabilise and cohere across the generations. But however limited, and perhaps temporary, the impact, it also affected their accessibility.

Table 4.5 confirms that a focal point of pressure on middle-class advantage was to be found in the battle for white-collar jobs. Here, following Kaelble, and in the light of the preceding discussion, the enhanced competitiveness of those from working-class homes would seem to be grounded in the increasingly credentialist and bureaucratic imperatives underpinning recruitment to this growing sector of the economy, for which they, in turn, were increasingly better prepared.[79] That the impact of these institutional pressures was not confined to the battle-lines between the two major classes, but also influenced relationships inside the working class, is suggested by the overall decline in the advantage of skilled men's sons over those with labouring backgrounds in gaining membership to the skilled service sector – centred on the developing bureaucracies of the railway companies, Post Office and police force.

A straightforward indication that men from inferior class backgrounds were gaining on their social superiors in terms of their technical ability to take advantage of these new recruitment imperatives can be gauged by turning to evidence of changes in the literacy rate between social groups. As Figure 4.3 shows, in the first half of the nineteenth century class differentials were marked, but by 1914 rudimentary literacy skills were possessed by almost all the population.

However, at several points across the occupational spectrum, and not just in sectors undergoing bureaucratisation, similar reductions in

Table 4.5 *Disparity ratios showing the relative chances of the sons of middle-class men and working-class men gaining entry to (a) business (b) white-collar positions (workers' sons chances set at 1); of skilled workers' and unskilled workers' sons moving into (c) a trade (d) factory work (e) mining (f) skilled services (unskilled workers' sons chances set at 1); of the sons of semi- and unskilled workers gaining access to (g) semi-skilled service occupations (unskilled workers' sons chances set at 1)*

	a	b	c	d	e	f	g
1839–54	9.0:1	6.5:1	4.7:1	6.2:1	2.9:1	2.2:1	3.5:1
1859–94	8.6:1	7.3:1	4.4:1	4.7:1	2.7:1	1.1:1	3.3:1
1879–94	7.0:1	4.5:1	3.1:1	4.2:1	3.1:1	1.3:1	2.7:1
1899–1914	5.6:1	4.0:1	2.3:1	3.7:1	1.7:1	1.2:1	1.7:1

Figure 4.3 *Literacy rates of grooms by class and period*

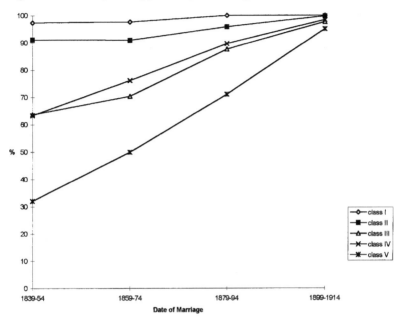

social closure were being achieved. The contraction of the handicraft sector coincided with a rising flow of its sons upwards but also, against the general trend, downwards into class V, while at the same time the sector itself became more accessible to outsiders. More points to 'the influence of better education, which combined with rising real wages among the lower paid must have strengthened the ability of the latter's children to enter, and to finance, apprenticeship training'.[80] Probably as important was the process of long-term restructuring, whereby technological developments in industries such a shoemaking, tailoring and building,[81] together with the continuing erosion of apprenticeship, gradually undermined the craft basis of a substantial part of the sector's membership.[82] Such pressures were also felt inside the factory sector, and they intensified towards the end of the century when, in the wake of the depression in prices and profits which had begun in the 1870s, employers launched an offensive against the trade unions, the main plank of which was their attack on craft privilege.[83] One response to this was the development of all-grades unions, which may in itself have helped to break down the barriers between strata.[84]

The impact of bureaucratisation on the expanding sectors within manufacture may have been limited,[85] but the increasing scale of the factory and mining unit suggests the possibility of more impersonal recruitment.[86] It is also likely that the introspection of rural mining communities was, to an extent at least, broken down by the process of urbanisation and the development of road and rail communications.[87]

Urbanisation is, in itself, an important dimension of the shift between the old and the new, and, as suggested in the previous chapter, a potential facilitator of greater fluidity. It seems likely that the tendency towards an equalisation of class chances as far as access to white-collar employment is concerned was in part a reflection of this sector's 'strikingly urban' location.[88] From a different perspective, one of Booth's authors noted the tendency of the able migrant from the countryside to secure the better opportunities offered by the London labour market.[89] The implied relationship between migration and enterprise is made explicit in Sewell's work on Marseilles.[90] Many ex-countrymen possessed skills which were quickly adaptable to the requirements of the urban semi-skilled service sector, where class V men made big gains on men born into class IV. The transition from carter to cabman, and from farm hand to gardener was easily made.[91]

It is the urbanisation process which may also have been behind the growing ability of working-class sons to challenge for places amongst the petty bourgeoisie; the growth of towns perhaps undermining, for a short period at least, established structures of local power, while the urban sprawl provided space and markets for new concerns.[92] However, the small business family's increasing use of white-collar jobs to ensure a position of adequate status for their offspring suggests, as with handicraft, that this was as much a reflection of a parallel process of 'obsolescence'; the heyday of the mid-Victorian boom giving way to uncertainties created by the challenge of the multiples and the co-ops on the one hand, and incursion from the 'expanding ranks of semi- and unskilled shopkeepers' with easier access to capital and supplies on the other.[93] Ironically, the rising rate of working-class recruitment to white-collar positions suggests that the outcome of such a move was no more a guarantee of security than staying put, which, in turn, suggests that the growing anxiety detected in this sector towards the end of the period was well founded.[94]

CONCLUSION

This chapter has sought to explore the relationship between occupation and class in the process of mobility, and suggest ways in which the pattern of class mobility and social fluidity generated by economic development was underpinned by occupational change. In so far as the marriage data alone can reveal the degree of interplay between occupational and class identity there is no clear suggestion of the former undermining the latter. Wider strata and class affiliations were always relatively important, and were becoming more so over time.

The occupational evidence provides a good deal of support, at the structural level, for the existence of a labour aristocracy. Notions of a 'merging' with the lower middle class have little foundation, nor was this elite a closed shop. But both of these assumptions have, in any case, been modified by the theory's principal supporter.[95] Similarly, the data provides some support for the central component of the proposed trajectory of this elite. Avenues of advancement into the middle class did not close down, but the last quarter of the nineteenth century witnessed a significant decline in the stratum's ability to remain aloof from the rest of the working class.[96]

The mobility profiles of specific occupational sectors and groups were the product of many, often interrelated, factors. Among the most important, it was suggested, were the technical and institutional constraints on power over recruitment; the age, or work-life stage, of an occupational group's incumbents; the concentration of an occupation within a particular location or industrial environment; the salience, or otherwise, of an occupational tradition; and the existence of cultural and institutional links between occupations in different classes.

The role of occupational change in the temporal patterns of class mobility and fluidity was explained in terms of the shifting balance between old and new forms. Despite the acknowledged complexities of the processes of economic change which accompanied industrial development, the pattern of redistribution between primary, secondary and tertiary sectors was remarkably clear in its general direction.

Some of the complexities are revealed when the occupational developments which underlie the changing pattern of social fluidity are explored. Economic change not only sponsored sectoral expansion and contraction, but in doing so altered the composition, and with it the integrity, of classes. It did so mainly by encouraging the growth of intrinsically less tractable occupations and weakening the position of more established groups. This development was supported by institutional changes in recruitment, brought about by the gradual development of bureaucratic employment, and the decline of apprenticeship; the increasingly urban location of the population; falling class differentials in literacy levels; and the growing availability of capital.

5 Career Mobility

'But when we endeavour to trace the road by which each individual has travelled or is travelling,' reflected Charles Booth and one of his co-surveyors in 1897, 'the dynamic forces at work are impressed upon us.' 'Together with the permanence of the industrial type,' they observed, 'we become conscious of the incessant change that is taking place in the conditions of a large proportion of the individual lives. Restlessness, ambition, ability, folly, hesitancy, indifference or dullness', they concluded, 'carry men along, up and down, and down and up again, in the industrial as in other roads of life'.[1]

This image has ominous implications for an analysis of inter-generational mobility, particularly one based on marriage register data. A marriage certificate captures the mobility experience of two generations at a specific moment in their lives. Critics such as Sørensen argue that all such cross-classifications are misleading because they aggregate a collection of differing work-life patterns on either side of the relationship between parents and children.[2] But even those rising to the defence of the standard mobility table are likely to object that a snapshot taken at marriage is a distortingly early point from which to judge the full extent of social redistribution between the generations.

The primary purpose of this chapter is to shed some light on the representativeness of mobility at marriage, and, by extension, the whole notion of inter-generational transition, using evidence of intra-generational, or work-life, mobility. For the historian, diachronic perspectives on mobility are even harder to generate than the synchronic view which has so far predominated in this study,[3] and the evidence to hand is not extensive enough to allow a comprehensive study of career mobility on the same terms as the foregoing analysis of movement between fathers and sons. Nevertheless, it does afford a useful insight into the problem of inter- versus intra-generational mobility, and with it an assessment of Booth's assertion that the majority of Edwardian and Victorian working lives were far more unsettled than might be supposed from a reading of the cross-sectional data.

The snapshot problem is explored initially using the ancillary information carried by the marriage registers themselves, then by drawing on the evidence from a computer analysis of 479 career histories which have been taken from the 1,000 plus abstracts in the first volume of Burnett *et al.*'s anthology of working-class autobiography. The outcome of the secondary analysis of the registers supports most of the findings up to this point, although in one crucial respect – namely, with regard to the trend in fluidity – it suggests that some degree of qualification may be in order. As far as work-life mobility itself is concerned, it would seem that Booth was both right and wrong. The autobiographies reveal a great variety of experience. Many working lives were, indeed, punctuated by change and undulation. But more often than not such meandering occurred within more structured trajectories. Examples of completely incoherent careers were comparatively rare. Instead, the texts support the arguments of chapter 4 by revealing the gradual emergence of the bureaucratic career.

OCCUPATIONAL MATURITY

The marriage registers provide a perspective on work-life mobility because a proportion of them carry information about the groom's age. This allows the experience of those marrying later than the sample average of 27 years to be compared with that of the younger majority. However, as the nature of this information is far from unproblematic all findings resulting from it must be treated cautiously.

First, the proportion of grooms marrying beyond their twenties was small; slightly more than two in three signatories gave their age, but only one in five of these were 30 or more. At age 35, Goldthorpe's point of 'occupational maturity', the sample shrinks from 7,237 to just 842. Furthermore, the practice of entering one's age in the register was neither temporally nor socially consistent. In 1839–54 just one in three grooms volunteered this information, and it was not until the first decade of the twentieth century that it became customary to do so. This inconsistency is compounded by the fact that some classes were more forthcoming than others. Amongst the 1839–54 cohort only 18 per cent of elite grooms recorded their age compared to 30 per cent of those in classes II, IV and V, and 40 per cent of skilled working-class men, and disparities remained up until the turn of the century. Finally, and most importantly, this approach to work-life mobility remains an indirect one. A comparison of those who marry at different ages is one of separate samples of men, *not* a tracing of individual life-course patterns. We cannot know, therefore, whether the older man's position was recently acquired or of much longer standing. Moreover, such men are distinctive not just because of their age, but precisely *because* they married late. Delayed marriage was a practice associated with progress in middle-class careers and therefore introduces a class effect which would tend to exaggerate the relationship between age and success in samples of older grooms.[4]

That there was such a relationship, however, is not in doubt. This is clear enough from the variations in the sons' and fathers' marginal distributions in Table 2.1.[5] Here working-class occupations account for 84.6 per cent of the sons' division of labour, and 80.5 per cent of the fathers'; middle-class occupations, 15.4 and 19.5 per cent respectively. The difference could, in theory, be produced by a temporal shift in the social division of labour, but, given what we know about the evolution of the Victorian and Edwardian economy, work-life mobility is the obvious explanation.

The class distribution of grooms by age group (Figure 5.1) shows a steady rise in the proportion of men in middle-class positions throughout the life course. It also shows that the pattern as a whole stabilises at, or just after, 30, suggesting that those in the pre-1914 labour force reached 'occupational maturity' slightly earlier than their descendants.[6] This is confirmed by the experience of the autobiographers, whose mean age on entry to white-collar work was 28, while first-time businessmen averaged 31. Indeed, as a group, the authors tended to reach their 'optimal' class position at 30. On the other hand, there is an

Figure 5.1 *Distribution of grooms by class and age, 1839–1914*

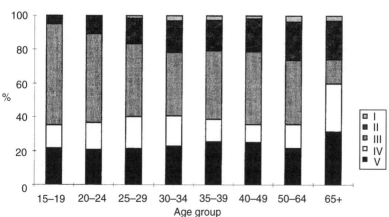

Social Mobility in England

Table 5.1 *Class distribution of grooms by class of father, 1839–1914: grooms aged under 30, upper figures; aged 30 and above, lower figures (percentage by row)*

Father's Class	Son's Class					n	%
	I	II	III	IV	V		
I	33.3	40.6	11.6	7.2	7.2	69	(1.2)
	44.4	16.7	29.6	3.7	5.6	54	(3.4)
II	1.1	44.9	31.1	13.9	8.9	877	(15.5)
	3.3	57.2	19.2	11.7	8.6	360	(23.0)
III	0.1	6.5	73.2	11.7	8.4	2626	(46.3)
	0.8	8.8	66.6	10.5	13.2	590	(37.6)
IV	0.0	6.6	36.7	44.1	12.6	708	(12.5)
	1.1	12.4	32.0	41.6	12.9	178	(11.4)
V	0.0	3.0	25.1	15.8	56.2	1389	(24.5)
	0.3	4.4	19.7	15.8	59.8	386	(24.6)
n	36	682	2812	966	1173	5669	
	44	306	611	241	366	1568	
%	(0.6)	(12.0)	(49.6)	(17.0)	(20.7)		
	(2.8)	(19.5)	(39.0)	(15.4)	(23.3)		

indication that the occupational plateau which began at this point only extended so far, before more undulating terrain was encountered towards the end of a working life. The numbers in the over 65 cohort in the grooms' distribution are small, but, reflecting the insecurity which attended old age in a free market economy, they suggest a dramatic shift towards the bottom of the class structure at this point.

AGE AND MOBILITY

A comparison of the mobility profiles of the under- and over-thirties (Table 5.1) suggests that concerns about the distorting effects of marriage-based studies of inter-generational change are exaggerated. The total mobility rates of these two cohorts differ only marginally, at 39.4 and 40.8 per cent respectively, and the most striking feature of the five-class analyses is their essential similarity. Drawing a line at 30 certainly reveals a number of important, although mostly expected, developments, but does not suggest the need for a radical overhaul of earlier conclusions about the relationship between major social groups and their *de facto* mobility chances.

The overall shift in the outflow pattern might best be described as centrifugal. As suggested by the grooms' distribution profile, age sponsored movement away from the middle of the social spectrum towards both poles. Most affected by this process was the territory above, where, as predicted, bourgeois stability was enhanced, presumably through the process of counter-mobility. Age encouraged an all-round process of class formation amongst the lower middle class, which, as well as sending almost 60 per cent of its sons into class II jobs by the time they had passed 30, also recruited two-thirds of its older membership internally. Even in this case, however, time failed to rescue a sizeable number of men who had become downwardly mobile earlier in their careers, and for members of the elite it actually increased their chances of rubbing shoulders with the working class.

Time spent in the labour market certainly brought more scope for working-class upward mobility, but the structural consequences were minimal. In the case of men from the semi-skilled sector the size of the group leaving the working class was twice as big after the age of 30 as it was before, but this still accounted for no more than one in eight of all men with class IV backgrounds. Invoking the modern criterion of occupational maturity makes little difference. After 35, the chances of a worker's son being found in a middle-class job were still less than 10 per cent.

In that other crucial dimension of working-class mobility – between different status groups inside the class – there were, again, only marginal changes associated with age. The total rate of internal mobility varied by just 0.5 per cent between the younger and the older samples. What developments there were resulted from the fact that age brought not only new opportunities but new pressures. The obverse of more chances for class advancement was an increasing threat of proletarianisation, as the skilled sector, with its emphasis on strength, acuity and dexterity, became less receptive. Apparently immune to the downward pressures of the more mature labour market, only the semi-skilled reaped the rewards of age without suffering its consequences, a later life-course perspective enhancing the highly heterogeneous image of this group.

The overall pattern of absolute mobility displayed by the older grooms, then, does not call into question the conclusions reached on the basis of the marriage register sample as whole. It need not follow, however, that the pattern of relative mobility was the same in both halves of the career. By and large, the shifts in the opportunity structure with age were conducive to the changing patterns of observed mobility, but at the same time the apparent counter-mobility of men originating in class II appears rather more decisive than the rise in working-class upward mobility across the career.

In the same way as they were used to compare the mobility regimes of different districts and different historical periods in previous chapters, any variation in the pattern of social fluidity by age-group will be revealed when the models for constant social fluidity and uniform difference are applied to the data. This procedure (Table 5.2) shows that there was effectively no difference between the two groups in these terms, the model for no change, or no difference, in fluidity fitting very well. If anything, the β parameters under the uniform change model suggest that the older population was very marginally *more* open than the younger, but, across the period as a whole, the nineteenth-century mobility regime would appear to have been little affected by progress through the life-course.

Table 5.2   *Results of fitting the constant social fluidity and uniform difference models to the data for grooms aged under and over 30, and parameter estimates for the model of uniform change in association between class origins and-destinations*

Model	G^2	BIC	df	p	Δ
CnSF	33.8	−108.4	16	0.01	1.2
Unidiff	32.2	−101.1	15	0.01	1.3

Parameter estimates of the model of uniform change by age group:	−30 set at zero	30+ −0.05

AGE AND TIME

What is of most interest in a comparative analysis of mobility by age-group, however, is the issue of change over time, and in particular the question of fluidity trends. In contrast to Goldthorpe's work on Britain since 1945, the marriage register sample suggests that English society became consistently more open between the first Reform Act (1832) and the outbreak of the First World War. But one vital factor stressed by Goldthorpe in relation to his findings was the importance of work-life stage. He too found some evidence of a trend in fluidity amongst men in mid-career, but argued that it was the pattern amongst older men, whose careers had stabilised, that was of greater significance.[7]

Historically, this issue appears more complicated. Twentieth-century models of occupational maturity, it would seem, cannot be applied so easily to the past and, as will be shown later in this chapter, it is only towards the end of the nineteenth century that the recognisably 'modern' career began to emerge. It is also in the dimension of change over time that an analysis of age and mobility based on late marriage is at its most fragile. Nevertheless, even if the light it casts on the relationship between fluidity and work-life mobility is, for both reasons, somewhat opaque, the experience of the older grooms is still worth considering.

As it turns out, the result of a test for trends in fluidity while controlling for the age of grooms is a mixed one. Given that log-linear analysis is a procedure sensitive to small samples with missing values, the first cohort has been dropped from the analysis in Table 5.3. What this analysis shows is that for the period 1859–1914, exchanging the no change model for the uniform difference model produces an improvement in fit in the case of both age samples. But while there is strong support for a trend where the younger men are concerned, the difference between the two models is not significant when it comes to the sample of older grooms, which means the constant social fluidity model is to be preferred in this case. However, according to Erikson and Goldthorpe, if there is still consistent movement in the β parameter values under the unidiff model, 'it would be unwise to discount this, even if the improvement in fit falls short of significance'.[8] Table 5.3 confirms that there is indeed such a pattern in these values, and that they move in a direction which indicates a gradual trend in favour of rising fluidity.

Table 5.3   *Results of fitting the constant social fluidity and uniform difference models to different age groups over three marriage cohorts, and parameter estimates for the model of uniform change in association between class origins and destinations*

Age group	Model	G^2	BIC	df	p	Δ
under 30	CnSF	57.3	−214.4	32	0.00	4.3
	Unidiff	21.1	−233.7	30	0.89	1.8
over 30	CnSF	31.0	−200.8	32	0.52	4.2
	Unidiff	29.9	−187.3	30	0.76	3.9

cohort*	β Parameter estimates	
Age group	3	4
under 30	−0.05	−0.30
over 30	−0.07	−0.09

Note:
* Parameters for cohort 2 (1859–74) set at zero.

The reason for the dampening down of this trend amongst the older grooms is not immediately evident from the observable pattern of mobility, which again varies little between the two samples. One area of difference concerns the process of working-class homogenisation. This was driven by increasing numbers of 'risers' within the class among the under-thirties, but by escalating rates of demotion among older men. Associated with this process, what appears to be a process of reverse counter-mobility makes the declining stability of the unskilled sector much less dramatic when looked at from a later life-course perspective. Nevertheless, when the test for fluidity is focused on the relationship between the three working-class sectors alone, a strong trend towards more openness is found regardless of when the career snapshot is taken.[9]

The other main point of divergence concerns mobility across the major class divide. In the older sample, increasing upward mobility brought the sons of working-class men gains in the competition for lower-middle-class positions over the second half of the nineteenth century. However, in contrast to the pattern among the younger men, these were reversed after the turn of the century when there was no further improvement in the rate of upward mobility. Specifically, this appears to have been caused by a fall in the rate of working-class mobility into a small business sector which was itself becoming increasingly stable over time. Neither of these developments is found in the sample of younger grooms; they are perhaps best explained by rising competition and greater concentration in this sector over the second half of the period. In these circumstances, the pattern of middle-class recruitment to business was reversed, as early entry was increasingly eschewed. Working-class recruits, on the other hand, would presumably have had fewest chances of long-term survival in what was often, as the autobiographers confirm, a highly precarious world.

Together with the occupational closure exercised in farming, it seems that the changing pattern of recruitment to the petty bourgeoisie ensured that men born into the lower middle class were, ultimately, able to maintain a more or less consistent level of advantage over working-class men in gaining access to middle-class jobs. There were, nevertheless, cracks elsewhere in the bourgeois edifice. By the end of the period, white-collar employment had become the most important route out of the working class among the older as well as the younger grooms, and in this sphere it is evident that competition for employment was becoming more open at all stages of the career (Table 5.4). Moreover, with the appearance of a tiny but growing number of workers' sons in class I positions towards the end of the period, quite large changes were even being made in the relative accessibility of positions of economic and social privilege.

WORK-LIFE MOBILITY

The contemporary career is the subject of an established and fast developing research field in sociology.[10] Unfortunately, the same

Table 5.4 *Disparity ratios showing the changing relative chances of the sons of middle-class men and working-class men gaining entry to (a) business, (b) white-collar positions, and (c) the sons of elite and working-class men gaining access to class I positions. Grooms aged 30 and over, workers' sons chances set at 1*

	a	b	c
1859–94	4.9:1	9.1:1	–
1879–94	3.4:1	3.9:1	68.2:1
1899–1914	11.6:1	2.1:1	31.6:1

cannot yet be said about its historical development. 'If social mobility analysis has been slow to pursue the origins of its conclusions', writes Vincent, 'career research has been virtually static.'[11] To a large extent this is once more a problem of sources. Dividing the marriage register sample in half according to the grooms' age may be an unsatisfactory approach to the problem, but sustained evidence of work-life mobility in the past is hard to come by.

Thernstrom used census material to investigate late nineteenth-century American career patterns. But this approach still provides only a limited number of snapshots of the career, suffers from the problem of diminishing returns and can say nothing about the subjective dynamics of mobility.[12] More recently, historians have begun to explore the potential of other sources which can overcome some of these limitations. Vincent, for example, has used Thompson's oral history sample to explore interwar careers, and new projects which utilise nineteenth-century company records and the research of family historians are currently in progress.[13]

A further, largely unexploited, source of career history is provided by autobiography. This is a source which, like all the others, has its limitations. Chief among these, and the reason it cannot substitute for survey data in the same way as the marriage registers can for a study of inter-generational mobility, is that autobiographers are exceptional people. This is accentuated by the particular nature of the texts used here, which are drawn from an anthology of 'working-class' auto-biography, and is most obviously reflected in their authors' success. Using the Registrar General's scheme, 60 per cent of the writers in the abstract sample finished up in a higher class than the one into which they were born, and 70 per cent experienced a net career gain. Two-thirds of writers could, by the end of their working lives, call themselves middle class and at least a quarter had gained access to the elite. The sample is clearly at its most revealing, then, as a study of upward mobility. However, by no means all the writers shared such good fortune, and there is no reason why the life histories of these men, whatever their outcome, should not reflect more general processes and developments in the structuring of the career.

The abstracts and texts used in this study span a period of over 250 years, the oldest author in the sample having being born in 1723 with some writers still alive in the mid-1980s. The sample has been divided into three birth cohorts, corresponding to three periods of substantive historical interest: 1723–1816, a span encompassing the classic period of the industrial revolution; 1816–64, a period of uneasy adjustment and consolidation culminating in the triumph of industrial capitalism and Britain's world economic supremacy; and 1865–1914, when that domination was challenged, relative economic decline began, and the state began to intervene directly in the sphere of education and social welfare.

In Table 5.5 the basic trajectories of the 479 men in the abstract sample are summarised. This takes the form of a three-point analysis comparing the writers' class of origin (his father's position at the time of the writer's fully-fledged entry into the labour market), with his first and last main occupations. Due to the small numbers involved, the semi- and unskilled categories have been collapsed into a single class IV. The five men born into the lower reaches of the elite have been excluded, although in the light of the poor performance of the marriage register elite it is interesting to note that all were downwardly mobile at both first and last job.

As noted, the patterns of work-life mobility displayed occur in the context of a strong overall rise in upward mobility between generations. This reflects the nature of the source, but, it should not be forgotten, is a trend also found in the marriage register sample. Within this, the principal feature is the way in which, as upward mobility increased, the routes by which access to the middle class was achieved changed. In short, transition via the career began to give way, especially in the last period, to direct entry. There might then be movement inside the bourgeoisie, but the crucial shift was the substitution of middle-class for manual positions at first job.

The key to this was the dramatic expansion of movement into white-collar positions. Among those born before 1816 a trade was the first job of 41 per cent of men, but after 1864 this dropped to 22 per cent. Before 1816 there were no examples of a man entering a white-collar position at first job, but in the later period a quarter did so. Master artisans made up 13 per cent of men in their final position at the beginning of the period but only 6 per cent by the end, when 30 per cent of men finished their careers in routine white-collar employment and a further 30 per cent reached professional white-collar positions.

Although there may appear to be some exaggeration in the strong profile of white-collar destinations – which would be natural enough among a collection of writers – there is quite a high degree of correspondence here with the pattern in the marriage registers. In the 1830s 22 per cent of upwardly mobile working-class men in the over-thirties age group were found in white-collar positions and by 1914 the figure was, as among the autobiographers, 60 per cent. Not as many made it

Table 5.5 Class distribution of autobiographers by father at writer's first occupation, by writer's first occupation, and by writer's last occupation, cross-sample, and by birth cohort, 1723–1914 (percentages–rounded)

Inter-generationally Stable

oc/c1/c2	y1	y2	y3	All
II/I/II	0	0	0	(0)
II/II/II	0	12	14	(10)
II/III/II	42	15	9	(20)
II/IV/II	30	27	25	(27)
All	(73	54	48	57)
n	24	31	21	76
III/I/III	0	0	0	(0)
III/II/III	3	0	0	(1)
III/III/III	15	13	16	(15)
III/IV/III	3	0	4	(2)
All	(21	13	20	17)
n	8	11	16	35

Inter-generationally Upward

oc/c1/c2	y1	y2	y3	All
III/I/I	0	0	0	(0)
II/II/I	0	5	18	(8)
II/III/I	9	7	18	(11)
II/IV/I	3	9	5	(6)
All	(12	20	41	25)
n	4	12	18	34
III/I/I	0	0	0	(0)
III/II/I	0	5	11	(7)
III/III/I	8	24	16	(18)
III/IV/I	5	6	5	(6)
III/II/II	0	0	10	(4)
III/III/II	36	40	18	(30)
III/IV/II	13	5	13	(10)
All	(62	81	73	18)
n	24	66	58	25

Inter-generationally Downward

oc/c1/c2	y1	y2	y3	All
II/I/III	0	0	0	(0)
II/II/III	0	0	0	(0)
II/III/III	6	7	2	(5)
II/IV/III	0	7	2	(4)
II/I/IV	0	0	0	(0)
II/II/IV	6	0	2	(1)
II/III/IV	3	5	2	(5)
II/IV/IV			2	(4)
All	(15	26	12	18)
n	(5	15	5	(25)
III/I/IV	0	0	0	(0)
III/II/IV	0	0	1	(1)
III/III/IV	13	2	1	(4)
III/IV/IV	5	4	5	(5)
All	(18	6	8	9)
n	7	5	6	18

Table 5.5 (Cont'd)

Inter-generationally Stable					Inter-generationally Upward					Inter-generationally Downward
oc/c1/c2	y1	y2	y3	All	oc/c1/c2	y1	y2	y3	All	
IV/I/IV	0	0	0	(0)	IV/I/I	0	0	2	(1)	
IV/II/IV	0	0	0	(0)	IV/II/I	0	2	8	(4)	
IV/III/IV	3	4	0	(2)	IV/III/I	0	7	12	(7)	
IV/IV/IV	30	21	16	(21)	IV/IV/I	7	18	18	(15)	
All	(33)	25	16	23	IV/I/II	0	0	0	(0)	
n	10	14	8	32	IV/II/II	3	2	8	(4)	
					IV/III/II	20	16	10	(15)	
					IV/IV/II	23	23	18	(21)	
					IV/I/III	0	0	0	(0)	
					IV/II/III	0	0	0	(0)	
					IV/III/III	13	5	6	(7)	
					IV/IV/III	0	2	4	(2)	
					All	(67)	75	84	77	
					n	20	42	43	105	

Key: oc = origin class, c1 = 1st class, c2 = 2nd class
y1 = born 1723–1815, y2 = born 1816–1864, y3 = born 1865–1914

into unequivocally professional situations, but a shift in this direction is very clear, and the shortfall can be explained by the fact that not all of the writers had working-class backgrounds, and some did not reach their destinations until well after 1914.

There are further indications that the autobiographers, their obvious success notwithstanding, are not such an unrepresentative group of men as they might seem. The trajectories reveal, for example, that no sons of master artisans experienced three-way stability inside the lower middle class, thereby confirming that the transformation from journey-men to employer was rarely an attainable aspiration in extreme youth. On the other hand, the pathway back via a trade was, not surprisingly, an important one for such men. Recalling a relationship first high-lighted in chapter 4, there was also a firm link between white-collar origins and semi-skilled positions at first job culminating in a return to class II by the end of the career. The continuing importance of three-way stability inside the skilled sector reflects a declining craft sector and the rising profile of mining, both well established in the marriage data. Although downward mobility was rare among this group, its con-centration in the periods of greatest economic uncertainty, particularly in the wake of the Napoleonic Wars and during the 1830s and 1840s, is further evidence that the writers could be as susceptible as any other men to the wider forces of economic and social change.[14]

Apart from the emphasis on success, the other peculiarity of the sample is the relatively high profile of men who were successful on the strength of their connection with the labour movement. This accounts for the apparently anomalous rise in the importance of indirect path-ways into the middle class between the first two cohorts. Men born in the first half and middle third of the nineteenth century were the first beneficiaries of the institutionalisation of the working class, which ironically involved their promotion out of it via representative work for the trade unions, and election to parliament.

THE EMERGENCE OF THE BUREAUCRATIC CAREER

These patterns, of course, reveal nothing concrete about what hap-pened to the authors in between first and last job. Not unexpectedly, the detailed career trajectories of the autobiographers range from the straightforward to the labyrinthine. On the one hand, there were men such as Francis Alfred Peet, son of a carpenter at the local estate works at Cole Green in Hertford. This was where he, in turn, was apprenticed as a carpenter in 1897, and where he worked, with the exception of his service in the Great War, until his retirement in 1948.[15] George Healey, on the other hand, entered the labour market in the silk trade in St Albans in 1837. His last recorded occupation, in his late forties, was as a maker of packing cases for Cadburys in Birmingham. In between he had been a domestic servant, a hotel porter, a travelling salesman of goods ranging from bonnets to Ostend butter, a waiter, a hatmaker, a factory labourer in the food, rope and cotton industries, an assistant to an egg merchant, a street seller, a bleacher of straw and tucking, a worker in a mat factory, a dairyman, a shoemaker, a shop assistant, a herbalist, and a cutter and packer for an india rubber company.[16] Peet had one job, and was intra-generationally class stable. Healey, who worked in St Albans, London, Essex, Oldham, Manchester and Birmingham, made at least 38 job moves, worked in 11 different industries, experienced life in four of the Registrar-General's five classes, and switched between classes on 23 occasions.

The question of who was more representative bears directly on Booth's claim that, within the late Victorian economy, industrial order coexisted with a large dose of occupational anarchy. We can consider this first in terms of the percentage of autobiographers whose experience took them into classes other than the ones in which they started and finished their careers (Figure 5.2). Overall, a not insubstantial quarter of the sample experienced such class-crossing undulation. However, only half of these moved along pathways which travel back and forth across the *major* class barrier, that is between bourgeois and

Figure 5.2 *Class undulation between first and last occupation*

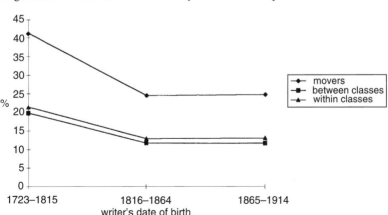

working-class occupations. And over time the picture is very clear: social flux inside the career was most definitely on the wane.

This evidence suggests that a substantial and increasing proportion of men moved along largely linear channels of progression. Nevertheless, such measurements offer only a crude indication of this process. In these terms 'undulation' might involve a single momentary shift, or a whole series of zig-zags. Looking at the pattern of work-life change in more detail, they reveal several distinctive models of career development in the nineteenth- and early twentieth-century economy (Table 5.8).[17]

First, three types of informal career can be identified: an *entrepreneurial* trajectory, involving a coherent progression into business from a starting point clearly connected, industrially and culturally, with the resulting enterprise. Typically, the category includes tradesmen who set up as manufacturers or retailers inside their trade, and shop assistants who become shopkeepers; *professional* careers are those originating in, based on and defined by possession of a recognised skill. The term is employed here in the broad generic sense of the capacities and assumptions which structure change rather than as a contemporary occupational definition. The model therefore incorporates the original professionals – craftsmen – as well as the more familiar clergymen, physicians and academics. It is noteworthy that, as categories of profession, these two worlds were not mutually exclusive. There are cases of men crossing from one to the other while remaining in the same industry. Robert Rippon Duke, for example, started out as an apprentice carpenter and joiner at the Buxton Estate in 1831, becoming its architect in 1862.[18] In addition there are those

Table 5.6   *Autobiographers' career typologies by period, 1723–1914*

| Career models | Writer's date of birth | | | | |
	1723–1815	1816–1864	1865–1914	All	n
Entrepreneurial	19.2	17.9	11.3	(15.9)	76
Professional	17.3	14.0	19.0	(16.5)	79
Union-political	0.0	14.0	7.1	(8.6)	41
Bureaucratic	0.0	4.8	16.1	(7.7)	37
Fractured	46.2	44.0	41.7	(43.6)	209
Shapeless	17.3	5.3	4.8	(7.7)	37
n	104	207	168	(100.0)	479

quasi-professionals – teachers, for example – who, at different levels, sought to ape their more established peers. Again, there are crossing points in the dimension of formality, as well as class. For example, there were seamen who became ships' masters and then sea captains,[19] or the gardeners who ended up as horticulturalists, herbalists or surveyors;[20] finally, the *union-political* model is one which is rather specific to the autobiographers. Typical here is the experience of John Hogan Jenkins, a shipwright elected local representative of and technical adviser to the Associated Shipwrights' Society, who in 1895 became president of the TUC, and in 1906, MP for Chatham.[21]

The *bureaucratic* career represents an externally structured, formally defined framework characterised by ladders of vertical progression. It was by no means fully and universally operationalised by credentialist entry and promotion through open competition in this period, but this was increasingly the case. It finds its clearest institutional expression where the state was the employer – in the Post Office, the Police and the Civil Service more generally – but also on the railways, whose organisation was heavily influenced by army and Civil Service templates. This model could also operate on a smaller scale in the form of a company career, where an employee entered on, or close to, the bottom rung of an established ladder with a particular firm as a boy and then, remaining with the same firm for the whole of his working life, experienced some degree of progression through the ranks and departments. At its most dramatic, such advancement might result in a position of significant managerial responsibility, as in Arthur Simpson's case,[22] or even a directorship, which J.A. Holt achieved after starting as an office boy.[23]

Where there was no overall trajectory, among what might be called the 'non-careers', two divisions present themselves. There are first those whose working lives were *fractured* by a distinct change of direction. In about half of these cases there was a single disjuncture involving no more than two occupations or forms of employment. Prominent here, and both characteristic of the sample, are men who suddenly convert and take up a religious calling, and men who move into journalism and writing.[24] However, the texts reveal a great range of experience under this heading, including the extravagant contrast in the career of Joseph Millot Severn, who began as a time-served carpenter but dropped his trade at 28 to become a 'professional' phrenologist.[25] The remainder of this group had their careers fractured more than once, but this fluctuation tended to cease at around 30, after which the individual settled down to a particular occupation or trajectory. Less often, inconsistency was experienced in the wake of a period of longer-term stability. The second type of non-career is the meandering or *shapeless*; more or less random motion through a series of largely unrelated jobs, or at best a sequence in which coherence is minimal and short-lived. George Healey is included in this category, although those experiencing such a lack of order in their working lives were normally more consistently associated with the lower reaches of the working class.

Once more, the changing distribution of career types over time throws up some strong patterns which, it has to be said, add further weight to the conclusion that Booth's observations can only be entertained with substantial qualification. On the face of it, the lack of patterning across the sample might suggest otherwise: the trajectories of as many as half of the autobiographers were devoid of an overall structure. Yet almost half of these were men who experienced just the one major shift, and the meanderers – the closest representation of Booth's undulators – make up less than 10 per cent of the sample.

Over time the situation moved impressively away from Booth's scenario. While the work histories of almost 20 per cent of writers born before the end of the Napoleonic Wars had been essentially shapeless, less than 5 per cent of Booth's contemporaries were likely to embark on such a trajectory. At the same time, although the fractured career remained commonplace, multiple breaks affected one in six men after 1865 compared to one in four at the beginning of the century.

In their place there was a growth in structured work-life mobility, and specifically in formalised, linear pathways. Representing the triumph of the 'modern' professional over the tradesman, the importance of professional trajectories first declined and then recovered. At the same time, the movement from high to organised capitalism in the era of international competition reduced the influence of the entrepreneurial mode. But the principal process evident in this analysis is the rapid expansion of the bureaucratic model in both its public and private guises.

CONCLUSION

The principal aim of this chapter has been to test the findings on inter-generational mobility at marriage against evidence of intra-generational, or work-life, movement, and to explore the changing structural dynamics of the career. Although there are considerable problems with using age at marriage as a proxy for career stage, the main conclusion must be that while a snapshot taken at marriage generates an incomplete picture of movement between the generations, in most respects the degree of distortion involved is not substantial. The basic framework of class relationships remained intact across the life course, as, for the most part, did the structures of advantage and disadvantage between individuals of different social backgrounds.

The one potentially serious anomaly concerns the matter of the temporal shift in the direction of increasing fluidity which is found to occur strongly in the sample as a whole, but not in such unequivocal fashion amongst the older men. According to statistical convention, the pattern of association between classes in this sub-sample is represented just as well by a model which posits constant social fluidity, an outcome which seems to favour Goldthorpe's contention that the stability of the post-Second World War mobility regime is more deeply rooted. Even so, a weak but consistent trend towards greater fluidity can still be discerned among the older grooms, and there are clear indications of falling barriers in particular relationships.

In earlier chapters it was suggested that changing employment practices were of key importance in opening up routeways between classes. This argument finds further support in the changing structures and, as the next chapter shows, mechanisms of the career. The use of autobiographical evidence for career analysis can be criticised from a number of standpoints. But the strength and clarity of the trends revealed by the texts, and their general compatibility with those derived from the marriage registers, cannot be denied. As far as it relates to the morphology of the career, this evidence suggests far less longitudinal instability than was claimed by Booth, at least in the period in which he was claiming it, and its main theme is the rising importance of formalised, structured pathways on the bureaucratic model. The development of categories of employment which 'make the modern world modern' may have been more impressive after the First World War but their origins are most definitely to be found in the pre-war period.[26]

6 Mechanisms and Meanings of Mobility

In this chapter, an attempt is made to pursue further both the assumptions which underlie a marriage-based study of inter-generational change and the emergence of the bureaucratic career by turning to the processes of work-life mobility: to the structures and dynamics of the individual career. Here, the actors behind the numbers and the tables come to the fore as strategies, motivations and understandings are explored. This perspective is relatively rare in modern survey research, despite the ready availability of evidence via tape recorder and questionnaire. Historical evidence of the mechanics and meanings of mobility is, of course, much harder to come by, but among the limited range of suitable materials available autobiography can provide a particularly rich insight.

These issues are explored here by following writers through the different stages of their careers, and listening to how they rationalised and made sense of their experiences. In the detail of their testimony, there is further evidence to support the impression given by the preceding analysis of career structures that formal, more impersonal and credentially defined structures were gradually challenging the role of direct and informal influences in the negotiation of a working life. It is also clear that the authors conceived of the movements they made in ways which do, by and large, correspond to the major social divisions assumed by the census stratification scheme employed in the rest of this study, that they indexed their achievements in *inter-* as much as intra-generational terms, and that, whatever its emotional significance, the event of marriage was, more often than not, a crucial watershed in career terms as well.

JOINING THE LABOUR MARKET

The most impressive feature of the autobiographers' entry into the world of work was the early age at which it occurred. A truncated childhood was the norm for the sons of shopkeepers and labourers alike, although its precise length was mediated, in hierarchical fashion, by class of origin: the higher one's background class, the later the confrontation with employment.

The transition from childhood to career could be abrupt, but for an equal number of men it was a two-stage process, beginning with a 'probationary' period of casual employment which would be followed by more formal entry into a regular job or trade. The main exceptions to this staggered format were to be found in agriculture, textiles and mining, where boys would generally move straight into ancillary occupations within each industry.[1] The mean age at which writers first came into contact with the world of work was 11. However, it could happen as early as five,[2] and 28 per cent of the sample began some form of full- or at least half- time work outside the home before they had reached ten years of age.[3] If probation was experienced, then it would last, on average, for three and a half years. A boy usually entered his first 'real' position, whether this was a formally apprenticed trade or not, at 13 or 14.

Not only timing of entry but the duration of probation were class-linked, and both in turn were associated with the length and quality of education received. The latest mean age of entry, and the highest proportion of writers experiencing some kind of post-elementary instruction, were to be found amongst men coming from middle-class backgrounds while the earliest mean entry age occurred among those with unskilled working-class backgrounds, of whom 40 per cent received less than five years of basic schooling.

Over time, the age at which either stage was experienced rose, although only in the post-1864 period (Figure 6.1). The period after 1815, characterised by the process of painful and uneven adjustment to the emergence an industrial-capitalist economy, was the one in which age at entry was at its lowest. Thereafter, there was something of a transformation. Previously, over a third of writers had been sent out to work before the age of ten. After 1864 this dropped to 7.5 per cent. Similarly, before 1865 40 per cent entered their first real job before 13, whereas more than 80 per cent of those born after this date entered after 13. At the same time the duration of the average probationary period contracted steadily, although as an institution it remained no less important.

The proportion of the sample population experiencing staggered entry into the labour market was, in fact, roughly consistent throughout. And while there was a qualitative shift away from the rurally-based employments of the earlier periods, there was no reduction in the tremendous variety of jobs which might be undertaken in

Social Mobility in England

Figure 6.1   *Mean age at entry to work and duration of probation*

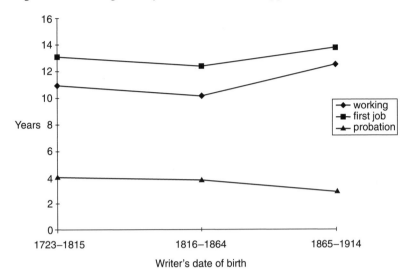

Years

1723–1815   1816–1864   1865–1914
Writer's date of birth

- working
- first job
- probation

this pre-career stage. Sidney Campion's pre-apprenticeship curriculum vitae from the early twentieth century reads: errand boy, delivery boy, machine operative, doctor's receptionist, seam presser and factory labourer.[4] The decline of the pre-career stage was also mitigated to some extent by part-time work, for children still helped out with the family business[5] or, classically in the late Victorian and Edwardian period, sold and delivered newspapers out of school hours.[6]

The growth of extended formal schooling was behind the rising age at first job and the contraction of the probationary period. Although the effects of Forster's Act, legislating for universal elementary education, are less obvious than when the boundaries of the period are drawn ten years later, the impact of educational reform from 1870 onwards are clearly reflected in Figure 6.2. Those receiving only a meagre dose of basic schooling – about 30 per cent up to 1865 – all but disappeared after this point. Instead, growing numbers received their full quota of elementary instruction, and most dynamic of all was the rising proportion of writers gaining entry to some form of further or higher education, in the main to teacher training.[7] This, and the appearance of a very small number of university-trained writers, accounts for the latest age at entry into work rising from 17 to 26 in the latest period. Overall, the 'secondary' sector remained

Figure 6.2   *Types of education experienced by period*

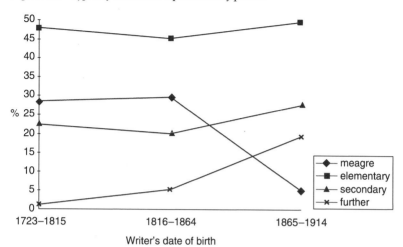

stable, but this hides a rise in the numbers experiencing Board-sponsored, post-13 instruction, or evening classes.

The rising profile of school is also strikingly evident from the breakdown of motivating factors and facilitating agencies behind labour-market entry in Table 6.3.[8] Until 1865, and especially during the 1816–64 'adjustment phase' of economic development, the overriding force behind movement into the labour market was the demand of the family economy. Sustained poverty, such as that which caused the young Benjamin Brierley to be chained to a stool in order to turn a bobbin wheel for his parents, and his mother to wish he 'should have followed the youthful departed',[9] was the most prominent of domestic push-factors. But equally the family unit could suddenly be destabilised by unemployment or the failure of the family business on the one hand,[10] and the ill-health, death or sometimes desertion of the breadwinner on the other.[11]

Reflecting Sanderson's arguments about the effect of industrialisation on working-class education, completion of schooling was the single reason most often given for joining the labour market in both the earliest and the last period. However, before 1816 economic hardship still accounted for well over a half of all labour-market entries, while after 1864 the luxury of completing at least one educational stage was enjoyed – sometimes endured – by 80 per cent of the sample.

Table 6.1 *Reasons for/mechanics of joining the labour market by period (percentage rounded)*

% of writers mentioning	Writer's date of birth				
	1723–1815	1816–1864	1865–1914	All	n
Why:					
Family business failure	5	15	10	(7)	5
General poverty	25	39	15	(26)	19
Death of parent	30	23	4	(18)	11
Schooling finished	35	15	82	(45)	33
Other	5	8	0	(4)	3
How:					
Work for father/mother	19	22	11	(17)	13
Work for father's employers	5	15	32	(18)	14
Parent arranges	29	33	11	(24)	18
Work for relative	10	4	0	(4)	3
Relative arranges	19	4	4	(8)	6
Workhouse	0	4	4	(3)	2
Independent mediation	10	11	29	(17)	13
Other	10	7	11	(9)	7

In part, the post-1864 shift reflects a general easing of economic conditions, as real incomes rose and mortality rates fell, as well the institutional and statutory reorganisation of education, which brought more opportunities and, in the 1880s, compulsory attendance. This does not mean that the demands of the family economy were no longer felt, however. In some cases they were not so much displaced as deferred, as Cecil Harwood found when, on passing the 'labour exam', his parents decided that he should leave school early to go out to work.[12]

Constraints on circumstances also continued to thwart post-elementary intellectual ambition. Like John Tough a hundred years before him, and David Barr half a century later, James Cruickshank, who left school in the early 1880s, could not extend his education beyond 13 without independent financial assistance.[13] Thomas McLauchlan, a child of the 1890s, could not follow in the footsteps of his schoolteacher brother because, as his father put it, 'there was one gentleman in the family and he couldn't afford to make another'.[14] On the other hand, there is a clear sense, as time went on, of parents recognising that there was value in education. It was, for example, Cruickshank's father's ambitions for his son which put the possibility of further education on the agenda. Arthur Goffin, an above-average scholar, had the option of leaving in 1890 at age 11, but his parents made sure he stayed on until 14.[15]

The dominant facilitators of a boy's transition into regular work were their fathers. All told, 50 per cent of the autobiographers obtained their first authentic position through his direct agency. Classically, as in Anthony Errington's case, a boy might be bound in apprenticeship to his father.[16] Alternatively, a position would be found with the parental employer. James Cruickshank, for one, was fortunate enough to obtain a clerkship at Piries' Paper Mill in Bankhead, Aberdeenshire, where his father was foreman,[17] and although Arthur Goffin's mother wanted her son to work in a solicitors' office, his father, a printer's reader, demurred and 'spoke for him' at the Caxton Works from which point his 'name was down'.[18] A third way in which a father could directly organise his son's passage was for him to arrange employment beyond the family work situation, which mainly involved the binding of sons to unfamiliar trades.[19]

The influence of family networks more broadly accounted for the original placement of a further 22 per cent of writers. David Barr was apprenticed as a shoemaker to his eldest brother,[20] William Johnston was a learner in a cousin's cartwright shop,[21] and Thomas Hardy was bound to his shoemaker grandfather.[22] The assistance of the extended family was particularly important when a father had died, or deserted the family. In John Brown's case, his father's death in 1806 left the ten-year-old boy and his family in the care of an uncle, who promptly drank and gambled the family into bankruptcy and then ran off to sea.[23] Recognising her son's unhappiness in the work he had to carry out to help sustain the family economy, Brown's mother subsequently sent him to live with her own mother, who arranged for her grandson to follow the trade of his choice.

Mothers tended to come into their own on such tragic occasions, but were no means without influence when the family remained intact. It was J. Wardle's mother who decided he should leave Harpur Hill Lime Works near Buxton for farm labour, on account of the 'uncultured, wicked boys' he was obliged to work with.[24] And when, to her delight because of the enhanced economic benefit it might bring to the family, Jack Lanigan passed the school leaving exam in 1900, it was his mother who kitted him out in 'new' second-hand clothes and went out with him in search of employment.[25]

The main change indicated by the figures in Table 6.3 is a sharp rise in 'independent' mediation of labour market entry, at the expense of family influence in the wider sense. In particular, this reflects the growing opportunities provided by public bureaucracies for entry via open competition in the form of examination and interview, which men like T. Lloyd Roberts, William Bowyer and Thomas Raymont took up.[26] However, while families in general became less important in the process of negotiating a boy's access to the labour market, parental authority often remained vital. As Arthur Gair's account of the way in which his apprenticeship at Hetton Engineering Works in 1909 was brokered shows, a father's influence was often no less vital in the factory than it had been in a craft economy. It just tended to be more subtle.[27]

Among those who took independent routes there was little to fill the supportive vacuum. T. Lloyd Roberts, who worked his way up in the Civil Service after beginning as a boy copyist in the Post Office Savings Bank, complained that 'no reference was made at school to careers for young people'.[28] Born in North Wales in 1881, he got to know of the Civil Service through the boy next door who had been sent away to school, and only found out about the examinations via an advertisement in the *Liverpool Daily Post* offering tuition. In the early years of this century Bowyer sat an examination for a temporary clerkship in the Post Office, complaining that the expected assistance from father and family was not forthcoming:

I had no friends or relations who would find a post for me. Even my former neighbour had found a distant relative to put him in an architects' office as a pupil ... had to depend on myself.[29]

For others who found work for themselves, the sanction and approval of parents remained an important reference point. Charles Bacon had to seek his parents' permission for an extension to his hiring on a farm where he was very happy, and when he left the next year his new employer came to see his father with the offer of a position.[30] Thomas Jordan was offered a full-time position with the newsagent he had worked for as a delivery boy while at school, but his father was adamant, again for reasons of family economy, that he should follow him down the pit.[31]

GETTING ON

Men moved between jobs for a huge variety of reasons, and behind the negotiation of individual work-life trajectories there often lay a complex series of motivating and facilitating factors. One specific change might be explained simply, or in several ways. John Leatherland, for example, moved from ribbon to velvet weaving because he disliked the work. But he also found the social side of his working environment uncongenial, trade was slack and so his wages were affected adversely, and his health was suffering.[32]

Rather than just aggregate stated reasons – which exaggerates the effect of more involved or longer trajectories – a better way of obtaining a global sense of the relative importance of different factors, and of changing priorities over time, is to calculate the proportion of writers giving particular explanations for movement over their lifetimes (Table 6.2). A number of patterns are thrown up by such an analysis, but what is of particular interest for this study of, predominantly, *inter-generational* mobility based on marriage register evidence is the continuing significance of family influence in the mediation of trajectories, and the conjunction of the event of matrimony with career considerations.

As with Leatherland, simple dislike of the work or the situation was the most likely reason for a move. Even here there was great variation upon the theme. James Murdoch left farm service in 1821 because he objected to the subordination involved.[33] Bowyer moved from the Post Office Registry to the Civil Service because he felt oppressed by its time and motion 'detectives'.[34] David Barr disliked the long hours at shoemaking which left him no time to study.[35] John Wood, a school teacher, objected to the imposition of domestic service duties by his Principal.[36] Arthur Goffin, a compositor made up to clerical manager, missed the noise of the shop-floor and could not settle to desk work,[37] while many others – George Healey among them – found factory work too physically demanding.[38]

Closely connected to this category of explanation were disagreements with employers and those in authority at work. Youngsters such as John Saville suffered from the violent and sadistic temperaments of their masters.[39] Cecil Harwood fell out with his boss when he was offered the services of a prostitute as an inducement to accept the position of manager at the Ostend Charabanc Company.[40] John Hodge left his supervisory post at the Singer Sewing Machine company in Glasgow rather than carry on a feud with the works under-manager over Hodge's refusal to discipline miscreant workers in another department.[41] The hostility of, or contempt for, workmates was another work-related reason, and particularly common in the accounts of the more pious and intellectually ambitious of the authors.[42]

Social Mobility in England

Table 6.2 *Reasons for/mechanics of job mobility by period, 1723–1914*

% of Writers Mentioning	Writer's Date of Birth				
	1723–1825	1816–1864	1865–1914	All	n
Why Move:					
Dislike of work situation	44	36	50	(43)	39
Employer discipline	32	26	32	(29)	27
Dislike of workmates	32	23	11	(22)	20
Money	44	36	43	(40)	37
Social ambition	32	26	36	(30)	28
Vocational ambition	24	13	29	(21)	19
Adventure/environment	40	41	39	(40)	37
Informal promotion	16	23	64	(34)	31
Formal promotion	4	10	25	(13)	12
Ill health	52	46	14	(38)	35
Trade slack/economic pressure	44	38	21	(35)	32
Employer dies, moves, folds	40	46	25	(38)	35
Temporary contract	20	23	11	(18)	17
Seasonal work	12	21	18	(17)	16
Employer directs	24	26	46	(32)	29
Sacked/victimised	40	46	29	(35)	32
Strike	0	5	7	(4)	4
War service	4	0	50	(16)	15
Family considerations (parental)	24	13	39	(24)	22
Family considerations (own)	12	21	29	(21)	19
Marriage	4	16	7	(10)	9
How Move:					
Family influence	44	29	43	(38)	35
Help of friends/workmates	24	18	18	(20)	18
Tip/word of mouth	16	18	32	(26)	24
Benefactor/patronage	20	26	14	(21)	19
Migrate	24	26	11	(21)	19
Informally solicit	16	36	25	(27)	25
Informally solicited	0	13	4	(7)	6
Make application	4	10	46	(20)	18
Via advert	4	5	32	(13)	12
Labour exchange	0	0	18	(5)	5
Interview/exam	4	13	46	(12)	11

Ill-health was another, unsurprisingly, prominent motivation behind change. The autobiographers succumbed to their fair share of diseases, and some had to bear physical infirmities which caught up within them at various moments. But again work was often instrumental in causing or exacerbating illness and injury. The noxious effects of the industrial process in the Sheffield and Birmingham metal trades affected James

Murdoch and Thomas Jackson respectively.[43] George Mallard's career on the railways was finally ended in 1901 by his fourth accident, and Thomas Jordan, previously a miner, was condemned to casual labour due to the combined effects of malaria and gas poisoning during the First World War.[44] Work-related illness could be mental as well as physical, particularly, it would seem, in the later period among white-collared careerists. T. Lloyd Roberts, a Registrar at the Welsh Board of Health, and Edward Balne, a Higher Executive Officer at the Admiralty, both took early retirement from the Civil Service after suffering nervous breakdowns.[45]

Alongside and after ill-health the other major involuntary factors sponsoring job change were the death or failure of an employer, trade slumps and economic pressure, and the migration structures built into particular jobs. Prominent among those affected by the latter were soldiers, domestic servants and those inside the new bureaucracies. Alan McEwan, who enlisted in 1863, mentions 12 postings in his 22-years in the army.[46] Thomas Arthur Westwater made 23 job moves in his 52-year career on the railways of the North-East, a third of which were unrequested transfers.[47]

Boredom, generating a largely unfocused desire for challenge and excitement, and usually combined with *wanderlust*, was another principal voluntary motivation behind movement.[48] For many, like Thomas Hardy and George Mallard, London was the magnet.[49] A third of the 479 visited London having been born in the provinces, and half of these stayed to finish their working lives there. For others, like Charles Bacon, the lights of Leicester, just 10 miles from where he worked on a farm, were bright enough.[50] As in Bacon's case, the rationale for migration to the city usually included economic considerations.

The instrumental search for more remunerative employment was given by 40 per cent of the 100 writers as a reason for job change. This exceeded the proportion mentioning social ambition as a motive, although the desire for greater income could be combined with ambitious sentiments. Ambition is not as straightforward a motivation as it might at first appear. Among the testimonies two main dimensions present themselves. First, and the more prominent, was the desire for social advancement, itself often associated with a craving for independence. David Barr's consistent justification for moving between employments was 'to take another step up the ladder', but his aim was 'to be my own master'[51]. The second was concerned with the intrinsic satisfaction to be gained from a particular occupation, and the desire to progress, and sometimes to gain status, in terms of acquired skill or expertise. As one would expect, such vocational ambition was particularly prevalent among tradesmen such as George Mitchell, who moved eight times between 1846 and 1851 in order to gain the experience needed to fulfil his quest to become a highly skilled mason. Yet it was also a professional calling which found William Bowyer leaving his clerical post in Whitehall to become a Keeper at the Victoria and Albert Museum.[52]

The influence of family could last a long time, and was most direct as a facilitator of movement. However, particularly early on in a son's career, parents still tended to play a determining role. Edward Cain followed his father down the pit in 1905. He lost his first four jobs at various collieries in the North-East because of his father's drunkenness, and did not finally escape his influence until he joined up in 1914, aged 20.[53] When, in 1907, William Bowyer neared the cut-off point for temporary clerkships at the Savings Bank, he wanted to follow the example of friend who had borrowed 50 pounds in order study full-time for a post as Surveyor of Taxes. Accepting that this was out of his reach, he asked to borrow the examination fee of 2 pounds for a Second Division Clerkship. When his father refused, his mother came up with the money by way of a bequest from an aunt she had nursed in Teignmouth.[54] John Hodge, in partnership with his brother, left what had been a flourishing and expanding business because his mother was constantly interfering, and had undermined a solid concern by giving credit out of pity to poor customers.[55]

More broadly, family matters affected movement right through the life course. Homesickness was not confined to youth. And in the days before compassionate leave, children returning to tend dying parents often lost their jobs. As to the conjugal family, Westwater offered no resistance to one of his transfers because, during a sticky patch in the marriage, his wife was agitating for alterations to their house which he could not afford and thought unnecessary.[56] And when the autobiographers themselves became parents, the rhythms of the family life cycle could determine job movement. The increasing size of Robert Spurr's family, for example, was the reason he went into business on his own account in the mid-1830s.[57]

Marriage has a low statistical profile as a reason for movement, but this is partly because, for most, it would only happen once. What the figures hide is the quality of movement often associated with taking a partner. Marriage was a mark of 'settling down' emotionally, but also economically, and with sometimes pivotal consequences for a career. For Robert Spurr, it was the cue to throw off the immaturity which had previously prevented him from 'facing up to the serious realities of life'.[58] According to William Fairbairn, 'The important event of a marriage, and the altered conditions and circumstances which it involves, are such as to open a new epoch in every man's history'.[59] In his case it was the stimulus to realise his ambition to achieve independence, so the move into business actually came after the ceremony. However, Edward Brown's engagement immediately turned his thoughts to obtaining a better paid position, and so he diverted his love of study 'away from personal whim' and towards a programme of self-education leading to examinations for membership of the Chartered Institute of Secretaries.[60] Arthur Goffin decided he must defer marriage while he went off in search of security and advancement. 'I had contracted ties which meant responsibility,' he writes. Remaining at home 'would mean restricting my efforts at improvement. A better position would mean something for us both later on.'[61] Roger Langdon and Cecil Harwood's proposals were only accepted on condition that they secure a stable economic position before their weddings. Langdon's fiancée told him to find a permanent position on the railways or with the Post Office, while Harwood had to be in a steady job which would bring in as much as his intended could earn. The one duly applied for, and obtained, a position on the Bristol and Exeter Railway, while the other, previously a painter for a beehive maker, started his married life as an inspector with the Anlaby Motor Company in Hull.[62]

The relative importance of different explanations clearly changed over time, and in ways that quite closely reflect the developments in occupational structure and social expectations associated with a maturing capitalist economy. Most strikingly, ill-health declined dramatically as a factor in the period after 1864, so too did an employer's death. Macroeconomic pressures, although hardly disappearing, are rarer among those growing up to work in the late nineteenth- and twentieth-century economy than among those working in the more unstable conditions of early industrial Britain. Also in decline as a reason for movement was the temporary engagement, a reflection of the shrinking profile of tramping artisans on contract work, and of agricultural workers on seasonal hirings.

By contrast, there are a number of factors which became steadily more important. An early indication of the twentieth-century shift towards family-centredness perhaps, the demands and concerns of the writers' own families was one.[63] Presumably an expression of the growth of trade unionism, strikes were also cited more often as time progressed. A further factor in the last period was war service, as men left their work to fight in the twentieth century's two major conflicts. However, most prominent of all is the increasing importance of promotion, both formal and informal, in the process of job change. Both indicate the expanding influence of bureaucratic employment structures. The former ties in with the rising profile of employer-directed movement, while the latter may be an expression of a more generalised 'career' consciousness, growing in the wake of the bureau-cratisation of the more dynamic sectors of the economy.

The net effect of these shifts over time was to increase the rate of voluntary, or unforced, movement. At the same time the dynamic rise of the bureaucratic career was, in this regard, a mixed blessing. For while there was a virtual guarantee of 'progress', it took place within and at the behest of the constraining structures and demands of the 'organisation'.

Motivation is one side of the job-change equation. On the other lie the process and mechanics of entry and placement. It is in this dimen-sion of occupational change that the continuing influence of the family was most important. The input could be direct and simple. After nine years at South Hetton Thomas McLauchlan became a miner at Dawdon Colliery because his father knew the official and arranged the necessary recommendation.[64] Arthur Gill was invited to join his brother's firm as a specialist showcard, ticket and poster writer, with a view to taking a share of the business.[65] On the other hand, members of the immediate or extended family could be involved as the prime movers in a rather more intricate and indirect process of contact and patronage. David Barr was able to leave shoemaking for a job at Staveley station in 1847 because his sister, who was in service, worked for the parents-in-law of a vice-chairman of the Midland Railway Company, and he used his good offices on Barr's behalf.[66] When Thomas Jackson was thrown out of the plating trade by 'commercial panic' in 1816, it was his cousin's petty-bourgeois contacts that rescued him. Herself the wife of an innkeeper, she was friendly with the daughter of a coal merchant whose clerk had just died, and a success-ful interview was arranged.[67] Harwood, as noted, was able to get the stable job with a transport company that fulfilled his fiancée's con-ditions for marriage, but this was because his brother, a policeman, was owed a favour by his boss, who just happened to be a partner in the Hertford and District Motor Service company.[68]

It was not only the influence of parents, siblings and the members of the extended family into which one was born that mattered. Although more rare, members of a writer's own family could play a crucial role. William Farish moved from warping to supervisory work as a clerk and timekeeper on railway bridge construction because his wife knew the stonemason involved in the project from the days when she lodged with him and his wife during her millinery apprenticeship.[69] Not only partners, but children, too, could assist. When Edward Rymer left his position as a union organiser in Hanley, it was his son's employer who offered him a job as a datal worker at Wombell Main colliery near Barnsley.[70] Chance acquaintance and the 'tip off' also retained a high profile, and even increased in importance in this period. Barr, for example, left the railway quite quickly, and a little later in his life experienced a protracted period of unemployment. This was ended when, having stood in one day for a local preacher friend of his during a service, he was approached by a member of the congregation who later introduced him to a relative in the insurance business.[71] Mallard's progress between navvying jobs in the 1850s, and Bacon's movement, during the 1890s, from farm work into a series of jobs prior to his going into business, were both conducted largely on the basis of hearsay and chance tips. Likewise, the influence of friends and workmates remained important, as the experience of William Hart, Emmanuel Lovekin and William Miles, in each of the three periods respectively, demonstrates.[72]

However, in line with tendencies already noted in other dimensions of work-life change, the major shift in the matter of job facilitation was away from the informal mechanism, and towards the more formalised and structured modes of engagement characteristic of a modern economy. The profile of the benefactor, instrumental in Thom's attempt to live by the pen, and in Wood's return to school teaching, fell. So too did the importance of patronage, which had assisted, along with those already mentioned, Wardle, Purkiss and Joseph Wilson. There was less direct soliciting of work from employers, and the informal procedure of simply being offered employment was less often experienced. Fewer men chose, or were forced, to take to the road to find work.

In place of these measures, there was strong rise in the proportion of writers making formal applications for jobs, attending interviews and sitting examinations. Labour exchanges are first mentioned in the later period, by Harwood among others,[73] and with development of urban labour markets printed advertisements were among the means by which a rising proportion of writers, including Gill, Rooney, Lanigan and Edward Brown, heard about openings.[74] To an extent all these changes are reflective of the rising influence of bureaucratic recruitment and employment structures. But most telling of all in this regard are the expanding numbers of men whose careers were mediated by internal appointments and transfers.

LEAVING THE WORKING CLASS

The foregoing has not sought to tie up forms of explanation for movement with any specific type of destination. Of particular interest in this regard are the motives and mechanisms underlying transitions to middle-class positions (Tables 6.3 and 6.4), which, given their generally successful trajectories, were a form of mobility experienced by a high proportion of writers.

In line with the findings of much European work on this sector, the autobiographies paint a picture of the nineteenth-century petty bourgeoisie which highlights the often precarious existence of families with small business interests. As suggested by the mobility profiles in the marriage registers, the incidence of direct inheritance of what were frequently volatile or marginal concerns was low.

In a less direct sense, however, families were still among the most important facilitators of movement into this sector. George Herbert

Table 6.3   *Reasons behind, and facilitators of, movement into first business,*
1723–1914

Why	% Mentioning	How	% Mentioning
Trade slump	13	Borrow capital	18
Money	10	Assistance of friends	18
Social ambition	10	Assistance of family	15
Employer dies	8	Used savings	15
Vocational ambition	8	Inherit directly	12
Sacked	8	Sold property	9
Hobby developed	8	Inherit directly	3
Family considerations	6	Gambling Benefit	3
Disagreement with employer	6		
Dislike work	4		
Marriage	4		
Illness	4		
Boredom	2		
Victimisation	2		
Strike	2		
n	48	n	34

Table 6.4 *Reasons behind, and facilitators of, movement into white-collar positions, 1723–1914*

Why	% Mentioning	How	% Mentioning
Social ambition	13	Appointed within	20
Illness	13	Exam/interview	16
Dislike work	11	Patronage	16
Perceived advance	11	Apply	14
Promotion	9	Informally solicit(ed)	9
Victimised	7	War	7
Money	7	Tip	7
Trade slump	4	Advertisement	5
Marriage	4	Hobby developed	5
Boredom	4	Family assistance	5
Vocational ambition	4		
War	2		
n	54	n	44

was lucky enough to be set up as a shoemaker in Banbury by his plush-weaver father, while William Smith simply took over his sister's provisions shop when she moved on to the proprietorship of a public house.[75] And like William Johnston, who took on his father-in-law's croft and gardening business, it was possible to marry into success.[76]

A more common route in, though, was via a partnership, which was often established between siblings. The example of the showcard writer Arthur Gill, and of John Hodge – later first president of the Iron and Steel Federation and a cabinet minister, but who first ventured into the grocery business with his brother in his twenties – have already been mentioned. Ernest Shotton was employed as a clerk in his brothers' casting business, but when, in 1905, he was head-hunted by a local firm they offered him a quarter share in the company.[77] Partnerships could also offer means to greater business security, as in John McAdam's case,[78] or expansion. Both William Farish, with his brother, and Ben Brierley, with his brother-in-law, enhanced their interests by combining resources.[79]

The mechanisms by which access to the small business world were achieved were many and various. There was no one dominant mode of facilitation. Friends were as important as families, whether as partners or providers of funds. John Bedford Leno, for example, was able to set up in business as a printer after his journeymen peers put on a benefit concert for him at the local town hall which raised 40 pounds.[80] Equal numbers borrowed more formally using agents, or obtained credit from suppliers. Samuel Marshall was able to buy the farm on which he was the manager by combining the assistance of good friends and money lenders.[81] Gifts and borrowing apart, other immediate solutions to the problem of raising capital included a gambling win or the selling of possessions.

For one in seven first-time businessmen, the accumulation of funds from saving provided the basis for the transition. Confirming the relatively low average age at which business was first experienced, however, this need not have been a particularly long and drawn out process. Edward Davis, advised by his Quaker superintendent to invest his earnings with a Birmingham friendly society, decided that with a new wife to support he should leave the pearl button trade for his own confectionery shop at 22.[82] Following an abortive building project, it took the 20-year old David Barr just a year or so to build up the funds to buy a small farm.[83]

Another prominent route into business, one where mechanism and motive are difficult to untangle, concerns the rather more gradual development of a supplementary occupation, or hobby, until it became the sole economic activity of the individual. Supplementary employment has been largely ignored in the history of work.[84] Yet it was a widespread and enduring practice, the economic, if not so much the social, consequences of which could be highly significant.

Extra income was gleaned from a tremendous range of activities, from sub-letting rooms, through petty dealing, to teaching, writing and preaching. William Smith's supplementary work as a postman brought him a pension.[85] Confident that he could fall back on his pig-breeding sideline, Cecil Harwood volunteered for redundancy rather than see a man with a wife and children thrown out of work.[86] By day, and until 1886, a coal miner, George Marsh spent his evenings at home on joinery work, which eventually paid for a holiday on the Isle of Mann. He filled the rest of his spare time doing some glazing, selling produce grown in a home-built hothouse, and, at the other end of the process begun by Harwood, butchering pigs at two shillings a time.[87] Partly because there was always more scope for such activities in the countryside, they tend to become less conspicuous later in the period, although they never entirely disappear.

They also provided the basis for a fully-fledged business in a number of contexts. Davis's savings were partly augmented from the cakes he made in his spare time. John Shinn, a cabinet maker, found his supplementary commitments as an organist and choirmaster taking up more and more of his time until, in 1864, he decided to drop his original trade and set up as a musical instrument retailer and teacher.[88] Joseph Livesey started hawking cheese after his doctor prescribed it to supplement his diet after illness. Discovering that the profit he made exceeded his wages from weaving, he continued, and a successful business as a cheesemonger was the eventual result.[89]

Turning more directly to the question of motive, it is again the sheer range of stated explanations for taking the plunge into business which is impressive. Pure social ambition was among the more prominent of these, but was only mentioned by 10 per cent of men. A similar proportion were concerned with vocational ambition, and a further 10 per cent with cruder material considerations.

However, what is most striking is the extent to which disaster was the sponsor of independence. In the case of Thomas Wilkinson Wallis the death of his employer provided the opportunity to take over the business and become a master carver and guilder himself.[90] For several others, setting up on one's own account was a response, and often the only alternative, to unemployment. This was the stark choice which confronted William Hart, suddenly an ageing liability in the West India Dock Company after 44 years at his trade.[91] The 1847 slump in the Kettering weaving trade, which threw him out of work and closed all vacancies for journeymen, forced John Leatherland to turn to small-scale manufacturing.[92] And William Smith was extremely fortunate to have the option of his sister's shop when the London to Holyhead road, on which he worked as a turnpike supervisor, was rendered obsolete by competition from the Great Western Railway at the beginning of the 1850s.[93]

Social ambition was more closely associated with transitions into the white-collar environment. And if it is read into the motives of those who simply state that they moved into the sector because they were promoted, or those who give an indication that movement was perceived in terms of an 'advancement', then it becomes by far and away the most common form of explanation.

Interestingly, an illness or injury disqualifying a man from manual work was often behind the taking of a white-collar position in the earlier periods, which may reflect the ambivalent status of 'book work' *vis-à-vis* the trades.[94] On the other hand, there is evidence, in the testimonies of men like Thomas Hardy in the mid-eighteenth century, John Brown in the early 1800s, and John Hodge 50 years later, that in certain contexts the pen was considered superior to the craft.[95] The ambivalence is shown in William Farish's reasons for resigning from the editorship of the *Cheshire Observer* in 1855: the papers' pro-prietors, he complained, 'appeared to have a notion that there was no difference between wielding the pen and using the spade, and that it was as easy to vamp up an article for the press as to cobble a boot.'[96]

As to the mechanisms of entry, the white-collar sector reflects most clearly of all the above noted shift towards more formalised and impersonal structures of recruitment. Taken together, the internal appointment, examination and interview, were in the ascendancy, while family and friends had a markedly lower profile as facilitators than they did among the businessmen. Patronage could still play an important role in individual cases, even in more modern employment contexts. Edward Balne, for example, started a long and distinguished Civil Service career at the Naval Stores Department in 1916 following the intervention of an Executive Officer in the Admiralty who had visited him in hospital where he was recovering from injuries sus-tained at Gallipoli,[97] while Edward Brown's move from a learnership with the Post Office in Bromley to a clerical position in the local gas company was achieved with the assistance of the chief clerk of the former who lodged with the chief clerk at the latter.[98] Nevertheless, as the spectre of the organisation grew, the importance of the influential contact, at least in an overt sense, was clearly on the wane.

BOWING OUT

The leaving of the labour market is a subject upon which the auto-biographies are less forthcoming. In part this is necessarily the case, for a proportion of the writers were still working as they wrote, and some did not cease until they died. Among the abstracts, although the date of death may be given, there are fewer details of timing at this end of the life course. And from the read sample, those authors who did 'retire' offer a more limited insight into the reasons behind their exit from work, and the ways in which they sustained themselves econ-omically in this phase of their lives, than the other dimensions of their work-life mobility. Nevertheless there are clear patterns in the data, which move in predictable directions.

The major contrast is between those born before and after 1865. Among the former there was generally only a limited conception of retirement, which for most was viewed and experienced as a con-dition into which one was forced by illness and infirmity.[99] Without any guaranteed or substantial means of support it was imperative to work as long as possible. Thomas Dunning ran a newsagent and stationery business until his death in 1894, when he was in his 82nd year.[100] George Marsh, born in 1834, waited until he was 72, when he thought he had enough put by, before risking the disposal of his cab concern.[101] John Shinn, a man theoretically eligible for a state pension, gave up his music business and resigned from his post as church organist in 1915, aged 78. However, he was 'compelled' to carry on teaching music, and was still doing so in 1923, aged 85, for fear 'of being left badly at the end'.[102]

Even those clearly untroubled by such a prospect seemed reluctant to let go. William Chadwick finally retired as Chief Constable of Stalybridge in 1899, three years before his 80th birthday,[103] and William Sutton was still in post as the manager and secretary of Kenilworth Gas Company on his 86th birthday in 1903.[104] Joseph Wilson of Great Horton was running a cotton mill in the early 1920s, even though he was only one year short of 90.[105]

Until 1908 there was no free provision for the elderly short of the Poor Law, and even then such a measure was, at a maximum of five shillings a week, strictly supplementary. Without a business to hang on to, or the capacity to set one up as a marginal form of protection in the manner of William Hart, the future could take on a grim aspect. John Tough was 75 when failing health caught up with him in 1848. When his employers, a firm of hosiery manufacturers whom he had served faithfully for $37\frac{1}{2}$ years, subsequently failed, the blow was compounded, for with them went hope for financial support.[106] Edward Rymer, a life-long miner and union activist, was forced out of the pit at 63 when his sight failed. One of the campaigns he had been involved in before his forced retirement in 1898 was the agitation which resulted in the establishment of the Miners Permanent Relief Fund. However, because his infirmity was not caused by work, he was unable to benefit from his efforts. And while his comrades at Monk Bretton did him proud with the very substantial sum of 20 pounds to help him on his way, he was left to reflect on the bitter irony of his position:

'after a brave, hard and faithful struggle to help in building up such a grand benevolent asylum for injured miners, widows, orphans, the aged and worn out toilers of the mine ... here I am in my present condition, left by this same society to grope about in darkness, to starve or die of want, or end my luckless days in the workhouse.'[107]

In contrast, among those born after 1864 retirement was, for most, an established and predictable stage in the life course. The profile of illness and insecurity was much lower, and the timing of the post-work phase was either freely determined by the individual, or structured by the organisation he worked for. That the length of a working life had clearly undergone a degree of standardisation is evident in the figures for mean age at finishing work from the abstract sample, which dropped from 69 to 65 in the later period. The major dynamic behind this change was, once more, the rise of bureaucratic employment structures, incorporating, most crucially, the granting of pensions. For most of those born before 1865, if enough had not been made or saved to maintain independence, then family and friends were all that stood between an old man and public charity. But Edward Purkiss and E.G. Robinson, leaving the Post Office at 60, and Westwater, retiring from the railway at 65, could look forward to a period of relative economic security. And a Civil-Service pension allowed William Miles seven years of happiness with his second wife, visiting country and seaside.[108]

On the one hand, pensions clearly offered choices. Rather than stand down from his directorship at Piries' Paper Mill into management when the firm amalgamated in 1922, James Cruikshank took the option of retirement at 52 on a company pension.[109] Balne's $26\frac{1}{2}$ years' pensionable service with the Admiralty, which entitled him to £235 a year plus a lump sum of £750, gave him the option of early retirement in 1948 when the nervous toll of his position became too much to cope with.[110] However, psychologically, retirement could bring new problems. Cruickshank, now 'a fish out of water', felt cut off in his prime, 'just as the harvest was due to commence'.[111] Others, like T. Lloyd Roberts, felt suddenly confronted with a void which they had no idea how to fill.[112] Westwater sold up and moved away from Stockton because, deprived of his work, he felt he had 'lost his place'.[113] Some remained disillusioned and effectively faded away, but most refocused their lives. Harry West knew that the immediate sense of relief would probably be followed by feeling of loss and futility, and so decided to learn a craft.[114] Robert's 'salvation' came in the form of study with the Workers' Educational Association.[115] And Westwater found a new outlet for his confrontational personality in the setting up of a rival branch of the Old Age Pensioners Association in his new home town of Halifax.[116]

However, a number of writers found that the only way to offset the boredom was to rejoin the labour market. Robinson, formerly a Post

Office inspector, spent a year as a telephone clerk for the London Telephone Service.[117] Arthur Gair, ex-chief engineer with the Ryhope Coal Company, spent 13 years after his retirement in 1953 as a shop salesman and invoice clerk with a firm of builders and plumbers' merchants in Sunderland.[118] In the nineteenth century such positions of lower status and comparatively limited remuneration at the end of a career were rarely the stuff of hobbies. But, as Edward Balne found out, even in the middle of the twentieth century such work could be highly exploitative.[119]

TAKING STOCK

The question of how people made sense of their mobility experience is, on the basis of the evidence to hand, one of the most difficult to answer. Goldthorpe and his co-investigators were able to frame, and put directly to a sub-sample of their respondents, a series of questions designed to elicit information about how far an individual's awareness of mobility or immobility coincided with their observed trajectories according to the categories of the research, how they accounted for their experience, and how significant was this dimension of their life compared to others.[120] To expect definitive answers to the same kinds of questions from autobiographical testimony, written for a variety of reasons by men with varying preoccupations and of variable analytical capacities, is unrealistic. Rather, it is a question of distilling impressions from the authors' attempts to take stock of their lives, reading between the lines where commentaries are still less direct, and being wary of distorting influences. By comparison with contemporary research the results are crude, and any conclusions must necessarily be tentative. But even in this aspect patterns emerge which are broadly confirming of the assumptions made in the use of the class schema, and of the tendencies and trends noted throughout this study.

Because of the additional problem of small numbers, it is safer to concentrate on the experience of mobility largely in terms of the major division between working and middle class. Inter-generationally, the patterns of mobility which predominate in this regard are working-class upward mobility, working-class stability and middle-class stability. The fact that most of those stable from lower-middle-class back-grounds were counter-mobile over the life course means that, intragenerationally, the great majority of men were either upwardly mobile from the working class to the bourgeoisie, or started and finished in manual positions.

Judging awareness of mobility is less straightforward than might be supposed. That individuals indexed their achievements in terms of inter-generational relationships is clear from the near universal practice of prefacing life histories with genealogical snippets, and from the more detailed concern with identity through family history shown by men such as Langdon, Wallis and West among others. It is even more strikingly confirmed by the degree of concern, and pride, shown in the achievements of offspring.[121] Yet direct and developed comparisons of class position with the preceding and following generations were rare. More often it was a question of noting lifetime success in its own terms, and, given that origins had been established at the outset, leaving any contrast with those who went before as read.

In these terms, the contrast between the mobile and the immobile was encouragingly marked. Those crossing class barriers were overwhelmingly aware of having made a significant social shift. John Brown's early disappointments left him feeling deprived of his true station. Thereafter, he was conscious of his progress 'steadily onwards towards the goal of my ambition', which was to throw off dependence and 'establish myself in the just estimation of society'. With his proprietorship of a billiard hall and coaching establishment in the 1850s, 'it became patent to the world I had done exceedingly well'.[122] William Farish, one-time handloom weaver and son of the same, had become a well-established coal and builders' merchant by his forties, and by 1860 could afford to spend time and money on displaying his social status. 'As we all needed occasional recreation, and being comparatively well-to-do', he boasted 'I now added to my other dignities that of "gig respectability".' His later elevations to Sheriff, and then Mayor, of Chester was, for him, confirmation that 'honour and fame from no condition rise'.[123]

Moving in the opposite direction, Robert Loisan, a one-time insurance clerk fallen into vagrancy, hawking and petty crime, offered a verse from Shakespeare by way of a summary of his life: '"There is as a tide in the affairs of men/ Which taken at the flood, leads on to fortune:/ Omitted, all the voyage of their life/ is bound to shallows." I may have to sink lower yet', he added, 'I almost think that is impossible, however'.[124]

By comparison, those who were immobile were mostly silent on the matter of social achievement, while those who experienced inter-generational stability but intra-generational mobility tended to fall between the two extremes. None who were both inter- and intra-generationally stable inside the working class indicated that they had experienced significant advancement in class terms. For the desperately poor, like Willie Thom, there was little time to think of much beyond the basic problem of survival.[125] But others, like Mallard, who in shifting from labouring work to employment with the Great Western Railway felt he had improved only in appearance, were more explicitly aware of their social immobility.[126] So too were James Ashley and Henry Price, who had both been born into the lower middle class, but had themselves begun in the working class and failed to climb back out of it.[127]

Of all the different interpretative dimensions of a life story mobility ideologies – the ways in which trajectories were explained – were perhaps most susceptible to the external influences of publishers and markets. They were, nevertheless, also strongly reflective of experience. The upwardly mobile in general, and not just those spreading the gospel of 'improvement', tended to account for their achievements in terms of personal effort; in a willingness to persevere and to take opportunities when they came their way. By contrast, among those failing to make any significant improvement, or who were downwardly mobile, explanations were offered more sparingly, implying, as Price does, that it was simply a question of fate. Alongside the hand of fate, it was the will of God which were most often invoked by authors in this category.

In the first two periods the testimonies of the successful abound with Smilesean rhetoric. Farish, with more than a hint of false modesty, began by noting that 'Any small success in life which I may have achieved has not been the result of either brilliant talents or special genius, but rather of the simple, ordinary practice of industry, thrift, and economy'.[128] Like many others, John Brown chose, more classically still, to infuse his story with the sanctimonious air of a morality tale, finishing off his account thus:

> I pray you, gentle reader, mock me not; but truly, I am vain enough to believe that this autobiography of mine ... embodies also a tangible moral: one which, if rightly read, may be addressed, in turn, to friendless youth, to struggling manhood, and to prosperous old age. 'Even in this world, there is sometimes a reward vouchsafed to faith and perseverance.'[129]

Apart from providence, which was in any case more a function of faith than luck, most played down the role, often at least as important as effort, of simple good fortune. James Watson, for example, was given the press and types which allowed him to set up as a printer and publisher by a friend, but chose instead to stress that the humblest workman might render himself effectual 'if he brings to the task honest determination and unfaltering perseverance'.[130]

The real purpose of propagandists like Smiles was to persuade working men – the vast majority of whom were never going to come close to emulating the heroes of *Self Help* – that real and worthwhile improvements could still be made by following the same prescription.[131] The message did get through to some, such as Isaac Anderson and George Healey, who began, and at the time of writing, were still engaged in manual labour, although Anderson had, in fact, progressed to foreman of his labouring gang, and Healey's temporary occupation of positions on the lower margins of the middle class has already been noted.[132] But the great majority of men, who were stable inside the class, betray no commitment to the Smilesean credo.

Over time there were both marked and subtle shifts in ideological substance. In the first place, writers were less inclined to provide any justification at all for their experiences. But among those who did, the tendency to see one's fate as part of the divine scheme of things almost disappeared. With it also went 'pure' Smileseanism. Upward mobility was still explained in terms of personal industry, but the overtly moralistic tone and providential underpinnings were dropped.

A further, and related, development in the last period is that education was as likely to be the subject of such toil as work. For men such as Gair, Roberts and Edward Brown it was a question of striving to gain the necessary post-school credentials to get on.[133] In his progress from Drain Examiner with Salford Town Council to District Sanitary Officer which began in 1909, Jack Lanigan attended evening classes at Manchester College of Technology. Every minute of his working day was spent thinking about his homework, and in the evening he worked on it through to the early hours, when he would have to rely on candlelight because his brother-in-law insisted on the gas light being extinguished when he retired to bed. 'Determined to win through', he writes, it was a regime of 'sweat by day working, sweat by night studying'.[134]

As to the wider social, cultural and political significance of mobility and immobility, this is an area in which judgements must be at their most tentative. In several respects the testimonies indicate the type of connections between different levels of experience which might be expected. But equally there are contradictory indicators which suggest that the relationship between mobility and the spheres of consciousness and action is a complex one.

There are clear examples of a lack of movement generating social resentment, and focusing political interest. Lanigan, abused at work and then disillusioned by unemployment, felt 'something quite foreign to my happy-go-lucky side of life' welling up inside, that 'the seeds of bitterness and rebellion were being sown'.[135] Westwater, until promoted to Signalling Inspector in his sixties, was a very frustrated individual at work, who concentrated his energies on labour politics. And Price, in no doubt about which of the 'two nations' he belonged to, was convinced that effective change in the interests of working men could only be brought about by trade union action and state intervention.

On the whole, however, apart from those who saw success in narrowly economic or vocational terms, the immobile tended, rather more than the upwardly mobile, to relegate the profile of work in their accounts, and to concentrate instead on interests and achievements in the non-work sphere. In the early period, especially, spiritual aspiration could be both a priority and a surrogate. William Hanson, it will be recalled, started and finished his life as a weaver, and felt that in this sense his work 'was done'. The same was not true of his religious energies, however.[136] John Plummer, a stay-factory worker who wrote anti-union tracts, rubbed shoulders with some illustrious patrons, and saw the salvation of his class in education, clearly felt 'elevated' in a cultural sense.[137] Several found a substitute in the local political arena. Before his promotion, politics was not only a matter of conviction for Westwater. For when he was removed from Stockton Council in the early 1950s he lamented bitterly that his life's energies, which otherwise 'might have been put into getting somewhere', had been wasted.[138] Like Rooney, the immobile tended also to spend more time discussing family matters. And the achievements of family could also provide fulfilment. Men like James Ashley, the hat shaper, for example, clearly got much pleasure from his son's university appointment at Lincoln College, Oxford; this after he had been turned down for a fellowship at All Souls 'because of class reasons'.[139]

This is certainly not to say that the family was unimportant to upwardly mobile men. When Arthur Gair was appointed Chief Engineer at Ryhope his first description is of the house that came with the job, reporting that his wife was thrilled when she saw it. The subject of sons' and daughters' futures was, in fact, more often mentioned in their accounts.[140] But when businessmen eulogise their wives for their emotional and practical support in the struggle to get on, it is the successful outcome which is as often as not being stressed. And in James Cruickshank, a company careerist, there is a clear hint of resentment at the constraints imposed by 'domestic responsibilities' – which is all that is heard about his family – when they force him to leave his overseas representative job for an office-bound managerial position.[141]

The only area of non-work engagement mentioned more often by the upwardly mobile is politics. For those ascending into the petty bourgeoisie civic responsibilities were treated almost as a natural corollary to, and certainly a confirmation of, their economic achievement. The colour of their politics – Livesey, for example, was a free trader in the 1840s, and Barr a Liberal voter turned Tory councillor over the provisions of the 1870 Education Act – tended to reflect the individualistic nature of their success.[142] In the rather different context of a dependent and not altogether secure white-collar environment in the early years of the twentieth century, one gets the strong impression that a similar self-image underpins Edward Brown's fervent commitment to free trade.[143]

Different politics were expressed by those who benefited from different mechanisms, the collectivism of those whose fortunes were associated with the labour movement being the obvious example. But the standard relationships between routeways and convictions did not always hold. In the civil servant T. Lloyd Roberts's espousal of welfarism there is an early example of a connection, more commonly visible in the post-Second World War period, between those who depend on the opportunities provided by public bureaucracy and statist politics.[144] And from an earlier period still, William Farish's respect for Ernest Jones and the Peterloo Committee, and John Leno's co-operative leanings, are a reminder that not all 'self-made' businessmen were wedded to purely capitalist politics.[145]

Edward Brown's insecurity is a reminder that mobility itself is not always a process conducive to fulfilment and tranquillity. Men rising out of the working class often betray an air of uncertainty which contrasts with the confidence of those from middle-class backgrounds who regain their class position over the course of a career. In the criticisms of establishment privilege levelled by Chadwick, Raymont and Roberts there are also hints of both resentment and status inconsistency.[146] Cruickshank concluded that 'anyone emerging from obscurity to a place in the sun was forced to have many ups and downs: he was bound to come up against those born with the silver spoon'. Yet, 'of the type which rises from the ranks', he continued 'the danger is that they develop a masterful domineering nature, born of their very struggles'.[147]

Some men, on the other hand, clearly recognised that there were risks as well as rewards in mobility. Not all who had the opportunity had the inclination. Writing about a life which began at the end of the eighteenth century, the draper Albert Adams, thankful that he had 'managed to clip the wings of ambition when she pointed me to soar on to untried fields', counselled against the single-minded pursuit of wealth and social status, wishing men would recognise 'that enough is as good as a feast'.[148] One hundred years later, the editor of the *Mount Review* wrote in tribute to the retiring postal sorter Edward Purkiss,

> There is a school of thought ... which looks on promotion, in the narrow sense of the word, as the be all and end all of human endeavour, and who will dare to say that the glittering prizes ... are not worth striving for? But Ted's promotion idea flows in a different direction. 'Promotion by all means, but let it be towards the happiness and well being of our fellow men.'[149]

CONCLUSION

Distilling a detailed perspective on the meaning of mobility from auto-biographical testimony is a process fraught with difficulty. It is clear that the authors recognised and understood the principal cleavages in social space which are assumed in the categories and organisation of this study. At the same time, the texts reveal the relationship between mobility, social consciousness and action to be a complex one. Smilesean rhetoric was often evoked to 'explain' the successes of the upwardly mobile in the middle of the period, while the immobile were generally more fatalistic. Ideological justifications are less evident among later writers who tend to concentrate more on the educational basis of their achievement. A lack of movement could generate resent-ment, radicalisation and political commitment of a collectivist nature. Others bypassed it by seeking out fulfilment and achievement beyond the world of work or in the successes of their children. When the upwardly mobile became involved in politics, their particular affiliation often reflected the mechanism by which success had been achieved, but this was not always the case. Confirming the arguments of Lipset, and of Sorokin before him, upward mobility could also generate insecurity and resentment as well as satisfaction.

In so far as they cast light on the importance of inter- for intra-generational change, the writers do appear to have indexed their own achievements, if only subconsciously, against both their fathers' and their sons'. Fathers retained a high profile as negotiators of labour market entry, as did the family more generally in mediating movement throughout the life course, a process in which informal communication, connection networks and personal 'influence' continued to play an important role. There are also clear correlations between class of origin and the timing of various work-life transitions, from entry though to retirement. The impression that a marriage-based snapshot is only partially distorting is borne out further by the importance attached to the event of marriage in terms of the economic as well as the emotional preparations involved.

In most respects, however, the influence of the parental family, as the informal and direct agency in the progress of children, was starting to be undermined by the advance of bureaucratic recruitment imperatives centred on the new service and white-collar sectors of the economy. In this context the role of the family was to become no less important, as the battle to seek out an advantage switched from the labour market to the realm of education.[150] But what this and the preceding analyses suggest is that for at least the limited period of the later nineteenth and early twentieth centuries the middle class had yet to fully appropriate the 'new institutional devices of the nominal meritocracy'.[151] It was in this temporary lacuna created by the process of readjustment that the sons of working-class men found themselves equipped and able to steal back some ground from their more privileged peers.

7 Marriage Markets and Women's Role in Social Mobility

In this chapter, we return to the event which gives rise to this study's main body of evidence. Marriage provided the principal setting for conjugal relationships and household formation, without which there can be no mobility between generations. However, anthropologists, demographers and historians have long emphasised the fundamental importance of intermarriage itself in the definition and reproduction of social structures.[1] Indeed, some would go as far as to argue that the marriage relationship is a better litmus test of class formation and fluidity than occupational inheritance. F.M.L. Thompson, for example, takes the view that:

> The social identities of marriage partners … are among the most sensitive and acute indicators of community or class feelings. Who marries whom, without courting alienation or rejection from a social set, is an acid test of the horizons and boundaries of what each particular social set regards as tolerable and acceptable, and a sure indication of where that set draws the line of membership.[2]

Before now, the historical record of social and marital mobility in Britain was virtually interchangeable. The predominant focus in the historiography, most notably in the work of Stone,[3] and the various contributions of the Cambridge Group for the History of Population and Social Structure,[4] is on pre-industrial marriage patterns. But the data collected by Foster, Crossick, Gray, Penn, and Mitch, together with more closely defined studies of elite marriage, such as those of Hollingsworth and Thomas on the peerage, mean that we also possess more knowledge about this aspect of mobility in the Victorian and Edwardian period than any other.[5]

Most of this material suggests that it was easier to become mobile through marriage than in the labour market, leading some to argue that the marriage market could act as a significant social solvent. Synthesising the available evidence, Thompson's conclusion is that the

marriage patterns of the working classes made them 'the most individualistic and least hidebound' members of nineteenth-century society,
and that they became more so over time. By the end of the century a
gently liberalising aristocracy had begun to follow suit, but 'the middle
classes', he writes, 'in all their different layers were ... if anything
becoming increasingly selective and exclusive right down to 1914'.[6]

Before these propositions can be considered, however, we must be
clear about what can be meant by marital, or connubial, mobility. The
social nexus created by marriage has three distinct dimensions to it,
each revealing a different perspective on the interactions and boundaries between classes. The respective viewpoints of the partners themselves provide two of these dimensions. That of the bride raises the
controversial issue of women's mobility. Women have featured only
fleetingly in this study so far because, as in many other areas of their
history, evidence of women's occupational mobility in the past is
scarce. The space for bride's occupation on the marriage certificate
was normally left blank, and a record of her mother's was not
required. However, some argue that women's *social* mobility is not, in
fact, defined by their own occupational experience, but rather by the
status of her husband in comparison with that of her father. If this
claim is accepted, women's (marital) mobility can be analysed in historical perspective because the marriage certificates invariably provide
the occupational title of the bride's as well as the groom's father.

The male outlook on marriage is defined by the same relationship,
but in reverse: in other words, a groom's father-in-law's social position
compared to his own. Following the same logic which links women's
social status with that of their fathers and husbands, men's marital
mobility is a process which has been neglected by contemporary
mobility research, while only Gray, among the historians, has considered it. Yet even if the term 'mobility' is questionable in this case, a
man's choice of partner is surely not without social significance.
Marshall *et al.* have written that the study of class formation should
include the mechanisms making for the stabilisation of demographic
collectivities.[7] A comparison of the occupational mobility and
marriage patterns of grooms provides both a measure of their socialisation within a destination class, and a further indication of whether
career mobility, in the wake of marriage, was likely.

The final component of connubial mobility comprises the relationship between the partners' families, as indicated by the comparative
status of the bride and the grooms' fathers. It is this which has
received the most attention in British research, and is of particular

interest at this point because it involves two samples of men who should certainly have reached 'occupational maturity' in Goldthorpe's terms. Although not equivalent to a comparison of completed careers across the generations in one family, it might therefore be considered that this perspective offers some indication of how the process of class realignment would look with the age factor controlled for.

WOMEN AND SOCIAL MOBILITY

Theoretical Considerations

Women's mobility has been the subject of an acrimonious debate among British sociologists. At issue is Goldthorpe's defence of 'men only' mobility studies, on the grounds that a 'conventional' approach to the question of class and gender remains largely valid.[8] This approach is rooted in the argument that the family constitutes the basic building block of the class structure, and as males remain the principal labour market participants within families it is they who determine their social destinies. Consequently, women's subordinate position in the economy means that their class identities are effect-ively generated by their fathers before they marry and their husbands when they do.

Critics argue that this ignores the rapid growth of female labour market activity since the Second World War, the fact that not all women marry, and the high incidence of separation and divorce in contemporary society.[9] Yet Goldthorpe contends that the character of women's work, which is still much more likely than men's to be part-time, discontinuous and poorly paid, has not fundamentally altered their position of dependency. This being the case, considerations of gender remain, in his view, largely irrelevant to the study of class inequalities. Married women's employment, he argues, typically forms part of a family strategy contingent upon the husband's career, and thereby tends to confirm rather than cut across existing lines of class division.[10] Similarly, although male career prospects are conditioned by the overall pattern of female employment, this is but 'one of the exogenous factors shaping the structural context within which men's class mobility occurs', and, moreover, one from which men from dif-ferent class backgrounds have benefited alike.[11]

The main modification which Goldthorpe has conceded to his critics is a recognition of the significance of women's marital mobility.

In other words, the logic of accepting that most women do derive their class identities from the male head of the family demands that 'a full account of class mobility must take in the mobility that occurs as a result of women *marrying*: that is to say, as a result of their moving from their family of origin ... to enter a conjugal family'.[12]

This is an approach which is easily replicated using the marriage registers, and it can be argued that there is at least as much justification for its application in the nineteenth century as at the end of the twentieth. 'Historically', writes Sewell, 'women's place in society typically has been determined more by family roles as daughters, wives or mothers than by occupational roles' so that their social mobility 'was governed above all by the *marriage market*'.[13] There seems little doubt that this view was also shared by most women at the time. This includes the mother of one respondent in Paul Thompson's 'Family Life and Work' survey of interviewees born in the 1890s and early 1900s who 'gave all the boys a chance for a trade', but refused her daughter a dressmaking apprenticeship on the grounds that 'a girl married for her future'.[14]

The registers provide no solution to the problem of women who never married, a group which ranged between 10 and 14 per cent of the female population across the sample period, nor those affected by a husband's death or desertion, although, as Anderson points out, the effects of marital dissolution were partly offset by remarriage.[15] In any case, this still means that the experience of the vast majority *is* accessible. According to the official view, this was unlikely to include participation in the labour market. The 1911 census records that fewer than 10 per cent of married women had jobs.[16] This is certainly a distorted picture, as many more than one in ten working-class wives engaged in some form of economic activity.[17] However, the fact that much of this activity either escaped the enumerators' gaze or was not reported might be seen to indicate its relative lack of *social* importance, an argument which has been extended to explain the omission of women's occupational descriptions in the marriage registers themselves.[18]

The ubiquity of women's work is confirmed by Vincent's recent re-analysis of Thompson's oral history survey, but so too is the fragmentation of the female career.[19] The minority of women who experienced settled and structured employment invariably had their progress truncated by marriage or first pregnancy. One in four of these careerists subsequently returned to the labour market, but with their horizons reduced to the casual jobs occupied by the remainder of their peers.[20] In Penn's view, such an analysis cannot take account of the local importance of female participation in particular cases such as the Rochdale textile industry.[21] Yet, in a similar context, Liddington and Norris note that there was 'an assumption, common to both sexes, that a woman's work and wages were temporary and/or supplementary to a man's'.[22]

By and large, then, history would seem to be bear out the main assumptions of the conventional framework. Yet it simultaneously casts doubt on the claim that gender issues are of merely marginal relevance to class analysis. Davidoff and Hall's celebrated account of the formation of the Victorian middle class, for example, shows how patriarchal gender relations provided a crucial cultural cement binding together otherwise disparate social identities, and how the public profile of the middle-class male was fundamentally underpinned by the servicing role of females in the domestic realm.[23] Likewise, the work of Savage *et al.* records how middle-class convergence in the first half of the twentieth century was aided by gendered strategies of exclusion and demarcation in the labour market which worked to articulate and stabilise male middle-class careers.[24]

Wives and Families

The relationship between the female labour market and men's careers in the twentieth century will be revisited in this study's concluding chapter. In the meantime, the autobiographies can provide some sense of the ways in which women, as wives and mothers, affected the economic and social trajectory of nineteenth-century families.

The importance of wives in workshop production is apparent enough from the testimonies of early nineteenth-century tradesmen autobiographers, whose success, solvency and even – as in John Brown's case – liberty could depend on a spouse's skills.[25] In the 1830s, Brown was committed as a debtor to Cambridge County Prison when his boot and shoemaking workshop was burgled and his creditors called in their loans. He was released after six weeks when he had cleared some of his debts working on boot orders from the brethren of his Oddfellow's Lodge. Having cut out the legs, his wife would take them home to close them and complete the seams, while he threaded the soles and fixed the buttons. Such accounts strongly support the view that women, without being breadwinners in their own right, could fundamentally influence a family unit's economic fate.

The general success of the autobiographers makes it difficult to judge questions of class bias in this regard, but the significance of a wife's incorporation in her husband's work is most clearly revealed by writers who inhabited the world of small business. The catalyst for Edward Davis's transformation from a worker in the pearl button trade to prosperous confectioner in the 1850s, for example, was his marriage to a baker's daughter.[26] Charles Bacon, the proprietor of a successful haulage firm in Leicester in the early years of this century, made his wife an equal partner in the business, declaring that he would never have got on had they not 'sailed our ship together'.[27] A hundred years earlier Joseph Livesey's wife took over his market stall so that he could develop a business which would eventually take him full time into the wholesale cheese trade, this while she continued to wind bobbins for the three looms which made up the family's main trade and nursed the first of their 13 children. Little wonder her husband recommends to his readers 'the truth of the old saying "In taking a wife you had better have a fortune *in* her than *with* her"'.[28]

Present-day studies have likewise found that the contribution made by a wife's own capital, contacts and resources to the fate of the household is most tangible in the case of petty-bourgeois families.[29] However, it also argued that simply by performing domestic labour and offering general encouragement a wife enhances her husband's prospects.[30] As Davidoff and Hall point out, though, it is at this level that the process of incorporation is most obscured by its location in the private sphere, making historical evidence particularly difficult to generate.[31]

Here the light cast by the autobiographers is somewhat opaque as few authors were willing to deconstruct this aspect of their lives in much detail. Some fail to mention their wives at all, and among those that do there is a preference for general eulogising or affectionate but succinct acknowledgement of support and forbearance. Where influence is detectable in these terms, no particular class leaning is evident, although it is again among men making their way in business or the professions that it is most palpable.

Good household skills were certainly prized for the comforts they could bring to a home, and occasionally the connection between the stability of home and work is revealed.[32] For example, Albert Adams, a draper's assistant forced to leave a happy family home on the death of his mother, only felt settled again when he set up his own marital abode, at which point he also decided to go into business.[33] More obliquely, the newly married William Farish writes of the difficulty he had in finding a house both 'convenient for my work and suitable to our means', problems that were overcome in part by his milliner wife's 'economical hand ... in furnishing'.[34]

On the theme of counsel and encouragement Livesey writes that 'Whenever I was cast down she was the one to revive my spirits', while Bacon recommends that 'love, honour and obey' should be changed to 'love, honour and consult'.[35] However, the texts also offer more specific examples of a partner's advice impacting on her husband's career. For example, it was as a direct result of his wife's intervention that Jack Lanigan finally passed the exams to become a district sanitary inspector in May 1914. Not only did she secretly put back part of the money he had given her for housekeeping to pay his exams fees, but it was she who spotted that it was his English which had let him down in his two previous attempts.[36] Thomas Raymont's promotion to Professor of Education at University College Cardiff in 1905 came soon after he published an influential textbook on educational theory, but it was his wife and her friend, both graduates of the Froebel Institute, who had persuaded him to write it.[37]

In conventional theory the family takes centre stage in the process of class formation because of the role it plays in transmitting assets between generations, yet, as Witz has noted, there has been a curious neglect of the part played by women in this, particularly as bearers of cultural resources.[38] As far as historians are concerned, these mechanisms remains poorly understood, and care must be taken when visiting modern models on past realities in the case of such a time-sensitive institution. It is, nevertheless, indicative that while the autobiographers usually wrote sparingly and intermittently about their partners, they are invariably more forthcoming about their mothers.

Edward Rymer's declaration that his mother was his 'only true friend and protector', and Benjamin Brierly's declaration that he would not contemplate marriage to anyone who lacked any of his late mother's qualities, even down to her Christian name, may smack of over-sentimentality, but the deep sense of devotion expressed by so many writers also testifies to pivotal role of many working-class mothers in holding their families together in the face of adversity.[39] As was seen in chapter 6, this role could, on occasion, extend to a very direct influence on the process of social reproduction in terms of a son's career choice and placement. However, there is also evidence that mothers in particular intervened in more abstract, although no less telling, ways: as teachers, advisers, moral guides and inculcators of ambition. John Leatherland, for example, a Kettering weaver who became a journalist in the 1850s, writes about his mother's Christian teaching and literary taste, both of which she passed on to him.[40] Likewise, Albert Adams, John Shinn, John Bedford Leno and Ben Brierley were all in part educated and inspired to read by encouraging mothers who kept books in the house. Ernest Shotton mentions the long-lasting moral example set by his mother, which shaped his approach to life and clearly influenced his business activity, and Arthur Goffin's mother remained an important source of financial advice as he completed his printing apprenticeship and became a journeyman.[41]

So women, both as wives and mothers, helped shape the class fates of family members in ways and through means which are not fully accounted for by the conventional framework. On the other hand, with the partial exception of the small business milieu and possibly some professional groups, the autobiographies do not reveal any consistent class bias to these influences. Moreover, while mothers may have set their sons on paths which eventually led to significant upward mobility, wives seem, in the main, to have played a more consolidating role, sustaining rather than transforming their husband's career prospects.

WOMEN'S MARITAL MOBILITY, 1839–1914

Origins and Destinations

Thus the evidence of the autobiographies provides further support for those who argue that the construction of social identities and mobility trajectories are fundamentally 'gendered' processes. But it is no less compatible with the contention that the primary context of women's social mobility was marriage. How far, then, did the pattern of social stability and exchange displayed by women in this context compare with the outcome of male occupational mobility?

Women's marital mobility enjoys a relatively high profile in historical research on the continent, where there is widespread agreement that women were more mobile in the marriage market than men were in the labour market.[42] Mitch has recently provided some evidence for the mid-Victorian period in Britain which points in the same direction, leading him to conclude that marital mobility acted as a significant check to forces making for increased stratification.[43] Studies of contemporary society, including the Nuffield study, have generally

Table 7.1   *Marital mobility of women by class and inter-generational class mobility of men, outflow rates, 1839–1914 (percentage by row)*

Father's class	I	II	III	IV	V	n	Δ
			Son's class (upper figures)				
			Daughter's husband's class (lower figures)				
I	42.8	33.2	15.9	4.3	3.8	208	5.8
	40.9	38.9	14.4	4.3	1.4	208	
II	2.7	50.2	25.8	12.2	9.1	1782	10.7
	2.7	39.5	33.7	12.5	11.5	1787	
III	0.3	6.8	72.8	10.3	9.8	4277	11.2
	0.4	9.4	61.7	14.6	14.0	4277	
IV	0.4	7.4	33.2	45.6	13.3	1186	17.6
	0.2	10.4	44.0	28.3	17.2	1167	
V	0.0	2.9	21.3	14.1	61.7	2757	9.1
	0.1	4.2	28.8	14.3	52.6	2718	
All	1.5	13.9	44.9	15.6	24.0	10210	0.15
	1.5	14.0	45.0	15.5	24.0	10157	

found a similar but smaller disparity, on which basis Goldthorpe argues that women's marital mobility makes virtually no difference to his overall findings.[44]

As Table 7.1 shows, this pattern is repeated in the marriage register sample which indicates that almost 50 per cent of women married a man whose class position was different to that of their father's. This compares with the 37 per cent of men who experienced class mobility in the labour market. In every class daughters were less constrained than sons, the largest disparities occurring in between the two extremes of the class structure.

There was, as Thompson suggests, 'considerable downward traffic' among lower middle-class women. Indeed, the whole of the difference in the rates of inter-generational stability displayed by class II sons and daughters was accounted for by unions with working-class men. However, the evidence does not support an image of 'almost complete social exclusiveness' in the case of upper-middle-class marriage.[45] It is true that the daughters of gentlemen and professionals married into their own social circle at a rate that is 20 times the figure we might expect on the basis of random assortment, and that their chances of making an elite match were 80 times greater than those of women from any part of the working class. Nevertheless, a clear majority still managed to slip through the elaborate series of constraints and procedures designed to ensure only respectable attachments, thereby exposing themselves to the kind of vilification heaped upon Sophia Galton by her brothers in the wake of an apostastical marriage to a clerk in their father's bank.[46] Even if class II contains a proportion of men who might properly, were more details available, be accorded class I status, this would still not account for the 20 per cent of elite women who actually married across the major class frontier.

The rate of middle-class marriage by workers' daughters was, in contrast, only half as great. Although working-class brides were more upwardly mobile than their brothers, the overwhelming impression remains one of massive working-class endogamy. The greater mobility of working-class women was therefore expressed, essentially, in *intra*-class terms, making women more than men the agents of class solidarity in basic demographic terms.

Although, in this sense, the differences between men and women were quite substantial – the daughters of skilled working-class men, for example, were 50 per cent more likely than sons to be downwardly mobile – the essential similarity in the general form and focus of the male and female distributions is striking.[47] Not only did the barrier between the working and middle classes remain formidable, but the internal division of the working class around the axis of skill, although certainly blurred, remained pervasive.[48]

In contrast to the findings of the Nuffield study, it is clear that at least part of the reason for women's greater mobility is that the marriage market was genuinely more open than the labour market. In other words, the fact that women were more likely than men to move is not simply a reflection of structural imperatives, such as the availability of husbands in different classes. This is obvious enough from an inspection of the marginals in Table 7.1, which indicates that men and women shared a virtually identical distribution of opportunities in class terms. A formal test confirms that the patterns of fluidity underpinning the male and female tables were divergent. Had they been comparable, in fact, the total mobility rate of women would actually have been 6 percentage points lower and the men's 6 points higher.[49]

Cross-sample absolute rates of marital mobility, then, offer an important qualification to earlier assessments of demographic class formation on the basis of males' labour market experience, but can hardly be said to undermine its basic conclusions. Marriage was certainly an additional social solvent. It reduced occupational, skill-based and class identities. It did not, however, disturb the skyline of the social topography. Its most marked contribution in this sense was to confirm the difficulty experienced by the lower middle class in severing contacts with the masses. The other chief significance of women's mobility by marriage was the role it played in both confirming and extending the wider demographic class identity of those masses.

Trends in Women's Marital Mobility

The simple indication of total mobility rate (Figure 7.1) shows that the chances of women becoming mobile, always greater than those of their brothers, were increasing throughout the nineteenth century. By the 1880s as many women married away from their immediate class background as married in, and by the early years of the twentieth

Figure 7.1   *Total mobility rates of men and women, 1839–1914*

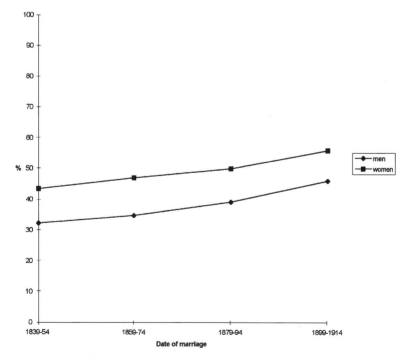

century the figure was approaching three in five. The much reduced advantage held by women over men in contemporary society appears to be rooted in the 1870s, which is when consistent acceleration in the male mobility rate began to close the gap.

Beneath this trend (Table 7.2) there were variations in men and women's experience. Women's mobility through marriage had contradictory effects on the integrity of the middle class, being at one and the same time anagency for increasing intra- and inter-class mixing. From a working-class perspective, the marriage market mostly confirmed developments in the labour market. Working-class brides remained more prominent than their brothers in forging links with the middle class, but while these links got closer with time they were never particularly strong. Women continued to cross internal social boundaries more effectively than men, but over time their contribution to the homogenisation process was less emphatic.

Although Thompson had in mind a more finely-tuned set of distinctions that this analysis can cater for, there is no sign here of women's mobility through marriage contributing to a stronger sense of structural differentiation within the middle class.[50] If anything, the opposite seems to have occurred. Elite sons and daughters struggled alike to maintain status from the 1860s onwards. But while class I men found it increasingly difficult to avoid the decline into manual employment, their sisters were able to limit the damage by entering into unions with lower-middle-class men. In this sense, they were agents of bourgeois integration.

The occupational dimension to this pattern gives contrasting indications. The daughters of those describing themselves as gentlemen or independently wealthy became more likely to marry into business, but this is mostly accounted for by unions with farmers and probably reflects the combination of a contracting gentry with the influx of new men on the land.[51] The daughters of professionals, on the other hand, married increasingly into both the white-collar and business sectors, and in the case of the former found a growing proportion of partners amongst the quasi-professions. But they also made more matches with industrialists, a development which offers tentative support to Rubinstein's account of the rhythms of interaction between different forms of wealth in the nineteenth century.[52]

Lower-middle-class women continued to undermine the persistence of their male peers in the labour market. In contrast to the daughters of the elite, their rates of marriage with working-class men were higher at the end of the period than at the beginning. The difference

157

Table 7.2 *Marital mobility of women by class and inter-generational class mobility of men, outflow rates by period (percentage by row)*

Son's class, left-hand column; daughter's class, right-hand column

Father's class	Period	I		II		III		IV		V		n		%	
I	1839–54	36.7	33.3	43.3	31.7	20.0	15.0	5.0	10.0	0.0	5.0	60	60	(2.1)	(2.1)
	1859–74	53.5	50.0	30.2	33.3	12.5	7.0	4.7	4.2	4.7	0.0	43	48	(1.7)	(2.0)
	1879–94	46.6	45.7	25.9	47.8	4.3	20.7	5.2	2.2	1.7	0.0	58	46	(2.5)	(1.9)
	1899–1914	36.2	37.0	31.9	44.4	18.5	19.1	2.1	0.0	10.6	0.0	47	54	(1.9)	(2.1)
II	1839–54	2.1	2.9	44.9	39.7	36.1	29.9	10.9	10.3	11.5	11.8	488	468	(17.1)	(16.6)
	1859–74	3.5	3.6	52.8	39.7	32.6	23.1	10.6	11.3	9.9	12.9	415	433	(16.5)	(17.7)
	1879–94	3.3	1.8	52.1	40.2	32.5	25.2	13.8	11.6	7.1	12.3	436	455	(18.2)	(19.3)
	1899–1914	2.1	2.5	51.7	38.3	33.6	24.4	13.5	17.2	7.9	8.8	443	431	(17.5)	(17.1)
III	1839–54	0.4	0.1	5.0	6.9	80.7	67.1	5.2	10.7	9.0	14.9	1134	1160	(39.9)	(41.1)
	1859–74	0.3	0.4	6.3	8.9	75.4	62.9	8.1	11.7	9.8	16.3	1034	1038	(41.7)	(42.3)
	1879–94	0.5	0.2	7.5	11.1	71.9	61.6	11.1	15.6	9.3	11.2	968	949	(41.5)	(40.2)
	1899–1914	0.4	0.5	8.4	11.0	63.4	55.1	16.6	20.4	11.1	13.2	1141	1130	(45.3)	(44.8)
IV	1839–54	0.4	0.4	6.4	8.3	30.5	45.3	24.0	47.8	22.0	14.9	249	254	(8.7)	(9.0)
	1859–74	0.0	0.4	5.2	8.6	33.0	48.6	27.3	46.7	15.5	14.8	270	245	(10.9)	(10.0)
	1879–94	0.0	0.7	8.9	10.1	33.9	42.5	30.3	45.4	17.1	11.1	280	287	(11.9)	(12.1)
	1899–1914	0.3	0.3	8.5	13.1	34.6	41.2	30.2	43.7	15.2	12.9	387	381	(15.3)	(15.1)

Table 7.2 (Cont'd)

Son's class, left-hand column; daughter's class, right-hand column

Father's class	I		II		III		IV		V		n		%	
V														
1839–54	0.0	0.0	2.4	3.9	18.1	25.2	8.4	8.2	71.1	62.8	918	878	(32.2)	(31.1)
1859–74	0.0	0.1	2.8	4.8	19.9	27.9	12.2	11.6	65.2	55.6	724	689	(29.2)	(28.1)
1879–94	0.0	0.0	3.1	4.2	21.5	29.1	17.7	17.9	57.7	48.9	610	626	(25.9)	(26.5)
1899–1914	0.2	0.2	3.6	4.2	28.9	36.0	23.0	23.6	44.4	36.0	505	525	(20.0)	(20.8)
n														
1839–54	38	36	340	340	1312	1295	311	311	848	838	2849	2820		
1859–74	43	43	331	334	1112	1111	344	319	656	646	2486	2453		
1879–94	39	41	359	365	1044	1039	405	401	505	517	2352	2363		
1899–1914	36	35	391	385	1120	1124	535	543	441	434	2523	2521		
%														
1839–54	(1.3)	(1.3)	(11.9)	(12.1)	(46.1)	(45.9)	(10.9)	(11.0)	(29.8)	(29.7)				
1859–74	(1.7)	(1.8)	(13.3)	(13.6)	(44.7)	(45.3)	(13.8)	(13.0)	(26.4)	(26.3)				
1879–94	(1.7)	(1.7)	(15.3)	(15.4)	(44.4)	(44.0)	(17.2)	(17.0)	(21.5)	(21.9)				
1899–1914	(1.4)	(1.4)	(15.5)	(15.3)	(44.4)	(44.6)	(21.2)	(21.5)	(17.5)	(17.2)				

was marginal, and those marrying down may later have been reinstated through the medium of their husband's upward mobility. But the chances of their moving into the adjacent world of the master artisan and, by process of accretion, returning to the petty-bourgeois circumstances of their previous existence were declining: working-class husbands were increasingly drawn from communities defined by factory work, mining or service sector employment rather than the craft workshop.

The changing fortunes of working-class brothers and sisters shadowed each other most closely at the bottom of society, from where, particularly among those squeezed out of agriculture and swept up by the expanding urban economy, a universal process of upgrading took place. The main point of variation was to be found in the changing circumstances of those originating in class IV. Indexed by the marital mobility of its daughters, the demographic identity of the semi-skilled sector, while never very strong, slowly increased throughout the course of the nineteenth century. Simultaneously, an always small but rapidly growing proportion of class IV brides were marrying out of the manual ranks altogether.

Over time, then, the effect of women's mobility on the class structure was ambiguous. It largely confirmed, in some respects emphasised, but also complicated the evolving relationship between the classes in the labour market. On the whole, a woman's chances of marrying out of the class into which she was born were higher in the early decades of the twentieth century than they had been 75 years previously. But of course this need not mean that the marriage market became more open over time, and in order to complete the 'full picture' of English social mobility in this period we need to know whether the trend towards greater fluidity found for males in the labour market was a broader-based phenomenon.

The test procedure for changes in the association between brides' fathers and brides' husbands across cohorts is exactly the same as the one applied to grooms and their fathers in chapter 3, and so, essentially, is the outcome (Table 7.3). The model for uniform change is a significant improvement on the no trend model, and while the trend toward greater fluidity is fairly weak early on, and seems to stall over the mid-Victorian period, it picks up again very strongly in the final cohort. Whether we take men or women as our reference point, English society was more open in 1914 than it had been in 1839.

Table 7.3 *Results of fitting the conditional independence, constant social fluidity, and uniform difference models to women's marital mobility over four marriage cohorts, and parameter estimates for the model of uniform change in association between class origins and destinations*

Model	G^2	BIC	df	p	Δ
Con. Ind.	3364.0	2774.0	64	0.00	22.1
CnSF	97.3	–345.5	48	0.00	3.3
Unidiff	73.1	–342.3	45	0.01	2.2

β Parameter estimates of the model of uniform change by cohort*	2	3	4
	–0.07	–0.07	–0.25

Note:
* Parameters for cohort 1 are set at zero.

The Dynamics of Marital Mobility

Various explanations for the greater fluidity of the marriage market have been put forward. Sewell suggests that patriarchal bias led fathers to place more emphasis on a son's prospects. Mitch argues that parents were also being practically minded in doing so, sons being better placed to provide them with financial support in old age.[53] Boys were therefore drawn by mutual expectation towards their fathers' trade, a pressure which was compounded, it is suggested, by the more direct influences fathers could bring to bear on occupational choice. These included the transmission of specific skills and attitudes and, as indicated by the testimony of the autobiographers, the pivotal role – ranging from informant to employer – that fathers often retained in the process of placement. On the other hand, and partly in consequence, it is argued that daughters were left more to their own devices. Moreover, because sexual and emotional attraction are essentially matters of personal taste, and because marriage generally occurred at least ten years later than entry into the labour market, the decision about whom to marry is seen to be less susceptible to background influences than career choice.[54]

The influence of work-related factors in differentiating between men and women's horizons is strongly suggested by the larger gap between occupational and class identities found among women. It will be recalled that 62 per cent of men shared the same class position as their fathers, and 43 per cent the same occupational title. By comparison 51 per cent of women entered socially endogamous unions but only 24 per cent married men in the same occupation as their fathers.

Sewell argues that the cosmopolitan nature of an urban centre like nineteenth-century Marseilles tended to accentuate the importance of personal inclination over parental pressure where marriage was concerned, and the contrasting rates of endogamy in classes I and IV would seem to bear him out.[55] The elite, among whom there was least variation in the succession rates of men and women, was based largely in the countryside, where greater cultural constraints were presumably exercised on 'the notorious unruliness of romantic love'. Class IV, on the other hand, is dominated by urban-based service occupations.

It is also likely that urbanisation was one of the main factors underpinning the trend towards more fluidity in the marriage market over the course of the nineteenth century. The fact that the trend gathers strength in the cohort of brides who got married at the turn of the century and beyond may reflect changes in women's own experience of the labour market. The rising number of jobs for young, single women in clerical and secretarial work, and in services and retailing, brought with them more freedom and access to wider social circles. Some, such as those in the department stores or at post office counters, involved working with the general public, and in office work contact between male middle-class bosses and female working- or lower-middle-class employees was common.[56]

Family influence may have been weaker where marriage was concerned, but according to Vincent, 'there is some evidence that girls were more subject to their parents' influence', and, as the previously related experiences of Cecil Harwood and Roger Langdon would tend to confirm, 'more concerned to enquire into the financial prospects of their suitors'.[57] A daughter's marriage, it seems, could be just as much of a life-cycle investment, or insurance against financial liability, as a son's career, and the marriage data clearly show aspirant working-class brides searching out the most tangible form of security available. Most of the difference between male and female rates of upward mobility out of the working class is in fact accounted for by higher rates of marriage to husbands with some property or capital. The same priority is evident among the daughters of clerks and other white-collar employees within the lower middle class who sought out husbands from the petty bourgeoisie in preference to men from their own occupational sector.[58]

MEN'S MARITAL MOBILITY

Goldthorpe's adherence to the conventional framework leads him to disregard the issue of men's marriage choices.[59] Yet, while Joseph Livesey may not have approved, men could marry into money, property, security and status, any of which might have had a significant impact on their life chances. The figures for occupational endogamy indicate a gradual decline in the practically motivated tradition of craft-specific marriage about which Thompson writes.[60] However, like John Brown, more than a quarter of all craftsmen married within the trades more generally, which suggests that the question of 'shared outlook and customs' continued to figure in the marriage decisions of men and women from this sector. In a different context, we know that one way in which the non-inheriting sons of businessmen could maintain status was to look to white-collar employment, but others, according to Hout, sought a route to independence by 'marrying' a farm or a shop.[61] Thus the groom/father-in-law relationship would seem to be significant from both sides of the equation.

Admittedly, the textual evidence indicates that finding a material fortune through marriage was rare. Many of the autobiographers took the view that marriage was a serious turning point in their lives, but not many derived the type of direct economic benefit that William Johnston did by inheriting his father's croft and garden.[62] Vincent argues that for all that practical considerations mattered, affection was the final arbiter in the decision to wed.[63] Most writers, it seems, shared the same sentiments as Joseph Wilson, whose concern when he made the decision to tie the knot in 1857 was not his intended's status but that 'she was a grand girl, a good girl with a passionate love for me – a real helpmeet'.[64]

Nevertheless, even if emotional fulfilment was a husband's priority, and marriage bound a wife, whatever her social origin, to his economic destiny, it is still of substantive interest to ask how often that brought men into contact with women from different social and cultural milieux. In particular, the relationship between a man's occupational mobility and his choice of partner offers a sense of how far he was assimilated within the class he had reached at marriage, together with a further indication of whether his journey in the labour market was incomplete at this stage.

Grooms and Their Brides

When dealing with men's marriage patterns we are looking at a mirror image of the relationship involved in women's marital mobility. This means that the total mobility rate and the underlying pattern of fluidity must be the same for both distributions. However, the marriage patterns themselves will differ because the shape of the market in partners is not the same. In particular, the indexing of the brides by the class position of their fathers introduces a life-course effect which results in the pool of potential middle-class partners being larger, and that of working-class spouses proportionately smaller, where men are concerned.

We would therefore expect to see, in comparison with brides' marriage patterns, a net upward shift in the unions made by men, and Table 7.4 confirms this. Although the basic form of this distribution is very similar to that for brides, there was clearly more middle-class endogamy from the grooms' perspective, and working men's chances of marrying out of their class also exceeded those of working-class brides.

As to the question of marrying for social and economic advantage, there was an excess of upward over downward 'moves' among the exogamously inclined, but the difference was marginal. Working-class men were roughly twice as likely to marry a middle-class bride as the

Table 7.4   *Marital mobility of men by class, percentage by row, 1839–1914*

| Groom's class | Father-in-law's class | | | | | | |
	I	II	III	IV	V	n	%
I	54.8	31.6	11.0	1.3	1.3	155	(1.5)
II	5.7	49.6	28.2	8.5	8.1	1424	(14.0)
III	0.7	13.2	57.8	11.2	17.2	4569	(45.0)
IV	0.6	14.2	39.6	21.0	24.7	1574	(15.5)
V	0.1	8.4	24.5	8.3	58.7	2435	(24.0)
n	208	1787	4277	1167	2718	10157	
%	(2.0)	(17.6)	(42.1)	(11.5)	(26.8)		

sons of workers were to achieve middle-class status themselves, but this still left seven out of every eight working-class husbands with working-class wives. Only 8 per cent of men from William Johnston's background married the daughters of businessmen, and none, presumably, was then guaranteed an inheritance. Meanwhile, more working-class men than women were to be found making matches at the other end of the spectrum, as the shape of the market in partners also meant more daughters of unskilled men were available than potential husbands in that class.

While the middle class as a whole was more endogamous from the male point of view, prospects began to diverge internally over time. A rising rates of upward mobility through marriage for working-class brides implies, of course, an increase in hypogamy among middle-class males, and by 1914 marriage to working-class partners was as common a practice among lower-middle-class men as it had always been among lower-middle-class women. This was in marked contrast to the trend in upper-middle-class marriage, where, despite a gradual rise in the number of matches made with working-class women from the 1870s, a consistent majority of class I grooms managed to find class I brides, and altogether more than eight out every ten men married into the middle class as a whole.

Labour Markets and Marriage Markets

The endogamy of elite men also stands in contrast to the uncertain fortunes of grooms from elite backgrounds in the labour market, and it is to the issue of grooms' marriage choices in relation to their occupational mobility, and the possible implications of this relationship for the process of class formation, that we now turn.

Almost 60 per cent of elite men were the sons of class I fathers, and almost 60 per cent also married into class I families. This would seem to indicate a considerable degree of homogeneity. But if these two indicators are treated sequentially the perspective changes. Not only were more than two in every five class I grooms born in a different class, but so, in turn, were 40 per cent of their wives.

Here again, the critical issue is how much social significance should be accorded to men's marriage. One indication is provided by a comparison of the respective influence of fathers and fathers-in-law on a groom's own position. This suggests that fathers were considerably more important. Using the same example as Mitch in his work on mid-Victorian marriage patterns,[65] in 74 per cent of cases where both father

Table 7.5   *Three-way matrix showing the relationship between the*
social mobility and the social endogamy of grooms, 1839–1914
(percentage by row)

		Bride's class in relation to husband's father		
		Same	Lower	Higher
Son's class in relation to father's	Same	59.0	20.3	20.7
	Lower	31.6	58.9 (36.6/11.9/10.3)	9.5
	Higher	32.5	6.9	60.6 (40.2/13.4/7.0)

Bracketed figures:
row 2: class of partner lower than groom's origin class but – the same
as/below/above his 'current' position
row 3: class of partner higher than groom's origin class but – the same
as/below/above his 'current' position

of the groom and father of the bride were in class V the groom was
himself in an unskilled occupation. Where the groom's father was in
class V, but his father-in-law was in class III, this percentage drops to
45.3 per cent. However, when the situation was reversed, and the son
of a skilled man married the daughter of a labourer, the chances of the
groom being found in class V were less than one four.

In the light of this, it seems more appropriate to consider men's
marriage not so much as an optional and equivalent form of social
mobility to that taking place via the labour market, but as an indicator,
as kinship relations and friendship networks were used by the Nuffield
study,[66] of individual assimilation within, and the internal consistency
of, the five classes identified in this study. Thus, if a man mobile
between classes were to marry a women from his destination class, this
might be thought to indicate a firm process of socialisation which
would, in turn, assist the stabilisation of that class. But a mobile man
who took a wife from a similar background to his own might be considered to be in a more ambiguous position, and his destination class
more heterogeneous as a result.

In these terms, Table 7.5 shows that 40 per cent of men on the move
married in such a way as to consolidate the outcome of their mobility
by taking a bride from among families of their assumed class, while a
very clear majority married away from their class of origin in the same

general direction in which they had travelled in the labour market. On the other hand, the proportion of grooms who did not share their father's social position but, through marriage, retained significant ties with the class they had left behind was not insubstantial. A clear majority of those who were immobile in the labour market married women of their own class, but again two out of five chose brides from different backgrounds.

In Table 7.6 the analysis has been refined to show the marriage choices of grooms from each class in turn according to whether or not they were first- or second-generation men. In addition to a class-specific view of assimilation, this analysis offers a perspective on the permanence of the mobility achieved via the labour market at the point of marriage.

The figures provide yet another perspective on elite exclusiveness, highlighting, as they do, a marked discrepancy between insiders and *arrivistes*. Second-generation members of the elite married in overwhelmingly, rarely took brides from non-manual backgrounds, and, if they did, never countenanced liaisons with anyone who was not from a 'respectable' working-class background. Their rate of endogamy was not only the highest of all among the five class groups, but twice that of class I men from other backgrounds. The latter, whose membership certainly seems to have reduced the effects of origin on their ability to assimilate, were no less integrated than outsider groups in other classes, but nowhere else was the differential between first- and second-generation men so large.

The fact that more than a third of men with class I origins who reported having a lower middle-class occupation on the day of their wedding were marrying the daughters of upper-middle-class fathers would seem to indicate a strong possibility that their downward mobility was only temporary. On the other hand, almost half of those following this occupational trajectory took a bride from their new class, and they were also three times more likely than second-generation men to marry a working-class woman. For those whose decline took them across the major class divide few, if any, direct links with the past were retained through marriage. The size of the group downwardly mobile into classes III and IV but still able to persuade daughters from lower- middle-class families of their worth suggests that an elite background still conferred some advantage, but those who experienced the rare descent into unskilled manual employment seem to have been only marginally less well assimilated within their new class than men born and bred in it.

Table 7.6   *Groom's marriage patterns by class of origin and destination
(percentage by row)*

Groom's own class	Groom's origin class	Bride's father's class					
		I	II	III	IV	V	n
Class I	I	71.3	21.8	6.9	0.0	0.0	87
	II	40.4	48.9	8.5	2.1	0.0	47
	III	36.4	27.3	36.4	0.0	0.0	11
	IV	0.0	20.0	40.0	0.0	40.0	5
	V	0.0	0.0	0.0	100.0	0.0	1
Class II	I	35.3	47.1	14.7	1.5	1.5	68
	II	4.8	58.1	23.9	7.8	5.3	869
	III	3.6	35.6	41.1	11.6	8.0	275
	IV	2.4	35.7	36.9	9.5	15.5	84
	V	0.0	24.4	28.2	7.7	39.7	78
Class III	I	10.0	30.0	46.7	10.0	3.3	30
	II	1.8	22.4	53.1	10.9	11.8	441
	III	0.6	12.9	60.7	10.5	15.3	2990
	IV	0.3	11.2	58.0	17.3	13.3	376
	V	0.2	8.5	46.3	10.9	34.2	562
Class IV	I	0.0	37.5	50.0	12.5	0.0	8
	II	2.4	27.8	33.0	18.7	18.2	209
	III	0.2	11.1	54.4	17.3	17.0	423
	IV	0.4	14.5	37.3	25.9	21.9	517
	V	0.3	10.0	27.4	21.1	41.2	369
Class V	I	0.0	12.5	12.5	12.5	62.5	8
	II	0.0	14.6	30.4	11.4	43.7	158
	III	0.0	11.0	35.3	10.5	43.3	400
	IV	0.7	14.1	34.9	14.1	36.2	149
	V	0.1	6.8	19.7	6.9	66.4	1606

The number of downwardly mobile men from the lower middle class
who married the daughters of lower-middle-class men also suggests a
certain amount of lower-level counter-mobility. Nevertheless, those
who were in unskilled, and particularly skilled, working-class positions
on their wedding day took a relatively high proportion of partners from
their destination classes. For some reason – probably to do with its size
and diversity – outsiders seem to have been accepted more readily in
class III than elsewhere, and a majority of men who arrived here from
class II married women from their new class.

If the link between the lower- middle and skilled working classes is confirmed by marriage evidence, so too is the fact that relationships were stronger in one direction than the other. Those who were upwardly mobile into class II from class III maintained much closer ties with their origins, and with the working class more generally. The chances of an upwardly mobile son of a skilled worker marrying a lower-middle-class woman were three times greater than those of the men who stayed behind, but more took brides from their class III, and altogether 60 per cent married into working-class families.

In these and other respects the experience of men hailing from the skilled and semi-skilled backgrounds was similar, highlighting further the comparatively weak influence of origin on the latter. Once in class II, for example, it can be seen that the skilled held no real advantage in their marriage prospects over their semi-skilled peers, and skilled workers from class IV backgrounds were almost as endogamous as second-generation class III men.

Exogamy rates among class IV insiders were not much lower than those displayed by first-generation men: in either case more than three out of every four men married a woman who was not from class IV. This lends further weight to the notion that semi-skilled employment was often a staging post mid-way through the career, and, as most brides of semi-skilled workers came from either class III or class V, confirms its pivotal homogenising role in relation to the rest of the working class.

The marriage patterns of unskilled men played a similar role, confirming their particularly strong social and cultural attachment to the working class. A clear majority of those who moved away from the unskilled sector married women from a higher status family than their own, but over 90 per cent of matches were nevertheless made inside the working class. Even though their chances of marriage to a women from a middle-class family were between three and four times better than men who stayed put, 75 per cent of men with class V origins but found in a middle class job on their wedding day married working class women. By comparison, almost 40 per cent of middle-class men from skilled or semi-skilled working-class backgrounds took middle-class brides.

In sum, these analyses highlight, as does Goldthorpe's more developed work on the relationship between mobility and the structure of primary relations, the potential complexity of the process of class formation. Marriage was likely, but by no means certain, to reflect the outcome of labour market mobility, and although the majority of mobile men married in the same direction as they moved, those who married a women from their destination class were actually in the minority. Given that second-generation men were, in all cases bar one, substantially endogamous, most classes contained a large core of, presumably, well-assimilated men. Nevertheless, marriage does seem to have added a degree of socio-cultural diversity to every class.

MARRIAGE AND FAMILY INTERACTION

The social relevance of marriage at the level of the relationship between families would seem perfectly clear. Yet those who have found discrepancies between rates of occupational and marital mobility argue that choice of spouse was subject to less parental pressure than initial choice of occupation.[67] In order to assess the value of this relationship as an indicator of social distance it is therefore necessary to be clear about how far the institution of marriage really was a family affair.

Thus far, the indications are somewhat contradictory. The preceding analysis suggested that men's own careers were the prime influences on their choice of partner, but that background still played a significant role. The weight of family pressure within this is impossible to measure,[68] although received wisdom would suggest that it found its strongest expression amongst middle-class and elite groups, where considerations of inheritance, as well as propriety, could loom large.[69]

The autobiographies indicate that less formal control could be exerted by working-class parents.[70] But this did not mean that they had no influence at all, nor that it was only daughters who were monitored.[71] Even if his priority was love, the aforementioned Joseph Wilson still felt it his duty to consult his parents on his choice of bride. Satisfied, in the first instance, that she 'was of a good family', they duly gave the match their approval.[72] The sustained hostility of Joseph Gutteridge's family to his marriage to a girl from a poor family, and the opposition of the Metcalfes and the Betts, superior artisan families, to their sons' unions with factory girls, further testify to an important degree of wider family concern in the outcome of liaisons at this level.[73]

Whether approval was sought, given or withheld, the basic outcome of the pattern of intermarriage in these terms is by now a familiar one. The classes mixed more often in marriage than through the labour market, and did so in part because the marriage market was more fluid than the world of work.[74] However, the degree of variation is not

enough to warrant anything more serious than qualification of earlier
findings about the basic pattern of relations and associations between
classes.

Given the greater availability of suitable matches, perhaps the most
surprising outcome of this analysis is that there was not more stability in
the higher reaches of the class structure. Yet this picture is very similar
to the one found by Penn in nineteenth-century Rochdale. His local
'bourgeoisie', comprising manufacturers, proprietors and directors,
could usually shore up their children with a non-manual spouse of some
kind, but here too only a minority contracted endogamous unions.[75]
Rather, it was children from working-class families – sons and daughters
alike[76] – who took advantage of the swollen market in middle-class
partners. However, while some, such as those who had grown up in craft
families or whose fathers worked in the skilled service sector, managed
to marry out of their origin class at a rate of one in five, the average
figure was closer to one in seven,[77] and of the 16,000 men and women in
the sample who came from working-class homes, just 90 married into
families from the professional or propertied elite.

It is, however, the question of change over time, and in particular
whether an extended life course perspective casts a different light on
the fluidity of social relations, that is most interesting about a comparison of men who had presumably completed their careers. To
begin with the pattern of raw percentages (Table 7.7), it can be seen
that the picture is a much less dynamic one than those produced by
the preceding analyses of inter-generational occupational and marital
mobility. There were shifts in the pattern of exogamous alliances contracted by families from the skilled and semi-skilled working class, but
only among the unskilled was there a sustained and profound decline
in the rate of endogamy resulting in more intra- and inter-class
mixing. Middle-class endogamy rates show little pattern until the turn
of the century, at which point men and women from class II became
still less inclined to intermarry, while the elite, at least from the male
perspective, appears to have been becoming more exclusive.

In this there would appear to be some support for Thompson's
assertion that, at the end of the century, 'the upper middle class elite,
mainly the most wealthy but including business leaders and leaders in
the professions below the private tennis-court level, distanced itself
from the rest of the middle classes'. On the other hand, one in four of
its sons still took a bride from class II, while the fact that a further
23 per cent married the daughters of working-class men in this period
would suggest that such events were not entirely confined to the pages

Table 7.7 Family interaction by class and period, 1839–1914. Left-hand column: groom's father class by bride's father's class; right-hand column: bride's father's class by groom's father's class (percentage by row)

Father's class	Period	I		II		III		IV		V		n		%	
I	1839–54	42.6	42.6	39.3	31.1	14.8	13.1	3.3	6.6	0.0	6.6	61	61	(2.2)	(2.2)
	1859–74	40.9	37.5	40.9	39.6	11.4	20.8	2.3	2.1	4.5	0.0	44	48	(1.8)	(2.0)
	1879–94	43.9	56.8	22.8	25.0	24.6	15.9	5.3	2.3	3.5	0.0	57	44	(2.5)	(1.9)
	1899–1914	51.2	40.7	25.6	46.3	16.3	13.0	0.0	0.0	7.0	0.0	43	54	(1.8)	(2.2)
II	1839–54	4.0	5.2	40.9	42.2	34.4	32.8	8.2	7.6	12.4	12.2	474	460	(17.2)	(16.7)
	1859–74	4.7	4.3	44.9	43.3	32.1	32.6	7.6	8.5	10.8	11.3	408	423	(17.1)	(17.8)
	1879–94	2.6	2.9	43.1	41.3	29.9	33.6	11.6	9.3	12.8	12.9	422	441	(18.7)	(19.5)
	1899–1914	5.8	2.6	35.3	35.9	34.3	34.5	13.2	14.2	11.4	12.8	431	423	(17.7)	(17.3)
III	1839–54	0.7	0.8	13.8	14.4	57.2	55.4	9.3	10.0	19.0	19.5	1098	1134	(39.8)	(41.1)
	1859–74	1.0	0.5	13.8	13.1	56.5	56.4	10.8	11.2	17.9	18.7	997	998	(41.8)	(41.9)
	1879–94	0.8	1.6	15.9	14.0	54.6	56.5	11.2	12.4	17.5	15.6	928	898	(41.1)	(39.8)
	1899–1914	0.6	0.6	13.2	13.5	56.3	57.0	13.8	14.7	16.1	14.2	1109	1095	(45.5)	(44.9)
IV	1839–54	1.7	0.8	14.6	15.5	47.1	40.5	19.6	18.7	17.1	24.6	240	252	(8.7)	(9.1)
	1859–74	0.4	0.4	14.3	12.9	44.6	44.8	20.3	21.2	20.3	20.7	251	241	(10.5)	(10.1)
	1879–94	0.4	1.1	14.9	17.6	40.4	37.4	20.0	19.8	24.4	24.1	275	278	(12.2)	(12.3)
	1899–1914	0.0	0.0	16.0	15.5	43.0	41.6	21.1	21.5	19.8	21.5	374	368	(15.3)	(15.1)

Table 7.7 *(cont'd)*

Father's class	Father's class						
	I	II	III	IV	V	N	%
V							
1839–54	0.5 / 0.0	6.3 / 6.9	25.0 / 24.6	7.0 / 4.8	61.2 / 63.7	851 / 885	(30.9) / (32.1)
1859–74	0.0 / 0.3	7.0 / 6.5	27.4 / 26.4	7.3 / 7.6	58.3 / 59.1	673 / 683	(28.2) / (28.7)
1879–94	0.0 / 0.3	9.9 / 9.0	24.3 / 27.1	11.6 / 11.2	54.2 / 52.3	598 / 577	(26.5) / (25.5)
1899–1914	0.0 / 0.6	11.2 / 9.8	32.2 / 35.9	16.4 / 14.8	40.2 / 38.9	499 / 482	(20.5) / (19.8)
n							
1839–54	61 / 61	460 / 474	1134 / 1099	252 / 240	851 / 885	2758 / 2758	
1859–74	48 / 44	423 / 408	998 / 998	241 / 251	673 / 683	2382 / 2382	
1879–94	44 / 57	441 / 422	898 / 935	278 / 275	598 / 577	2259 / 2259	
1899–1914	54 / 43	423 / 431	1095 / 1109	368 / 374	499 / 482	2439 / 2439	
%							
1839–54	(2.2) / (2.2)	(16.7) / (17.2)	(41.1) / (39.8)	(9.1) / (8.7)	(30.9) / (32.1)		
1859–74	(2.0) / (1.8)	(17.0) / (17.1)	(41.9) / (41.8)	(10.1) / (10.5)	(28.2) / (28.7)		
1879–94	(1.9) / (2.5)	(19.5) / (18.7)	(39.5) / (41.1)	(12.3) / (12.2)	(26.5) / (25.5)		
1899–1914	(2.2) / (1.8)	(17.3) / (17.7)	(44.9) / (45.5)	(15.1) / (15.3)	(20.5) / (19.8)		

Table 7.8   *Results of fitting the conditional independence, constant social fluidity, and uniform difference models to marital mobility between families over four marriage cohorts, and parameter estimates for the model of uniform change in association between class origins and destinations*

Model	G^2	BIC	df	p	Δ
Con. Ind.	2735.0	2147.0	64	0.00	20.4
CnSF	86.5	−345.8	48	0.00	2.7
Unidiff	71.2	−342.8	45	0.01	2.2

β Parameter estimates of the model of uniform change by cohort*	2	3	4
	0.01	−0.08	−0.19

Note:
* Parameters for cohort 1 set at zero.

of romantic fiction. Moreover, the high rate of lower middle-class hypogamy, which became stronger still among those getting married between 1899 and 1914, indicates that greater selectivity was not practised by the middle classes 'in all its different layers'.[78]

There are indications, however, that both the upper and lower middle classes were becoming more cohesive internally. Following the pattern established in the labour market, petty bourgeois families increasingly looked to the growing white-collar sector for suitable matches, while inside the elite, the expansion of the professions led to a dramatic increase in endogamy, but also in the number of professional alliances entered into by the sons and, to a lesser extent, daughters of the wealthy. Parents from the propertied sector of the elite seem to have remained more cautious with their daughters, the continuing cultivation of business alliances suggesting a concern with economic security before status.

Turning, finally, to the crucial question of relative mobility rates and trends in the openness of the class structure, the outcome from this perspective is, at the very least, not unsupportive of previous conclusions. Even though changes in the absolute pattern of movement were less pronounced in this dimension, and were once more supported by the changing shape of the alliance market, the model for uniform difference fits the data significantly better than the model for constant social fluidity. The Beta parameters associated with the former suggest a marginal rise in *inequality* over the first two cohorts, but thereafter, from the late 1870s onwards, a clear incremental shift in the direction of greater fluidity (Table 7.8). This is a finding based on a different set of social relationships from those found in the labour market, and therefore a different type of stratification. It does suggest, however, that the trend towards openness in English society was a more general phenomenon, rather than a product of different stages in the life course.

CONCLUSION

Constituting, to use Sorokin's words, an additional 'channel of social circulation',[79] the marriage market provides a further perspective on the pattern of interaction between classes and to considerations of openness. However, estimates of its significance for social mobility ultimately rest on judgements about the relative importance of the labour market as against other indices of class, and about the role of gender in the process of stratification.

If the conventional approach to class and gender is adopted – and, for the most part, there would seem to be good grounds for doing so in this period – then the social significance of marriage was far greater for women. Given their economic marginalisation, it was the marriage market which defined the prospects of the vast majority of women, and which therefore provided the principal vehicle for their mobility. This is not to argue that women were merely passive recipients of male-generated social identities, or that their impact on mobility and class formation was confined to their role as daughters and wives. It seems unlikely, however, that women, outside their marital mobility, affected the pattern of class inequality before 1914, although, as I shall suggest in the next chapter, this may have happened in the interwar period.

In marriage, women crossed class barriers more frequently than men did in the world of work, and in doing so were assisted by the fact that marriage markets were more open than labour markets. At one level, this suggests that gender played a complicating role in the process of demographic class formation, and qualifies the picture of class inequality drawn from the experience of men alone. That women held a more ambiguous position in the class structure is further suggested by the possibilities for middle-class mobility – via schoolteaching or civil service employment – for those who never married.[80] On the other

hand, it can be argued that women's marriage patterns largely confirmed the relationships between and within classes which are revealed
by men's economic mobility. Working-class women, for example, were
50 per cent more likely to move into the middle class than their
brothers, but still only one in ten did so. Most of their 'extra' mobility
was contained within the working class, thereby accentuating the
tendency towards homogenisation found in the labour market. Like
men, women became more mobile over time and, as in the labour
market, this reflected the increasing permeability of social barriers as
well as a redistribution of opportunities – partners rather than jobs in
this case – between classes.

Men also married across social divides rather more easily than they
moved over them at work, but again largely to the same general
pattern. In the logic of the conventional approach, it is difficult to
conceive of men's marriage in terms of mobility, even though some
individuals undoubtedly did transform their life chances in this way.
Nevertheless, men's marriage choices are still socially significant
because they are an indication of assimilation within, and thereby the
socio-cultural homogeneity of, classes. In this sense, too, marriage
complicated the process of demographic class formation, although
most men tended to confirm their mobility, or lack of it, by their
activity in the marriage market, and beneath the complexities thrown
up by this analysis established relationships between classes reappear.

A man's choice of bride may also suggest the likelihood of later
career mobility. Here the data show that a substantial core of downwardly mobile middle-class men did take a bride from their origin
class, which might indicate that the occupation they entered in the
marriage register was only temporary. Yet three out of four such men
married into families which were socially inferior to their own.
Another indication of career effect is provided by the relationship
between families through marriage, for here a comparison is, in effect,
being made between two 'occupationally mature' men. Again, this
comparison produces more mobility than occurred between fathers
and their marrying sons in the labour market, but the pattern of interchange clearly conforms to the same template. Yet the most notable
feature of this relationship is that here too, career stage notwithstanding, there is evidence of increasing fluidity in English society
from the mid-Victorian period down to the First World War.

8 Social Mobility and Class Structure in Historical Perspective

The issue of mobility speaks directly to the social historian's core concern with the structuring of society as a dynamic process of inter-action between individuals, social groups and institutions. All the more disappointing, then, that the subject has been largely neglected by historians in this country, and all the more important that recent calls for the study of social mobility to form the basis of a new agenda for social history are heeded. This book may be seen as a first system-atic attempt to lay the groundwork for such an agenda. It is a bench-mark study not just in terms of its subject matter but also in its methodology. In order to establish and explain the long-run pattern of mobility prior to 1914 it has employed a previously untried combina-tion of sources, and is among the first to subject such historical data to the powerful new tools of analysis developed within the dominant, sociological tradition in mobility research.

This cross-fertilisation of evidence and method is the only way to extract the historical study of mobility from the double-bind of presen-tism which has resulted from the power of the sociological tradition. While historians have been largely unwilling to engage with the lexicon of a 'foreign' discipline, the sociological study of mobility, for all its conceptual and technical sophistication, and despite the fundamentally historical nature of its concerns, has preferred to speculate about the past rather than investigate it. The findings reported here, which call into question one of the major assumptions about the long-term pattern of mobility in Britain handed down from sociology, suggest that this is a risky business. A proper understanding of mobility trends demands the right analytical approach, but it also requires us to take history seriously.

Having done so, however, we are left with the problem of how to reconcile two, apparently contradictory views of mobility in the making of modern Britain, one that stresses continuity, the other change. Accordingly, this concluding chapter begins, in the traditional way, with a distillation of this study's findings about the pattern of occupational and social mobility before 1914. But it then proceeds to explore where we might find a resolution to this discrepancy, and what this implies for the further study of social mobility, in both the past and the present.

THE PATTERN OF NINETEENTH-CENTURY MOBILITY

The evidence shows that Victorian and Edwardian society, while by no means immobile, was, nevertheless, one in which mobility was heavily structured. In contrast to the Smilesean rhetoric of a land in which opportunity was boundless, it was, in terms of its inhabitants' relative life chances, also a profoundly unequal society. The major barrier was between working-class families, dependent, in the main, on manual labour, and with little if any tangible property, and a heterogeneous middle and upper class of salaried employees, businessmen, professionals and landowners. This prevented all but a small minority of those brought up in working-class families from embarking on even the most modest of middle-class careers. The chances of crossing in the opposite direction were considerably greater, particularly for the sons and daughters of families on the lower margins of bourgeoisie, who, in terms of their origins as well as the destinations of their offspring, maintained close ties with the world of skilled labour. However, middle-class downward mobility made little impact on the social cohesion of the working class. Much more important from this point of view were internal divisions. For while workers and their children were largely cut off from the social territory above, the class to which they belonged was by no means an amorphous or homogeneous entity. Rather, it was one differentiated by the possession or otherwise of skilled status.

In terms of these basic inter- and intra-class relationships, English society looks to have shared many of the attributes of the nations of continental Europe.[1] There is, however, less correspondence in the comparative periodisation of European social mobility in the nineteenth century. Almost everywhere, it seems, there was a rise in the rate of mobility, attendant on the decline of the primary productive sector and the growth of the white-collar component of the middle class. Yet variability in the timing and scale of the expansion and contraction of different sectors in different economies necessarily precluded duplication of one country's path by another. In Britain, the comparatively slow decline of agriculture helped give rise to fairly even growth in rates of absolute mobility over the period of the long nineteenth century, while in Germany, for example, an abrupt transition away from the land was swiftly followed by a fall in the rate of movement over the manual/non-manual divide.[2]

In other respects, though, the sequence of change was more uniform. Both in Britain and across Europe the internal polarities of the working class were breaking down, as rates of interaction between men from the different skill sectors rose. The evidence shows, for the first time, how the process of homogenisation encompassed the labour market as well as the social relations of the working class, and how deep-rooted and persistent that process was. This trend, which is perhaps the most striking development in the pattern of change in mobility rates uncovered by this study, indicates that it was, in demographic terms at least, the *later* nineteenth century which witnessed the 'making' of the English working class. Broadening the perspective to incorporate the rarely explored mobility experience of women suggests that this was a process both assisted and complicated by gender, as women married more easily across boundaries both within and between classes.

The other principal outcome of the investigation of trends in the pattern mobility across the period relates to concerns of a rather different conceptual nature. The development of the nineteenth-century economy generated more mobility in this country, and, as in the middle decades of the twentieth century, this made for social aggregation as much as disaggregation. Yet, while this was a process driven in part by 'exogenous' economic and demographic forces, the application of log-linear models to the marriage data indicates that the rise in the rate of *de facto* movement was mostly reflective of increasing fluidity. In other words, mobility was to an extent 'forced' by the changing shape of the social division of labour, but an increasing 'exchange' of personnel between classes was much more important. In short, nineteenth-and early twentieth-century English society was becoming more mobile because it was simultaneously becoming more 'open'.

This development, as was illustrated in chapters 3 and 4, can be explained by a combination of factors: the occupational and institutional changes associated with British economic development, which altered the character and resources of classes; the achievement of mass literacy, which made for increasing competition for new types of employment; and by the increasingly urban location of the workforce, where older traditions were harder to apply and contacts and opportunities were more numerous. Crucially, informal mechanisms of training and recruitment were gradually being challenged by more structured, meritocratic, and bureaucratically mediated routes into the labour market.

FROM CONSISTENT TREND TO CONSTANT FLUX

The finding of a trend towards greater fluidity is not without support in other European historical studies, or, indeed, in twentieth-century research. It is, nevertheless, at odds with the results of Goldthorpe's influential study of mobility in twentieth-century Britain, which indicated there had been no change in the pattern of relative life chances between the 1940s and the 1970s, and disputes his broader contention that, in the long run, the 'genotypical' mobility regimes of industrial societies display only 'constant flux'.[3] Such a discrepancy can be explained in two ways: either it is a product of the contrasting data and organisational approaches, or it suggests that there have been two distinct eras of fluidity in modern Britain, and that these were joined by a period of disruption involving the generations missed by both Goldthorpe's research and this study.

As to the first type of explanation, those sceptical of this study's conclusions will doubtless suggest that the shortcomings of its evidence may mean that there is nothing to explain. Chief among these limitations is the snapshot problem, and the marriage sample's relatively youthful bias. In short, the trend towards fluidity in such a sample may merely reflect a life-course effect. Indeed, Goldthorpe himself found a trend towards increasing fluidity among his respondents after ten years at work, but that it disappeared when they were compared after the age of 35.[4]

The analysis of a subset of older grooms provided some support for this view, but was ultimately inconclusive, while the autobiographies indicated that men often made key social transitions – into business or white-collar employment – before the average age of marriage, sometimes as a preparation for, or condition of, their betrothal. Moreover, both the texts and the marriage data themselves suggested that

twentieth-century notions of work-life progression may be inappropri-
ate for much of the mostly pension-less nineteenth century.[5] In this
connection, William Sewell's justification of marriage registers as constituting 'a good sample of a broad and highly significant proportion of
the community, the settled young-adult population' is worth recalling.[6]
For when we come to consider the substantive historical issue of the
relationship between equality of opportunity and national economic
fortunes, it is surely with just this – prime-of-life – constituency that
such analyses should be concerned.

Reservations may also be raised in connection with the system of
classification adopted in this study, and the possibility that the apparent rise in mobility was just a reflection of its devaluation. In other
words, were the new opportunities inferior to the ones they replaced?
This is not an issue that is easy to resolve, particularly in view of the
often vague nature of the occupational descriptions in the marriage
registers. As argued in chapter 4, it does appear likely that 'obsolescence' made for easier access to some traditional sectors, but whether
this justifies their wholesale re-classification inside such a broad-based
scheme as the one employed here is a moot point. On the other hand,
the position of newer occupational groups seems to present less of a
problem. Railway engine drivers, for example, were wealthy enough to
merit inclusion in Hobsbawm's 'super-aristocracy' of labour,[7] policemen have been counted among the 'social superiors' of the nineteenth-century working class,[8] and, while their wages were not
especially high, postmen enjoyed the rare benefits of security of
employment and entitlement to a pension.[9] There has been much
debate about the position of clerks in the early years of the twentieth
century, but contemporaries such as Charles Booth seemed in no
doubt about the attractions of clerical work, while the weight of academic opinion suggests that most male white-collar employees did not
suffer 'proletarianisation' before 1920, if then.[10]

Ultimately, the more pertinent classification issue may, in fact, lie in
the contrasting dimensions of the scheme used here when compared to
the one employed in Goldthorpe's work. The latter is, for the most part,
more refined, but by combining semi- and unskilled manual workers it
actually subsumes an important dimension of the nineteenth-century
division of labour.

Turning to the second type of explanation for the contrast in findings
– concerning the question of a transition between two eras of mobility –
no sufficient empirical test of this hypothesis is available. On the face of
it, Glass's LSE survey of 1949 should be of some assistance in resolving

the issue. However, in addition to the familiar problem of different types of data and approaches to classification, insufficient chronological overlap makes a direct comparison between the marriage sample and this survey impossible. Glass's oldest cohort is an open-ended one, comprising men born before 1890, who were therefore contemporaries of the last cohort of grooms in the marriage sample.[11] A comparative test of trends would require a data series which began with an earlier birth cohort.

Glass's results have also been treated sceptically by some later commentators. This is because, over a period which, as a whole, witnessed an expansion in higher level occupations, the 1949 survey recorded an excess of downward over upward mobility, and found no sustained trend in the rate of mobility.[12] However, as Heath has pointed out, the 1972 Oxford enquiry's oldest cohort, born between 1908 and 1917, also exhibited higher rates of downward than upward mobility. Heath's reworking of Glass's data shows a rising trend in upward mobility among those born before 1900, ceasing for the following 1900–9 cohort, and then going into decline among those born between 1910 and 1919. Those born prior to and during the First World War, he writes, 'suffered some of the worst effects of the depression', a comparison of the division of labour in the 1921 and 1931 censuses confirming that 'This was no time of expanding opportunities.'[13]

Although this appears to lend support to the disruption hypothesis, the key issue here is how existing opportunities were distributed in relative terms. Glass's answer to this question, using indices of association based on the concept of 'perfect mobility', was that no discernible trend in fluidity could be found in the 1949 sample, a conclusion borne out by Hope's sophisticated attempt to compare the LSE and Oxford studies.[14] The same result is obtained when Glass's data are tested using the uniform difference method, which shows that the constant social fluidity model fits the data well. There are, however, some interesting fluctuations between cohorts, including a decline in fluidity in Glass's second 1890–9 birth cohort, which, crucially, is the first generation to fall beyond the marriage sample's coverage.[15]

Was this cohort the pivotal group linking an era of rising fluidity to one of trendless fluctuation? There is certainly enough circumstantial evidence to suggest it could have been. The last generation to be born during Victoria's reign grew up to face a series of events and changes, each with the potential to disrupt the pre-existing pattern of life chances. This was the group that went to school in a newly reformed and demarcated education system, had the formative stages of their working lives disrupted by a world war, and, as Heath suggests, made the remainder of their careers during a period of unprecedented economic turbulence.

As Ridge confirms, the period covered by the Glass survey was one in which academic qualifications became a more important determinant of occupational placement. However, as the relative importance of family background on careers declined, so the effect of social origins on educational success increased.[16] On the other side of the Channel, historians have identified a similar development as a central factor in explaining a process of social closure in the interwar period. As opportunities declined, and degrees became increasingly important for high status jobs, so the French elite protected their children by enrolling them at university.[17]

A similar connection between education and the constant social fluidity found in both the Glass and the Goldthorpe surveys has been made by Perkin. 'The middle classes', he writes, 'have a livelier appreciation of the value of education and of the opportunities for obtaining it than the working class, and in any movement towards a more meritocratic society will be more assiduous in acquiring the necessary merit.'[18] The statistics of interwar educational expansion bear out this conclusion, but only in part. It is certainly true that class disparities in access to both secondary and higher education remained wide between the wars, and that a steadily rising proportion of middle-class children were taking up both secondary school and university places. It also seems that the relative advantage held by middle-class boys in securing the latter did increase slightly. However, the social distribution of grammar school places actually became less unequal. Before 1910, the sons of middle-class families were almost seven times more likely to attend a grammar or a boarding school than working-class boys, while among those born between 1910 and 1929 the ratio fell to about four to one.[19]

These figures do not reveal anything about the different experiences or relative outcomes of a grammar school education, which were conditioned by hierarchies of resource and status within the system, the fact that working-class children were more likely to leave early, and social differentials in examination success.[20] However, it seems likely that working-class children did, at the very least, manage to hold their own within the new system, and that the more pertinent issue may therefore be the contrast between the old and the new. According to Reeder, it is unclear whether any working-class gains within the vertical and avowedly academic framework established by Morant after 1902 fully offset the losses caused by the proscription of the higher grade elementary schools. Although serving a similar constituency to the smaller grammar schools, these schools nevertheless drew a greater proportion of their pupils from working-class backgrounds.[21] It may be highly significant, then, that the new system came into operation just after most among the last group of men in the marriage sample had completed their schooling.

Just how much impact formal education had on mobility rates in a period when the vast majority of the population did not reach secondary level is unclear.[22] As Westergaard and Resler point out, the Glass study showed that while education clearly helped determine employment opportunities, grammar school-educated workers' children actually did worse than elementary school-educated middle-class children.[23] If the relationship between the two had been direct and straightforward, we would expect the apparent decline of class differentials in educational opportunity after the turn of the century to have produced rising rather than stable rates of fluidity in the interwar period. In his earlier work with Little, Westergaard tried to explain this anomaly in terms of the restrictions on career mobility brought about by the 'continued professionalisation, bureaucratisation and auto-mation of work'.[24] The gains generated by the increasing importance of education for mobility had been cancelled out, they suggested, by the simultaneous contraction of channels of advancement over the course of a working life. In particular, they pointed to the way in which, by the end of the nineteenth century, the growing scale and complexity of firms and organisations had reduced entrepreneurial activity, and how educational credentialism had replaced time-serving and patronage as the motor of progess within such enterprises.

This so-called 'counterbalance' thesis was rejected as an explana-tion of constant social fluidity by Goldthorpe because it was not explicitly formulated in terms of relative mobility chances and because his data indicated little change in the volume of upward mobility via career channels.[25] However, Goldthorpe's sample only allows him to compare men reaching occupational maturity between 1943 and 1972, which he does by dividing them into two large birth cohorts dominated by men whose careers were made in the relatively auspicious period from the mid-1930s onwards, and after the Second World War in particular. Given the uncertain circumstances in which the preceding generation left school for work, it is certainly possible that the stability found by Goldthorpe was a recent phenomenon, the product, perhaps, of a period of disruption to work-life mobility channels which may, in turn, have played a part in arresting the nineteenth-century trend in fluidity.

Just such a possibility is suggested by a new study of the emergence and development of bureaucratic career structures in Britain between 1870 and 1940.[26] Evidence from the employment records of four organisations – the Post Office, Lloyds Bank, the Great Western Railway and Cadburys – shows how career prospects were strongly defined by class. Career structures were generally constructed to allow mobility within rather than between social groups. They gave the best opportunities to those starting in white-collar jobs, who were, in turn, drawn largely from middle-class backgrounds. The study also suggests that Little and Westergaard were right about a declining trend in work-life mobility. Promotion prospects in each of the four organisations clearly began to worsen at the end of the nineteenth century. Whereas, for example, almost 40 per cent of Lloyds Bank clerks beginning their careers in the 1890s became managers, the proportion fell to just 22 per cent among those joining between 1910 and 1920. On the other hand, this seems to have been a general pattern, affecting middle- and working-class careers alike. A postman's chances of elevation to sorter or clerk began to decline with the 1870s entry cohort, and had halved by the 1890s. On the railways, what had been a four-year wait for promotion from the footplate to driving in the 1850s had increased to 16 years by the 1870s, and 21 years for those entering the service between 1910 and 1919.

Clearly, in so far as the trend in career mobility was generalised, it cannot have affected the prevailing pattern of relative life chances. Yet there is a suggestion in these figures that working-class careers were affected earlier than middle-class careers, which, if true, would have worked against the relative gains being made by the children of working-class families at the beginning of their careers. Second, however universal the crisis in promotion prospects, it seems to have been resolved to the particular advantage of the middle class.

At Lloyds, a recovery began with those entering the bank after 1915, and by the second half of the 1920s new employees could enjoy the same high promotion chances experienced by their predecessors. One factor here was the growing importance of post-entry credentials in the selection of candidates for promotion. Crucially, however, as concern about industrial unrest and the reactions of middle-class parents grew, the bank took the decision to employ women to carry out routine clerical and book-keeping duties, which, since women were not promoted, had the immediate effect of removing the career bottleneck for males. There are parallels here in the case of Cadburys, where an influx of women office workers in the 1920s and 1930s coincided with a sharp rise in the percentage of men finishing their careers in management, while in the Post Office, the amalgamation of previously separate male and female civil service grading systems in the 1920s brought about the downgrading of women clerks and the elevation of their male counterparts into the executive grades.

At the same time, it is not at all clear that – as Goldthorpe would have it – the outcome of the increasing interaction between women's work and male careers was socially neutral. Any gains for working-class men seem to have been short-lived or non-existent. The halving of a postman's prospects of reaching the position of sorter or clerk between 1860 and 1900 coincided with a marked rise in the number of female employees within the department, many of whom were brought into sorting and counter clerk categories after the absorption of the telegraph companies in 1870. Concentrated into the intermediate rungs of the employment ladder, women postal employees appear to have been used to form a buffer, protecting the status and ambitions of the middle-class male administrators at St Martin's le Grand, while simultaneously closing down the internal mobility prospects of working-class postmen and others in the 'manipulative' grades.

Such evidence is only suggestive. It comes from a limited number of what were, at the time, still unusual organisations and, therefore, offers what is, at best, only a partial view. It does appear, however, that career patterns were far from stable in the period preceding Goldthorpe's study, and that the nature and timing of change in this sphere, as in others, is not inconsistent with the halting and stabilisation of the trend in relative mobility. It may be, then, that the group of working-class men who got married in the period 1899–1914 can be seen as the last to have gained a relative advantage from the gradual bureaucratisation of work and the spread of basic educational skills. During the interwar period, with the consolidation of large-scale, impersonal capitalism, the bureaucratic career looks to have developed into a device of social closure rather than an expression of human capital.

CLASS FORMATION AND SOCIAL CHANGE

If the issue of mobility is to become a new agenda for social history, the current priorities of social mobility research itself require some attention. Criticisms of Goldthorpe's method often ignore both its power and his purpose, but there is, nevertheless, a certain amount of substance to claims that his recent preoccupation with the modelling of relative social mobility between generations has had a narrowing effect. This study has, for good reason, been guided by the conceptual and technical approaches developed by Goldthorpe. But in the process of applying them to historical evidence, it has also revealed how an understanding of the complex issue of change and persistence in mobility regimes demands a broader, more pluralistic research programme.

A revitalised agenda should, in the first place, give more attention to the dimension of intra-generational mobility, and, in particular, the relationship between careers and inter-generational change. This is an issue which continues to attract interest from critics of the standard approach to mobility within sociology, and which the findings and arguments advanced here suggest is crucial to the development of a constructive dialogue between students of mobility in different time periods and from different research traditions.

The subject of careers, highlights, in turn, an issue which also remains sidelined by the dominant tradition in sociological research: namely that of women and mobility. Reflecting their preference for the conventional approach to class and gender, Erikson and Goldthorpe concentrate on women's marital mobility, a perspective which, as it turns out, does not require them to modify the conclusions reached on the basis of male occupational mobility. While not seeking to deny the link between women's concentration in lower-grade employment and male career prospects, they see this as a separate gender issue because women's economic status means they derive their class position from their husband or father, and men of all classes benefit from female subordination.

Even in these terms, an historical dimension reveals a more complicated picture. Men may not, it seems, always have benefited equally from gender-based discrimination. The series of professional projects which underpinned the emergence of the modern service class in the early part of the twentieth century offered protection and status to middle-class males at a time when many working-class men were faced with rising competition from women and young workers in an increasingly bureaucratised labour market.[27] Nor is the question of women's marital mobility quite so straightforward in historical context, as several studies have now found more mobility and openness operating in nineteenth-century marriage markets than in the world of work.

But the conventional approach operates with too limited a conception of the relationship between class and gender. As Witz argues, and the example of the service class illustrates particularly well, the structure of occupational positions from which the class maps of social mobility analysis are drawn can only be explained with reference to an historical process of exclusion and demarcation involving gender. Furthermore, if the family is the social institution at the core of demographic class formation, the resources imported, invested and transmitted by wives cannot be simply be overlooked.[28]

One of the most important consequences of Goldthorpe's prioritising of relative mobility is that it has diverted attention away from the issue of mobility and class formation. Yet the pattern of demographic class formation, as revealed by the absolute rates of mobility, may have been crucial in creating the context in which the trend towards a more open society was halted in the interwar period. By the same token, it may also help to explain why, in contrast to the model proposed by the liberal thesis of industrialism, the period of rising meritocracy prior to 1914 did not check the onset of relative economic decline.

Political developments cannot simply be read as reflexes of economic and social change, but there seems little doubt that the homogenisation of working-class experience from 1870 onwards was implicated in the emergence of an independent form of working-class politics in the later nineteenth century. This connection was made some time ago by labour aristocracy theorists and others who wrote about the cultural 're-making' of the working class.[29] The evidence presented here, however, shows how deeply rooted this process was. Cultural change was embedded in a fundamental restructuring of the working class. This was cemented by the rise of an impersonal and bureaucratic form of capitalism and the territorial concentration of settled, urban working-class communities,[30] but crucially underpinned by the erosion of skill-based social identities through mobility between generations. In this context, the apparent failure of a more open society to generate greater economic competitiveness is understandable. The cultural, institutional and political consequences of the re-making of the working class, giving rise to a modern labour movement and a particular pattern of industrial relations, may simply have outweighed any beneficial effects to the economy of declining inequalities of opportunity.

It may also be possible to draw a link between the particular character of the pattern of demographic working-class formation and the particular nature of the labour movement as it developed in the early twentieth century. It is evident, for example, that the homogenisation process was gradual and incomplete. It was also more pronounced in some contexts than others, and was complicated by gender. Furthermore, while many of those caught up in this process were losers, consigned to a position inferior in status to what might have been expected on the basis of their family background, more were in fact winners who may have interpreted their upwardly mobility in a rather more individualistic way than the demographic class formation model implies.[31] This, then, is a pattern which is, on the whole, complementary to the generally moderate, reformist disposition of labour politics after 1900. At the same time, however, the much stronger increase in the downward mobility, which was greatest of all in the 1899-1914 period, corresponds well with Hobsbawm's picture of the skilled man radicalised in defence of his privileges, while the fact that the upwardly mobile travelled mostly into sectors associated with the rapid growth of general unions after 1910 suggests that success generated expectation as well as satisfaction.

Turning to how this pattern of class formation might inform the question of a shift in the mobility regime, the labour movement's role in the wartime economy, together with the period of postwar industrial unrest, sharpened perceptions of class division in Britain and mobilised the middle class and the establishment in defence of their interests.[32] As a result, the economy was deflated, Lloyd-George's welfare programme was severely curtailed, and from the point at which the postwar boom broke in the summer of 1920 and high unemployment set in, organised labour found itself on the back foot. It was in this context that the bureaucratisation of the labour market proceeded, threatening further the autonomy and status of skilled male workers while allowing the reconstruction and protection of middle-class careers.

Both Waites's work on the effects of the war on British society and Glass's data indicate that the process of working-class formation continued after 1914, and some have suggested that wartime gains for workers, the growth of egalitarian sentiments and the postwar success of the Labour Party are directly linked to the further homogenisation of working-class experience.[33] Nevertheless, enduring polarities between skilled and unskilled groups, and new tensions between men and women – in part derived from their different experiences of mobility – continued to influence the 'remaking' of the British working class in the interwar period, so that it remained an ambiguous process as far as the production of working-class consciousness is concerned. Indeed, this is reflected in the limitations on Labour's growth in the 1920s, as it continued to exist primarily as an institution for the defence of male trade union rights.[34]

The key point about the formation of the working class in the first two decades of the twentieth century, however, at least as far as this process relates to a change in the pattern of fluidity after 1918, may be that external appearances were as important as internal realities. Mckibbin has argued that the postwar middle-class backlash developed into a popular anti-working-class culture directed at the politics of organised labour and mobilised by the Conservative Party. People increasingly defined themselves in relation to what supporters of the Middle Class Union called 'the vocal working classes'.[35] But while the working class had become much more audible to other classes, it was now much more visible to them as well. Ironically, then, the fact of demographic, economic and urban working-class formation may have had a more coherent impact on middle-class consciousness. Meanwhile, its particular character may have helped to convince many workers that they belonged to the 'public' rather than their own class.

One can only proceed so far by inference, however. Demographic class formation is an elegant and straightforward notion, but its causal ramifications remain under-explored and cannot be assumed. The impact of mobility and immobility on cultural identities, political alignments and social action can only be properly assessed in the context of the subjective meanings invested in the experiences of individuals, and here there is much work to be done. Students of mobility in the past remain handicapped by the availability of evidence, but oral testimony, career histories and case studies of particular organisations offer much potential in more contemporary contexts.

Alongside this, there is the question raised by Goldthorpe long ago but never fully developed in his own work of 'other types of subjectively significant mobility' than class mobility.[36] The autobiographers suggest that success in some fields could divert attention from or compensate for the lack of progress in others, while in the developing bureaucracies of the early twentieth century the closing down of career routes involving class mobility coincided with the construction of other ladders within classes based around employment status and economic improvement. For example, only 14 per cent of postmen entering the service between 1860 and 1890 were promoted to inspector, sorter or clerk, yet an 'immobile' but loyal and well-behaved employee was promised security of employment, had his boots and uniform provided, received periodic rewards for efficiency, experienced a predictable and substantial rise in wages over the course of his career, and was granted a free pension at the end of it. Such 'gold watch' careers became quite widespread in the interwar period, and it is entirely possible that they played a stabilising role in the unstable economic climate of the 1920s and 1930s.[37] This, according to Vincent, was a generation which had to reconcile its aspirations with reality, but whose 'shadow careers' were to influence the way in which the next generation took its opportunities.[38] Such attitudes, echoes of which are found among the later autobiographers, suggest that the repercussions of immobility are no more straightforward or less important than the consequences of mobility.

Appendix 1: The Social Classification Scheme

CLASS I: PROFESSIONAL/HIGHER MIDDLE CLASS

Effectively the established middle class together with the odd member of the social elite proper (Earls, Barons, etc.). The two most distinctive groups within this category are professionals, and those describing themselves as 'gentlemen'.[1] Most prominent among the older professions are members of the clergy and the military. Medical men and lawyers, whose professions underwent rapid modernisation in this period, together with engineers and architects, are the main representatives of the newer professional groups. With the nineteenth century being a period of evolving boundaries in this sphere, the inclusion of particular occupations, as with the lower professionals in class II, depends on their date of entry in the register.[2]

CLASS II: INTERMEDIATE/LOWER MIDDLE CLASS

This is a highly heterogeneous class. It can be divided roughly between businessmen and white-collar employees, but these two categories break down further into a number of distinctive groups. Under business are included retailers, wholesalers, dealers, merchants, manufacturers and farmers. Clearly some members of these groups will be large and powerful operators who may properly belong to class I, but seldom do the registers indicate the size of the enterprise involved.[3] The major white-collar groups included here are clerks, salesmen and agents (moved up from class II in the Registrar-General's 1951 classification),[4] and lower or quasi-professionals – principally teachers, and managers of industrial and commercial concerns.

CLASS III: SKILLED WORKING CLASS

Definitions of 'skill' are notoriously difficult. In the technical sense, skilled occupations are usually accepted to be those involving significant periods of 'training' whether in the classic form of apprenticeship or through other methods such as 'migration' or 'following up'.[5] This is a somewhat inflated sector under the Registrar-General's schema,[6] first, because it includes some occupations normally classified as semi-skilled,[7] and second, due to the inclusion of several commercial, transport and service occupations whose classification is not straightforward. With the help of other occupational and

191

industrial sources, backed up by local studies where available, this sector has been refined and slimmed down a little. Nevertheless, a number of service and transport occupations, principally members of what has been called the 'uniformed working class' (postmen and policemen along with higher-grade railwaymen) have been retained, not least because in these cases literacy was a principal requirement of employment.

CLASS IV: SEMI-SKILLED WORKING CLASS

Semi-skilled occupations can be defined as those requiring proficiency in one or a restricted number of fairly basic, and mostly manual, tasks for which little training is required.[8] Although it includes machine-minders, this category is not the equivalent of the classical deskilled mass in Marx.[9] Encompassing much more than the growing factory proletariat, it is, in fact, dominated by occupations in the even more dynamic transport and service sectors.

CLASS V: UNSKILLED WORKING CLASS

For the most part this class includes all those describing themselves as a labourer of some sort. Industrial differentiation is difficult within this category because its incumbents tended not to elaborate beyond the basic term. For this reason, agricultural labourers, so defined, are also placed in this category.[10] Agricultural specialists, such as animal keepers, have been coded to class IV.[11] Also included here are costermongers, hawkers and other marginal or itinerant traders.[12]

Appendix 2: Class Outflow and Inflow Rates of Selected Occupational Groups, Percentage Rounded by Row (superscript figure denotes rates of occupational stability and self-recruitment)

	Outflow						Inflow					
	I	II	III	IV	V	n	I	II	III	IV	V	n
Clergymen	71^{42}	29	0	0	0	24	73^{45}	23	0	0	5	22
Doctors	38^{19}	38	13	6	6	16	56^{17}	44	0	0	0	18
Shopkeepers	1	53^{38}	30	9	8	319	4	59^{31}	25	6	6	386
Merchants	11	46^{26}	23	12	9	103	6	66^{40}	16	4	7	68
Publicans	2	35^{12}	39	18	7	108	0	48^{22}	29	12	12	32
Manufacturers	4	60^{36}	31	4	0	45	0	75^{50}	16	3	6	32
Clerks	9	30^{16}	36	20	5	64	9	37^{6}	35	15	4	171
Managers	0	40^{7}	47	7	7	30	6	61^{11}	17	17	0	18
Teachers	0	50^{9}	41	0	9	22	14	42^{5}	30	9	5	43
Bricklayers	0	4	73^{34}	11	13	140	0	10	62^{32}	7	21	148
Masons	0	7	72^{43}	13	8	90	0	14	77^{59}	5	5	66
Painters	0	14	67^{33}	13	6	78	2	16	65^{28}	7	11	105
Furniture makers	1	9	70^{39}	11	9	79	0	10	73^{38}	9	9	81
Carpenters	0	9	63^{30}	16	11	254	1	20	55^{35}	12	12	216
Tailors	1	10	67^{26}	11	12	113	0	13	68^{33}	10	9	87
Shoemakers	1	9	65^{30}	11	14	290	0	12	64^{42}	6	18	209
Millers	2	12	62^{27}	18	6	66	3	20	48^{31}	10	19	59
Bakers	0	10	69^{43}	15	7	73	3	16	59^{28}	15	7	111
Printers	0	18	64^{36}	11	7	28	0	23	56^{21}	15	6	48
Blacksmiths	0	7	64^{34}	12	18	155	0	12	65^{38}	7	15	138
Weavers	0	7	74^{50}	9	10	339	0	5	80^{61}	4	11	276
Cutlers	0	5	79^{57}	10	7	195	1	9	84^{65}	4	4	173
Nailers	0	2	78^{48}	7	13	116	0	7	84^{53}	5	5	105
Metal makers	0	6	75^{52}	10	10	242	0	7	70^{36}	7	16	343
Potters	0	5	85^{66}	8	3	264	0	6	80^{61}	9	5	287
Engineers	2	12	66^{29}	13	7	144	4	16	60^{23}	12	9	183
Railwaymen	0	8	67^{18}	10	15	61	2	15	41^{13}	21	21	87
Policemen	0	23	54^{17}	23	0	13	0	15	37^{7}	22	26	54
Postmen	0	8	46^{8}	23	23	13	0	15	55^{5}	5	25	20

	Outflow						Inflow					
	I	II	III	IV	V	n	I	II	III	IV	V	n
Quarrymen	0	4	27	50^{46}	19	26	0	6	18	42^{36}	33	33
Brickmakers	0	2	24	58^{51}	16	55	0	9	20	51^{48}	20	59
Metal workers	0	6	60	31^{29}	3	35	3	7	57	22^{15}	12	69
Textile workers	0	13	35	36^{24}	16	55	0	6	57	26^{24}	11	54
Brewery workers	2	6	48	35^{17}	8	48	0	35	23	23^{19}	19	43
Sawyers	0	3	23	52^{44}	22	64	0	6	12	62^{56}	20	50
Carters	0	8	39	37^{25}	17	130	0	11	32	28^{16}	29	206
Grooms	0	6	26	52^{26}	16	50	0	10	20	28^{14}	42	96
Cabmen	0	10	31	48^{24}	11	81	0	20	19	38^{19}	24	101
Seamen	0	0	25	63^{53}	13	40	3	14	14	33^{23}	36	92
Soldiers	5	24	33	33^{14}	5	21	0	15	40	21^{4}	25	83
Gardeners	1	8	33	49^{30}	10	175	1	17	16	38^{26}	28	201
Servants	5	5	33	44^{23}	13	39	2	17	22	41^{14}	19	64

Appendix 3 Occupational Sector Distribution of Grooms by Class and Sector of Fathers by Marriage Cohort

								Sons								
	Independent	Professional	Business	White-collar	Farming	Workshop	Capitalist	Factory	Mining	Service I	Industrial	Agricultural	Service II	Labouring	n	%
Fathers																
Class I																
1839–54	26.7	10.0	15.0	25.0	3.3	10.0	1.7	1.7	0.0	1.7	1.7	0.0	3.3	0.0	60	(2.1)
1859–74	27.9	25.6	16.3	14.0	0.0	2.3	0.0	4.7	0.0	0.0	0.0	0.0	4.7	4.7	43	(1.7)
1879–94	17.2	29.3	8.6	13.8	3.4	8.6	0.0	8.6	0.0	3.4	3.4	0.0	1.7	1.7	58	(2.5)
1899–1914	6.4	29.8	6.4	23.4	2.1	4.3	0.0	12.8	2.1	0.0	0.0	0.0	2.1	10.6	47	(1.9)
Business																
1839–54	1.9	1.3	33.8	3.1	4.4	26.9	2.5	8.1	1.9	1.3	3.1	0.0	4.4	7.5	160	(5.6)
1859–74	1.7	3.4	42.5	7.8	1.1	17.9	1.1	6.7	2.2	0.6	2.8	0.0	6.1	6.1	179	(7.2)
1879–94	1.1	1.6	35.7	11.5	2.7	14.3	2.2	4.9	2.7	2.7	4.4	0.5	9.3	6.0	182	(7.7)
1899–1914	0.0	2.8	30.7	14.8	2.3	14.2	0.6	8.5	2.8	5.7	1.7	0.0	8.5	7.4	176	(7.0)
White-collar																
1839–54	3.4	1.7	6.8	27.1	3.4	27.1	0.0	15.3	0.0	1.7	3.4	0.0	1.7	8.5	59	(2.1)
1859–74	1.9	3.8	17.3	28.8	0.0	15.4	0.0	7.7	0.0	0.0	3.8	0.0	9.6	11.5	52	(2.1)
1879–94	0.0	0.0	7.6	34.8	4.5	18.2	0.0	9.1	3.0	3.0	3.0	0.0	13.6	3.0	66	(2.8)
1899–1914	0.0	5.4	8.6	26.9	1.1	11.8	2.2	10.8	5.4	5.4	5.4	0.0	11.8	5.4	93	(3.7)

	Independent	Professional	Business	White-collar	Farming	Workshop	Capitalist	Factory	Mining	Service I	Industrial	Agricultural	Service II	Labouring	n	%
Fathers																
Farming																
1839–54	1.5	0.7	11.5	1.1	36.1	12.6	2.2	3.0	1.5	1.1	4.8	1.5	7.8	14.5	269	(9.4)
1859–74	1.6	0.0	7.6	2.7	45.7	8.2	0.5	3.3	3.8	2.2	3.3	0.0	8.2	13.0	184	(7.4)
1879–94	0.5	1.1	13.8	4.3	37.8	9.6	0.5	3.2	3.2	4.3	0.5	0.0	11.7	9.6	188	(8.0)
1899–1914	0.0	0.6	11.5	5.2	47.1	3.4	0.0	1.1	5.2	1.1	1.7	1.7	11.5	9.8	174	(6.9)
Workshop																
1839–54	0.2	0.0	3.6	1.2	1.9	61.0	2.6	9.0	3.3	0.9	2.6	0.2	3.4	10.2	580	(20.4)
1859–74	0.4	0.2	4.4	1.8	1.6	52.7	1.8	10.3	3.4	1.8	5.4	0.2	5.8	10.1	497	(20.0)
1879–94	0.3	0.0	4.5	4.0	0.5	46.3	1.0	12.1	4.0	1.5	4.5	0.0	7.8	13.4	397	(16.9)
1899–1914	0.2	0.4	5.1	5.8	0.9	36.3	0.9	11.3	3.8	3.1	7.5	0.4	13.1	11.3	452	(17.9)
Capitalist																
1839–54	0.0	0.0	0.5	1.1	0.0	8.7	68.5	3.8	3.8	1.1	1.6	0.0	2.2	8.7	184	(6.5)
1859–74	0.0	0.0	3.4	0.9	0.9	2.6	56.9	5.2	10.3	0.0	2.6	0.0	3.4	13.8	116	(4.7)
1879–94	0.0	0.0	4.3	0.0	0.0	6.5	47.3	10.8	10.8	2.2	8.6	1.1	4.3	4.3	93	(4.0)
1899–1914	0.0	0.0	2.1	4.3	0.0	4.3	27.7	6.4	2.1	4.3	14.9	0.0	6.4	27.7	47	(1.9)
Factory																
1839–54	0.0	0.0	2.6	3.6	0.0	11.9	1.6	67.4	4.1	0.0	3.1	0.0	2.6	3.1	193	(6.8)
1859–74	0.0	0.5	2.5	4.6	0.0	8.6	1.5	59.9	7.6	0.5	4.6	0.0	3.0	6.6	197	(7.9)
1879–94	0.0	0.0	4.3	3.6	0.8	9.5	2.0	57.7	4.3	2.8	5.5	0.0	5.1	4.3	253	(10.8)
1899–1914	0.6	0.0	3.2	4.7	0.0	10.1	0.6	41.8	7.9	1.9	8.2	0.0	8.9	12.0	316	(12.5)

Sons

| | Sons | | | | | | | | | | | | | | | |
	Independent	Professional	Business	White-collar	Farming	Workshop	Capitalist	Factory	Mining	Service I	Industrial	Agricultural	Service II	Labouring	n	%
Fathers																
Mining																
1839–54	0.0	0.0	1.2	0.0	0.0	5.6	1.2	4.3	73.5	0.0	2.5	0.0	0.6	11.1	162	(5.7)
1859–74	0.0	0.0	1.0	0.0	0.5	5.2	1.0	8.3	73.6	1.0	1.0	0.0	0.5	7.8	193	(7.8)
1879–94	0.0	0.0	2.7	1.6	0.0	5.3	0.5	11.2	61.7	1.6	2.1	0.0	3.7	9.6	188	(8.0)
1899–1914	0.4	0.0	0.8	2.1	0.0	4.6	0.4	6.6	70.1	2.5	3.7	0.0	3.7	5.0	241	(9.6)
Service I																
1839–54	0.0	0.0	0.0	6.7	0.0	33.3	0.0	6.7	0.0	33.3	0.0	0.0	0.0	20.0	15	(0.5)
1859–74	0.0	0.0	3.2	3.2	3.2	19.4	0.0	9.7	3.2	29.0	3.2	0.0	3.2	22.6	31	(1.2)
1879–94	0.0	2.7	2.7	5.4	0.0	10.8	0.0	5.4	5.4	37.8	2.7	2.7	13.5	10.8	37	(1.6)
1899–1914	0.0	0.0	4.7	4.7	0.0	15.3	1.2	16.5	8.2	20.0	4.7	0.0	9.4	15.3	85	(3.4)
Class IV																
1839–54	0.4	0.0	2.8	2.0	1.6	17.7	2.4	7.6	2.8	0.0	20.5	4.8	22.5	14.9	249	(8.7)
1859–74	0.4	0.0	3.3	1.1	0.7	13.7	1.9	11.5	3.3	2.6	17.0	2.6	27.0	14.8	270	(10.9)
1879–94	0.7	0.0	2.9	5.4	0.7	11.1	0.7	12.1	4.6	5.4	12.9	1.1	31.4	11.1	280	(11.9)
1899–1914	0.3	0.0	3.4	4.1	1.0	12.1	0.3	7.8	9.3	5.2	10.3	2.1	31.3	12.9	387	(15.3)
Class V																
1839–54	0.0	0.0	1.0	0.3	1.1	7.7	2.4	2.8	4.6	0.5	1.9	0.0	6.5	71.1	918	(32.2)
1859–74	0.0	0.0	1.7	0.3	0.8	6.5	0.8	4.0	6.8	1.8	3.3	0.7	8.1	65.2	724	(29.1)
1879–94	0.0	0.0	1.0	1.0	1.0	7.7	0.3	5.6	5.2	2.6	5.4	0.7	11.6	57.7	610	(25.9)
1899–1914	0.0	0.2	2.2	1.2	0.2	8.5	0.6	5.1	11.3	3.4	4.6	0.2	18.2	44.4	505	(20.0)

198

	Independent	Professional	Business	White-collar	Farming	Workshop	Capitalist	Factory	Mining	Service I	Industrial	Agricultural	Service II	Labouring
									Sons					
n														
1839–54	27	11	143	64	133	621	185	273	209	24	117	17	177	848
1859–74	22	21	161	65	105	438	94	278	256	46	125	13	206	656
1879–94	16	23	155	111	93	367	63	321	213	80	127	10	268	505
1899–1914	8	28	149	145	97	356	28	305	332	99	154	14	367	441
%														
1839–54	(0.9)	(0.4)	(5.0)	(2.2)	(4.7)	(21.8)	(6.5)	(9.6)	(7.3)	(0.8)	(4.1)	(0.6)	(6.2)	(29.8)
1859–74	(0.9)	(0.8)	(6.5)	(2.6)	(4.2)	(17.6)	(3.8)	(11.2)	(10.3)	(1.9)	(5.0)	(0.5)	(8.3)	(26.4)
1879–94	(0.7)	(1.0)	(6.6)	(4.7)	(4.0)	(15.6)	(2.7)	(13.6)	(9.1)	(3.4)	(5.4)	(0.4)	(11.4)	(21.5)
1899–1914	(0.3)	(1.1)	(5.9)	(5.7)	(3.8)	(14.1)	(1.1)	(12.1)	(13.2)	(3.9)	(6.1)	(0.6)	(14.5)	(17.5)

Notes

INTRODUCTION

1. Samuel Smiles, *Self Help*, London, 1859, p. 234.
2. See also his *Lives of Engineers*, 3 vols, London, 1861–2. On the 'literature of success', see J.F.C. Harrison, 'The Victorian Gospel of Success', *Victorian Studies*, December 1957.
3. Calculated from John H. Goldthorpe (in collaboration with Catriona Llewellyn and Clive Payne), *Social Mobility and Class Structure in Modern Britain*, Oxford, 1987, Table 2.1, p. 44. Unless otherwise stated, all subsequent references to this work are to the 2nd (1987) edition.
4. See, for example, R. Pahl, 'Is the Emperor Naked? Some Questions on the Adequacy of Sociological Theory in Urban and Regional Research', *International Journal of Urban and Regional Research*, 12, 1988.
5. See Patrick Joyce, *Visions of the People. Industrial England and the Question of Class, 1848–1914*, Cambridge, 1991; Gareth Stedman Jones, 'Rethinking Chartism' in his *Languages of Class*, Cambridge 1983; William Reddy, *Money and Liberty in Western Europe*, Cambridge, 1987.
6. See the discussion in Mike Savage and Andrew Miles, *The Remaking of the British Working Class*, London, 1994, chapter 1.
7. See, for example, Lawrence Stone, *The Crisis of the Aristocracy, 1558–1640*, Oxford, 1965; and Sidney Pollard, *Britain's Prime and Britain's Decline. The British Economy 1870–1914*, London, 1989. For case-study analyses of mobility within these debates, see P. Bearman and G. Deane, 'The Structure of Opportunity: Middle-Class Mobility in England, 1548–1689', *American Journal of Sociology*, 98, 1, 1992; and Y. Cassis, 'Bankers in English Society in the Late Nineteenth Century', *Economic History Review*, 38, 1985.
8. S. Thernstrom, *Poverty and Progress: Social Mobility in a Nineteenth-Century City*, Cambridge, Mass., 1964; and *The Other Bostonians: Poverty and Progress in the American Metropolis, 1880–1970*, Cambridge, Mass., 1973. Michael Sanderson, 'Literacy and Social Mobility in the Industrial Revolution in England', *Past and Present*, 56, 1972.
9. Mike Savage, 'Social Mobility and Class Analysis: A New Agenda for Social History', *Social History*, 19, 1994.
10. See n. 3 above.
11. See, for example, D. Rose's review of *The Constant Flux*, in *ESRC Data Archive Bulletin*, 54, 1993.
12. See chapter 1, n. 10.

CHAPTER 1

1. Anthony Heath, *Social Mobility*, London, 1981, p. 13. See also the review of social interests and mobility in Goldthrope, *Social Mobility*, chapter 1.
2. Karl Marx, *Capital*, Vol. III, Moscow, 1959, p. 587. Karl Marx, 'The Eighteenth Brumaire of Louis Bonaparte', in Karl Marx and Friedrich Engels, *Selected Works*, Vol. 1, Moscow, 1962, p. 255; 'Wages, Prices and Profit', *Selected Works*, Vol. 1, p. 444; his letter to Joseph Weydemeyer, 5 March 1852, in Karl Marx and Friedrich Engels, *Collected Works*, Vol. 39, London, 1963, pp. 60–6.
3. See Pitrim Sorokin, *Social and Cultural Mobility*, Glencoe, 1927, pp. 510, 524; and S.M. Lipset and R. Bendix, *Social Mobility in Industrial Society*, London, 1950, pp. 284–5.
4. See, for example, Goldthorpe, *Social Mobility*.
5. R.H. Tawney, *Equality*, London, 1938; D.V. Glass (ed.), *Social Mobility in Britain*, London, 1954.
6. See, for example, Mancur Olson, *The Rise and Decline of Nations: Economic Growth, Stagflation, and Social Rigidities*, New Haven, 1982. Also David Landes, *The Unbound Prometheus. Technological Change and Industrial Development in Western Europe from 1750 to the Present Day*, Cambridge, 1972.
7. For a extended summary of this debate, see Robert Erikson and John H. Goldthorpe, *The Constant Flux: A Study of Class Mobility in Industrial Societies*, Oxford, 1993, chapter 1. Also, John H. Goldthorpe, 'On Economic Development and Social Mobility', *British Journal of Sociology*, 36, 1985.
8. P.M. Blau and O.D. Duncan, *The American Occupational Structure*, New York, 1967.
9. See S.M. Lipset and H. Zetterberg, 'A Theory of Social Mobility', in Lipset and Bendix, *Social Mobility*.
10. Goldthorpe defines 'demographic' class formation as the formation 'of aggregates of individuals or families that are identifiable through the continuity of their class locations over time', *Social Mobility*, p. 330.
11. D.L. Featherman, F.L. Jones and R.M. Hauser, 'Assumptions of Social Mobility Research in the US: The Case of Occupational Status', *Social Science Research*, 4, 1975.
12. H.B.G. Ganzeboom, R. Luijkx and D.J. Treiman, 'International Class Mobility in Comparative Perspective', in Arne L. Kalleberg (ed.), *Research in Social Stratification and Mobility*, 8, 1989.
13. See D.V. Glass and J.R. Hall, 'Social Mobility in Britain: a Study of Inter-Generational Changes in Status', in Glass (ed.), *Social Mobility*, pp. 177–217.
14. Goldthorpe, *Social Mobility*, pp. 27, 327.
15. Ibid., chapters 2 and 3, pp. 327–8.
16. Ibid., chapter 2.
17. Ibid., chapters 6, 7, 8.
18. Ibid., 1st (1980) edition, p. 272. My brackets.
19. Ibid. 2nd edition, pp. 344–51.

20. Ibid., p. 323.
21. Keith Hope, 'Trends in the Openness of British Society in the Present Century', in Donald J. Treiman and Robert V. Robinson (eds.), *Research in Social Stratification and Mobility*, 1981, pp. 127–70; R.D. Penn and D.C Dawkins, 'Structural Transformations in the British Class Structure: A Log Linear Analysis of Marital Endogamy in Rochdale 1856–1964', *Sociology*, 17, 1983.
22. There are numerous studies of recruitment to particular elite groups. See, for example, P.E. Razzel, 'Social Origins of Officers in the Indian and British Home Army', *British Journal of Sociology*, 14, 1963, and also Charlotte Erikson's work mentioned in note 31 below. A broader study of the social composition of the British elite was conducted by Harold Perkin with the assistance of W.D. Rubinstein in the early 1970s. See Perkin, 'The Recruitment of Elites in British Society since 1800', *Journal of Social History*, 12, 2, 1978. See also, Rubinstein's work on millionaires, for example, *Men of Property*, London, 1981, chapter 4.
23. John Stuart Mill, *Principles of Political Economy*, ed. Sir William Ashley, London, 1909, p. 393.
24. Ibid., 1904 edition, p. 455.
25. Walter Bagehot, 'Sterne and Thackeray', *The Collected Works of Walter Bagehot. Vol 2, The Literary Essays*, ed. Norman St John-Stevas, London, 1965, pp. 307–8.
26. Arthur Marshall, *Principles of Economics*, ninth edition, 1961, pp. 217, 218, n. 1.
27. Harold Perkin, *Origins of Modern English Society*, 1780–1880 London, 1985, p. 225.
28. Harrison, 'Victorian Gospel', p. 162.
29. Patrick Joyce, *Work, Society and Politics. The Culture of the Factory in Later Victorian England*, London, 1980, pp. xvii–xviii.
30. Flora Thompson, *Lark Rise to Candleford*, London, 1984, p. 183.
31. Perkin, *Origins*, pp. 124–33, 424, 437. See also Charlotte Erickson, *British Industrialists: Steel and Hosiery, 1850–1950*, Cambridge, 1959, which showed declining rates of working-class recruitment to positions of ownership and management in both industries, and that the worst prognosis was to be found in steel, the more modern and progressive of the two.
32. The classic statement of this position is to be found in David Landes, *The Unbound Prometheus*, chapters 2 and 3. See also Peter Mathias, *The First Industrial Nation. An Economic History of Britain, 1700–1914*, London, 1969, p. 10.
33. See Sanderson, 'Literacy and Social Mobility'.
34. Thomas Laqueur, 'Literacy and Social Mobility in the Industrial Revolution in England', *Past and Present*, 64, 1974, pp. 105–6. Sanderson was in fact fully aware of his study's limitations and should be commended rather than criticised for trying to open up discussion on a subject hitherto neglected by historians. See his 'Rejoinder', *Past and Present*, 64, 1974.
35. Michael Anderson, *Family Structure in Nineteenth Century Lancashire*, Cambridge, 1971, pp. 26, 28.

36. See, for example, Brian Preston, 'Occupations of Father and Son in Mid-Victorian England', Reading University, Department of Geography, *Geographical Papers*, 1977. Also P.E. Razell, 'Statistics and English Historical Sociology', in R.M. Hartwell (ed.), *Industrial Revolution*, Oxford, 1970.

37. F. Engels, 'England in 1845 and 1885', incorporated into the preface of the 1892 edition of *The Condition of the Working Class in England*, reprinted in Karl Marx and Friedrich Engels, *On Britain*, Moscow, 1953, pp. 28–33; V.I. Lenin, 'Imperialism: The Highest Stage of Capitalism', in *Selected Works*, Peking, 1975, pp. 128–31.

38. E.J. Hobsbawm, 'The Labour Aristocracy in Nineteenth-Century Britain', in his *Labouring Men. Studies in the History of Labour*, London, 1964, pp. 273–5. 'An "artisan" or "craftsmen"', he continued, 'was not under any circumstances to be confused with a "labourer"'. He suggested, however, that between these two poles there existed an intermediate group which 'belonged to neither' but 'shaded into each'. More recently Hobsbawm has accepted that there may have been rather more interaction between skilled and unskilled, at least from the bottom up, than he originally thought; see 'Artisans and Labour Aristocrats?', in his, *Worlds of Labour. Further Studies in the History of Labour*, London, 1984, p. 265.

39. Hobsbawm, 'Labour Aristocracy', p. 295. The problem is not just one of evidence. If, as Hobsbawm argues, the aristocrats had merged with, or even gained a higher status than, sections of the lower middle class (pp. 273–4), then terms such as 'rising out of the working class' or 'promotion' become highly problematic.

40. Geoffrey Crossick, *An Artisan Elite in Victorian Society. Kentish London, 1840–1880*, London, 1978. This is based on his figures for intermarriage. The data on occupational change show no overall trend but suggest that some trades experienced both increasing incursion from below and declining recruitment from above.

41. R.Q. Gray, *The Labour Aristocracy in Victorian Edinburgh*, Oxford, 1976, chapter 5.

42. E.J. Hobsbawm, 'The Aristocracy of Labour Reconsidered', in *Worlds of Labour*, p. 251.

43. Hobsbawm, 'Labour Aristocracy', although in his later writings he seems to have moved to a less mechanistic position. As well as 'The Aristocracy of Labour Reconsidered', see 'Debating the Labour Aristocracy', in *Worlds of Labour*, pp. 221–6. Gray, *The Labour Aristocracy*, chapter 9. For a classic example, see Standish Meacham, 'English Working-Class Unrest before the First World War', *American Historical Review*, LXXVII, 1972.

44. Roger Penn, *Skilled Workers in the Class Structure*, Cambridge, 1985. Penn rejects the notion of an isomorphic association between the economic differentiation inside the working class and its social and political relations, arguing that, 'Far from there being rhythms of increasing and declining skilled endogamy, there would appear to be little evidence of any skilled social divide' (p. 187).

45. See, for example, Olson, *Rise and Decline*, pp. 82–3; Andrew Gamble, *Britain in Decline. Economic Policy, Political Strategy and the British*

State, Basingstoke, 1990, pp. 78–83; Harold Perkin, *The Rise of Professional Society. England since 1880*, London, 1989, p. 516.

46. Hartmut Kaelble, *Social Mobility in the 19th and 20th Centuries: Europe and America in Comparative Perspective*, Leamington Spa, 1985, chapter 4.

47. Reinhard Schüren, 'Intergenerational Occupational and Marital Mobility in German Cities in the Nineteenth and Early Twentieth Centuries', in Miles and Vincent (eds.), *Building European Society*. See also Jürgen Kocka, 'The Study of Social Mobility and the Formation of the Working Class in the Nineteenth Century', *Le Mouvement Social*, 111, 1980.

48. See Krzysztof Makowski, 'Social Mobility in Nineteenth-Century Poznan', in Miles and Vincent (eds.), *Building European Society*.

49. M.H.D. van Leeuwen and I. Maas, 'Long-term Mobility in a European City: Berlin 1835–1957', paper to the ISA Committee on Social Stratification, University of Trento, 1992; D.B. Grusky and I.K. Fukumoto, 'Social History Update: a Sociological Approach to Historical Social Mobility', *Journal of Social History*, 23, 1, 1989; A.M. Guest, N.S Langdale and J.C. McCann, 'Intergenerational Occupational Mobility in the Late 19th-Century United States', *Social Forces*, 68, 1989; M. de Seve and G. Bouchard, 'Long-term Social Mobility in Quebec: the Case of the Saguenay/Lac St Jean 1851–1951', paper to the ISA Committee on Social Stratification, Bielefeld, 1994; I.K. Fukumoto and D.B. Grusky, 'Social Mobility and Class Structure in Early-Industrial France', in Miles and Vincent (eds.), *Building European Society*; William H. Sewell Jr, *Structure and Mobility. The Men and Women of Marseille, 1820–1870*, Cambridge, 1985; M.H.D. van Leeuwen and I. Maas, 'Log-linear Analysis of Changes in Mobility Patterns. Some Models with an Application to the Amsterdam Upper Classes in the Second Half of the Nineteenth Century', *Historical Methods*, 24, 2, 1991.

50. See David Vincent, *Literacy and Popular Culture. England 1750–1914*, Cambridge, 1989.

51. The Act created the office of Local Registrar and made provision for the civil, as opposed to ecclesiastical, registration of births, marriages and deaths, and the central collection of data under the auspices of the General Register Office in London. It also provided for the administrative division of the country into Registration Districts based on the Poor Law Unions. See Thomas Erskine May, *The Constitutional History of England Since the Accession of George the Third, 1760–1860*, Vol. II, London, 1963, pp. 419–20.

52. Although 10,835 is the total sample size, the operational figure in cross-sample analyses of intergenerational change is smaller (10,210 in the case of fathers and sons). This is due to the fact that occupational information about one or more signatories is missing in a proportion of cases. This compares favourably with the size of the 1972 Nuffield survey, which generated 10,309 useable interviews, although the cross-sample mobility matrices are based upon 8,575 respondents, or 9,434 if agricultural categories are included. See the appendix to the first edition of *Social Mobility and Class Structure in Britain*.

53. B.R. Mitchell and P. Deane, *Abstract of British Historical Statistics*, Cambridge, 1962, p. 15. R.S. Schofield, 'English Marriage Patterns Revisited', *Journal of Family History*, 10, 1985. Michael Anderson, 'The Social Implications of Demographic Change', in F.M.L. Thompson (ed.), *The Cambridge Social History of Britain, 1750–1985*, Vol. 2, p. 28.

54. Occupational information does appear in some church registers prior to this date, but the practice was dependent on the initiative of individual parish priests. In the light of recent revisionist studies the whole notion of industrial 'revolution' must, in any case, be handled with care. See N.F.R. Crafts, *British Economic Growth during the Industrial Revolution*, Oxford, 1985; Maxine Berg, *The Age of Manufactures, 1700–1820*, London, 1985.

55. The Dissenters' Marriages Act, also of 1836, allowed dissenters to marry in their own chapels and permitted civil contracts to be taken out in the presence of the Superintendent Registrar. Prior to this, under Hardwicke's Marriage Act of 1753, the only legal marriages were those conducted by a minister of the established church. Only copies of specified certificates are made available, and these must be purchased.

56. O. Anderson, 'The Incidence of Civil Marriage in Victorian England and Wales', *Past and Present*, 69, November 1975, pp. 50–87.

57. See Vincent, *Literacy*, Appendix A. Until 1884, the Registrar-General published aggregate returns of the form of marriage, making it possible to identify areas in which rates of marriage outside the established church were low. Further inspection of the returns suggested no simple correspondence between the Anglican/non-Anglican/civil divide and occupational or class identity. One supportive complication is that the members of some nonconformist groups continued to marry in the parish church for some time after compulsion ceased. Vincent records that in the Methodist stronghold of Stoke, 82 per cent of partners in 1874 availed themselves of ceremonies in the established church. See also, Anderson, 'Incidence of Civil Marriage'. The sample was tested against the Registrar-General's returns for the proportions of marks and signatures for each Registration District. There being a strong correlation between literacy rates and social status, it was felt that an accurate literacy sample would also indicate that the occupational sample was reliable.

58. On the considerable problems associated with the interpretation and use of historical occupational titles, see R.J. Morris 'Fuller Values, Questions and Contexts: Occupational Coding and the Historian', in Kevin Schürer and Herman Diederiks (eds.), *The Use of Occupations in Historical Analysis*, St. Katherine, 1993. Also his *Class, Sect and Party. The Making of the British Middle Class: Leeds, 1820–32*, Manchester, 1990.

59. See chapter 7, pp. 147–9.

60. See A.B. Sørensen, 'Theory and Methodology in Social Stratification', in U. Himmelstrand (ed.), *The Sociology of Structure and Action*, Vol. 1, *Sociology: From Crisis to Science*, London, 1986.

61. Goldthorpe, *Social Mobility*, pp. 44, 52–3.

62. Frank McKenna, 'Victorian Railway Workers', *History Workshop Journal*, 1, Spring 1976, p. 32.

63. Goldthorpe, *Social Mobility*, pp. 52–3.

64. Sewell, *Structure and Mobility*, p. 319.

65. Following Thernstrom, this concerns men who were 30 years of age or older (*The Other Bostonians*, pp. 62, 87). See chapter 5 below.

66. See Thernstrom's work in Newburyport and Boston, for example.

67. See Colin G. Pooley and John C. Doherty, 'The Longitudinal Study of Welsh Migration to English Towns in the Nineteenth Century', in Colin G. Pooley and Ian D. White (eds.), *Migrants, Emigrants and Immigrants. A Social History of Migration*, London, 1991, pp. 148–50. Also, Hershberg, 'New Urban History', p. 16.

68. On autobiography as evidence, see Norman K. Denzin, *Interpretative Biography*, London, 1989; and David Vincent, *Bread, Knowledge and Freedom. A Study of Nineteenth-century Working Class Autobiography*, London, 1981. Paul Thompson argues that the issue of memory loss in the construction of life stories is less problematic than it might seem, and that, in some senses, the process of recall is enhanced by age. See his, *The Voice of the Past. Oral History*, Oxford, 1988, pp. 110–17. As regards verifying information about occupations, a small number of cross-checks were made by comparing a writer's account of his career with the records of the same individual appearing in local trade directories. No anomalies were found. Similarly, the occupational titles in a small sample of marriages, taken randomly from Birmingham parishes between 1841 and 1891, were checked against directory and census records. Out of a total of 38 individual traced between sources, 19 gave exactly the same title in each, and 12 gave slightly different or more elaborate descriptions of the same occupational activity (e.g. Alfred Cleaton was recorded as a gunmaker on his marriage certificate on 30 June 1861, and a pistol maker in the 1861 census, while Thomas Leonard was described as a steel toy maker at his son's wedding on the 26 March 1841, and as a watch, key and gilt toy maker in an 1841 trade directory). Of the seven who gave different titles in the different sources, only one (the case of Robert Hawke Foy, described as a ticket writer in White's Directory in 1851 and as an artist at his marriage in July of the same year) is suggestive of an attempt to enhance status. The remaining 6 would appear to be either cases of genuine mobility between the dates of record or dubious traces.

69. Pooley and Doherty managed to link only 53 individuals between the 1861 and 1871 censuses out of a total population of over 22,000, and a known migratory group of nearly 300 ('Longitudinal Study', pp. 162–3).

70. John Burnett, David Vincent and David Mayall (eds.), *The Autobiography of the Working Class. An Annotated, Critical Bibliography, Vol. I: 1790–1900*, London, 1984, pp. xviii-xix.

71. Ibid., p. xxxi. My emphasis.

72. Sorokin, *Social and Cultural Mobility*, pp. 3, 12.

73. See Sewell, *Structure and Mobility*, chapters 4 and 9.

74. Goldthorpe, *Social Mobility*, pp. 26, 39. The assumption that occupation is a good indicator of class is widely held in sociology. See, for example,

Blau and Duncan, *American Occupational Structure*, pp. 5–6. Also, Frank Parkin, *Class, Inequality and Political Order*, London, 1971. Citing Gosta Carlsson, *Social Mobility and Class Structure*, Lund, 1958, Thernstrom writes, 'The historical study of mobility requires the use of an objective criteria of social status. The most convenient of these is occupation. Occupation may be only one variable in a comprehensive theory of class, but it is the variable which includes more, which sets more limits on the other variables, than any other criterion of status', *Poverty and Progress*, p. 84.

75. It may be that, as in nineteenth-century Marseilles, the lack of any clear distinction in the registers marking off proprietors from wage earners was itself an indication of how masters and journeymen viewed the difference between them. See Sewell, *Structure and Mobility*, p. 49. See also Crossick's comments on the transition from wage earner to small master not necessarily being experienced as upward mobility: Crossick, *An Artisan Elite*, p. 114.

76. *Census 1951, Classification of Occupations*, HMSO, London, 1955. For further discussion of the suitability of this classification, see W.A. Armstrong, 'The Use of Information about Occupation', in E.A. Wrigley (ed.), *Nineteenth-Century Society. Essays in the Use of Quantitative Methods for the Study of Social Data*, Cambridge, 1972.

77. See Gordon Marshall, David Rose, Howard Newby and Carolyn Vogler, *Social Class in Modern Britain*, London, 1989, pp. 18–19; R.S. Szreter, 'The Genesis of the Registrar-General's Social Classification of Occupations', *British Journal of Sociology*, 35, 1984, pp. 522–46; Catherine Marsh, 'Social Class and Occupation', in Robert G. Burgess (ed.), *Key Variables in Social Investigation*, London, 1986, pp. 123–52. From the perspective of historical data, see Penn, *Skilled Workers*, chapter 8; and Simon Szreter, *Fertility, Class and Gender in Britain, 1860–1940*, Cambridge, 1996, part II.

78. Armstrong, 'Use of Information', pp. 202–3.

79. The degree of commensurability between the 1951 classification and the nineteenth- and early twentieth-century division of labour is high because the 1951 enumeration would still have had to deal with people who were economically active in an earlier period.

80. The relative merits of the 1911, 1921 and 1951 classification schemes are discussed in Armstrong, 'Use of Information', pp. 205–11.

CHAPTER 2

1. There seems little doubt that Smiles himself recognised that such rewards were out of the reach of most working men, regardless of how much they evinced the prized virtues held out as integral to success. See Harrison, 'Victorian Gospel', p. 163.

2. The decade of the *Registration of Births, Deaths and Marriages Act* also saw the volume of Parliamentary Papers double. The Statistical Office of the Board of Trade and the Statistical Section of the British

Association was established in 1832, and local statistical societies multi-plied, providing much of the evidence for Chadwick's *Report on the Sanitary Condition of the Labouring Population of Great Britain* in 1842. See Philip Corrigan and Derek Sayer, *The Great Arch. English State Formation as Cultural Revolution*, Oxford, 1991, pp. 129, 134–5; Edward Royle, *Modern Britain. A Social History 1750–1985*, 1987 p. 190; and Derek Fraser, *The Evolution of the British Welfare State*, London, 1973, chapter 3.

3.   Glass, *Social Mobility*, p. 188.
4.   See Goldthorpe, Social Mobility, pp. 25–6; Anthony Giddens, *The Class Structure of the Advanced Societies*, London, 1981, p. 107; Frank Parkin, 'Strategies of Social Closure in Class Formation' in his (ed.) *The Social Analysis of the Class Structure*, London, 1974.
5.   William Hanson, *The Life of William Hanson, Written By Himself (in his 80th year), and Revised By a Friend*, Halifax, 1883, p. 34.
6.   See Henry Burstow, *Reminiscences of Horsham, being Recollections of Henry Burstow, the celebrated Bellringer and Songsinger, with some account of the Old Bell Foundry, of Horsham Parish Church Bells, and of Famous Peals rung by Horsham Ringers. Together with a list of 400 and odd songs he sings from memory*, Horsham, 1911.
7.   Robert Roberts, *The Classic Slum. Salford Life in the First Quarter of the Century*, Harmondsworth, 1973, p. 13.
8.   See Edward G. Davis, *Some Passages From My Life*, Birmingham, 1898; Ernest Ambrose, *Melford Memories. Recollections of 94 years*, Long Melford Historical and Archaeological Society, 1972, p. 53.
9.   See chapter 1, p. 10.
10.   James Bowd, 'The Life of a Farm Worker', *The Countryman*, Vol. 51, part 2, 1955.
11.   Thomas Jordan, untitled typescript, from an interview conducted on 22 November 1976, Brunel University Library, pp. 15–16.
12.   The high degree of insecurity experienced by class I offspring is also found amongst elite groups in Lyons and Marseilles. See Pinol, 'Occupational and Social Mobility', Sewell, *Structure and Mobility*, pp. 243–5.
13.   See Crossick and Haupt (eds.), *Shopkeepers and Master Artisans*. Also Andrew Miles, 'Lower Middle Class Mobility in England, 1839–1914', *Bulletin de Centre Pierre Léon*, 4, 1993.
14.   See Crossick's speculation in 'Emergence of the Lower Middle Class', pp. 30, 38.
15.   See James Ashley, untitled typescript, written in 1908, Brunel University Library; Thomas James, *Some Experiences in My Life, by Thomas James, Plaindealings, Narberth*, Cardiff, *c.* 1930.
16.   Perry Anderson, 'Origins of the Present Crisis', in P. Anderson and R. Blackburn (eds.), *Towards Socialism*, London, 1965, p. 34.
17.   Roberts, *Classic Slum*, p. 13.
18.   See P.J. Waller, *Town, City, and Nation. England 1850–1914*, Oxford, 1983, p. 149.
19.   Mill, *Principles*, 1909 edition, p. 393.
20.   Ibid.

21.   On the uncertain notion of economic upturn in the third quarter of the nineteenth century, see G. Best, *Mid-Victorian Britain*, London, 1971; R.A. Church, *The Great Victorian Boom, 1850–1873*, London, 1972; Francois Crouzet, *The Victorian Economy*, London, 1982, pp. 54–8. On commercial expansion see, Charles More, *The Industrial Age. Economy and Society in Britain, 1750–1985*, London, 1989. In view of the ambiguous nature of economic change in nineteenth-century Britain the positing of simplistic cause/effect relationships between economic downturn and mobility patterns would appear somewhat risky. On the other hand, Thernstrom stresses the adverse effects of the Great Depression on the prospects of men originating particularly at the top but also at the bottom of Boston's social spectrum. See *The Other Bostonians*, Chapters 4 and 5. Pinol, 'Occupational and Social Mobility', comes to similar conclusions.

22.   See Henry Herbert, *Autobiography of Henry Herbert, a Gloucestershire Shoemaker and Native of Fairford*, Gloucester, 1866.

23.   See John Foster, *Class Struggle and the Industrial Revolution. Early Industrial Capitalism in Three English Towns*, London, 1974.

24.   On the debate concerning what constitutes the 'local' and the 'national', and the relationship between them, see A. Sayer, 'The Difference that Space Makes', in D. Gregory and J. Urry (eds.), *Social Relations and Spatial Structures*, London, 1985.

25.   Perkin, *Origins*, p. 424, also pp. 124–33.

26.   On the effects of industrial expansion on patterns of urban growth, see Asa Briggs, *Victorian Cities*, London, 1961, who argued that 'The first effect of early industrialisation was to differentiate English communities rather than to standardise them' (p. 32). He was responding to the opposite argument put forward by Lewis Mumford in his, *The City in History*, London, 1961.

27.   Even the Bethnal Green district contained a small proportion of farmers in its population: 3 per cent for the whole sample period; 6 per cent in 1839–54 and 1 per cent in 1899–1914. Jackson remarks that in Macclesfield, 'there were and still are many farms within the borough boundaries' (J.N. Jackson, 'The Population and Industrial Structure of Macclesfield', Manchester University PhD thesis, 1959, p. 235) and the figures for the Macclesfield sample confirm a weighty representation for the farming community in the wider registration district – amounting to 14 per cent across the whole period.

28.   The geographical coverage of the districts prevents the application of more exact settlement typologies or models of growth, as in Waller, *Town, City and Nation*.

29.   See R.G. Hagger, 'Pottery', in M.W. Greenslade and J.G. Jenkins (eds.), *A History of the County of Stafford*, Vol, II, *The Victoria History of the Counties of England*, Oxford, 1967, pp. 1, 12, 27. Also Raphael Samuel, 'The Workshop of the World: Steam Power and Hand Technology in mid-Victorian Britain', *History Workshop Journal*, 3, Spring 1977.

30.   See A.J. Taylor, 'Coal', in Greenslade and Jenkins (eds.), *A History of the County of Stafford*, pp. 68–108; M.W. Dupree, 'Family Structure in

the Staffordshire Potteries', Oxford D Phil, 1981, pp. 41–4. Also Lesley Howe, 'The Social and Economic Development of the North Staffordshire Coalfield, 1790–1918', Keele University MA thesis, 1972; H.A. Moseley, 'The Potteries Coalfield', Leeds University MSc thesis, 1950. On the expansion of the iron industry, which was mainly due to the demands of railway development, see Dupree, 'Family Structure', pp. 35–41; also A. Birch, 'Iron and Steel', in Greenslade and Jenkins (eds.), pp. 121–34.

31. J. Benson, *British Coalminers in the Nineteenth Century: a Social History*, London, 1989, p. 22.

32. See G.C. Allen, *The Industrial Development of Birmingham and the Black Country 1860–1927*, London, 1929, pp. 94–5, 97–8, 127, 141, 148, 183, 324–8. Also V.L. Davies and H. Hyde, *Dudley and the Black Country, 1760 to 1860*, Dudley Public Libraries, Transcript No.16; Musson, *The Growth*, chapters 5 and 10.

33. See Waller, *Town, City and Nation*, pp. 77–8, 149.

34. See S. Pollard, *A History of Labour in Sheffield*, Liverpool, 1959, Appendix B, pp. 331–4; Benson, *British Coalminers*, p. 14.

35. See Musson, *The Growth*, p. 92; Gail Malmgreen, *Silktown: Industry and Culture in Macclesfield 1750–1835*, Hull, 1985, pp. 1–27; Frank Warner, *The Silk Industry of Great Britain*, London, 1920, pp. 131–4; Jackson, 'Population and Industrial Structure', pp. 42, 50; C.S. Davies (ed.), *A History of Macclesfield*, Manchester, 1961, pp. 122–43; Jill Norris, 'Gender and Class in Industry and Home. Women Silk Workers in Macclesfield 1919–39', Keele University MA thesis, 1985, pp. 8–9.

36. See Waller, *Town, City and Nation*, pp. 41–2; Charles Booth (ed.), *Life and Labour of the People in London*. 2nd series, Vol. IV, *The Trades of East London*, London, 1892–7; Gareth Stedman Jones, *Outcast London. A Study in the Relationship between Classes in Victorian Society*, Oxford, 1971, p. 142, pp. 362–75.

37. See N.J. Tringham, 'Economic History', in M.W. Greenslade (ed.), *A History of the County of Stafford*, Vol. 14, *Lichfield, The Victoria History of the Counties of England*, Oxford, 1990, pp. 109–31.

38. Joan A. Dils *et al.*, *An Account of Early Victorian Wokingham. Town and Parish*, Oxford University Department for External Studies, 1985, pp. 7–20; Nigel K. Hammond, *Rural Life in the Vale of the White Horse, 1780–1914*, Reading, 1974, p. 148; Roy Spurgeon, 'Wokingham', in *Berkshire. Old and New*, Berkshire Local History Association, 1985; *Wokingham. A Chronology*, compiled by the Wokingham Society, 1978. Also John Orr, *Agriculture in Berkshire. A Survey made on behalf of the Institute for Research in Agricultural Economics, University of Oxford*, Oxford, 1914; Henry Farrar, *The Book of Hurst: the Story of Hurst and the Surrounding Villages of Twyford, Ruscombe, Woodley, Winnersh, Newland, Sandlesham and Sandford*, Buckingham, 1984; Angela Perkins, *The Book of Sonning: the Story of an English Village*, Chesham, 1977.

39. See D. Milburn, 'Nuneaton. The Growth of a Town', Nuneaton Corporation, Library and Museum Committee, 1963, chapters 2 and 3; E.A. Jackson, 'Nuneaton – a Study in Urban Development', BA Dissertation, Victoria University of Manchester, 1955, pp. 5–7, 20, 25–6,

37. Also William Page (ed.), *The Victoria History of the County of Warwick*, Vol. II, *Victoria History of the Counties of England*, London, 1908, pp. 137–82, 193–297.

40. On Cleobury Mortimer and agriculture in Shropshire, see B.S. Trinder, *A History of Shropshire*, Chichester, 1983, p. 100; W.W. Watts, *Shropshire. A Geography of the County*, Shrewsbury, 1919 p. 214; W. Smith and K. Beddoes, *The Cleobury Mortimer and Ditton Priors Light Railway*, Oxford, 1980; A.E. Jenkins, *Titterstone Clee Hills. Everyday Life, Industrial History and Dialect*, self-published, 1982, pp. 1, 22; R.T Rowley, 'The History of the South Shropshire Landscape', B Litt dissertation, University of Oxford, 1967; Edmund Vale, *Shropshire*, London, 1949. See also Stuart Davies, 'Rural Colliers of Wyre', *Folk Life*, Vol. 22, 1983–4; and D. Jones, 'The Forest of Wyre Coalfield', *The Mining Journal*, December, 1870. On the Samford district, see Herman Biddell, 'Agriculture'; and Dorothy Kemp, 'Social and Economic History. Part II', in William Page (ed.), *A History of Suffolk*, Vol. I, *Victoria History of the Counties of England*, London, 1911, pp. 395, 671.

41. See A. Armstrong, *Farmworkers. A Social and Economic History, 1770–1980*, London, 1988, pp. 147–8.

42. In fact, the total volume of movement was no greater in Stoke (34.4 per cent) and Dudley (32.8 per cent), than Cleobury Mortimer or Samford at 32.3 and 34.0 per cent respectively. However, Macclesfield at 43.4 per cent and Sheffield at 41.2 per cent were both considerably more dynamic.

43. The corresponding ratios in the other categories were: industrial 0.91–0.81; urban 0.72–0.73; rural 0.97–1.0.

44. Waller, *Town, City, and Nation*, p. 150. Hammond, *Rural Life*, p. 148, stresses the importance of transport development in breaking down village isolation. François Crouzet writes that farm workers' wages and living standards were markedly inferior not only to those of skilled tradesmen but also to those of 'the semi-skilled "hands" who formed the mass of factory workers, and even of ordinary town labourers'. See *The Victorian Economy*, London, 1982, p. 73.

45. Huntley and Palmers employed 5,000 people in Reading by 1914. The population of the town increased from 15,000 in 1851 to 84,000 in 1901. Waller, *Town, City and Nation*, p. 5. See also Stephen Yeo, *Religious and Voluntary Organisations in Crisis*, London, 1976.

46. Thompson, *Lark Rise*.

47. K.D.M. Snell, *Annals of the Labouring Poor: Social Change and Agrarian England, 1600–1900*, Cambridge, 1987, p. 387. Although the fact that Farfrae was on his way to the USA in search of a better life when he stopped off in Casterbridge suggests that Hardy was under no illusion about the limited prospects for upward mobility in nineteenth-century rural England. Thomas Hardy, *The Mayor of Casterbridge*, London, 1978, p. 49.

48. From 1.5 per cent to 11.0 per cent.

49. The proportion of working-class sons leaving their class in Samford rose by just over one percentage point – from 3.2 to 4.4 per cent – between 1839–54 and 1899–1914.

50. Between the 1859–74 and 1899–1914 cohorts, the proportions remaining class stable fell from 73 to 70 per cent in Cleobury Mortimer, but from 67 to 54 per cent in Samford. It was arable, and particularly wheat, farming that was hit hardest in the wake of overseas competition from the 1870s onwards. See Howard Newby, *Country Life. A Social History of Rural England*, chapter 5. By comparison, 'Shropshire, with its many dairy and sheep farms, was less affected by the agricultural depression of the late 19th century than regions where there was more arable cultivation'. Trinder, *History*, p. 105.

51. Stedman Jones, *Outcast London*, p. 177. It was, however, not simply an exchange of the well-off for the poor. Waller writes of the shifting frontiers of Bethnal Green's clerkly suburbs 'as well-paid manual workers seeped into their neighbourhoods'. By 1901 clerks comprised fewer than 3 per cent of the district's population. Waller, *Town, City, and Nation*, p. 151.

CHAPTER 3

1. Landes, *Unbound Prometheus*, p. 546.
2. See Introduction p. 1, chapter 1, p. 9 and chapter 2, p. 28.
3. Goldthorpe, *Social Mobility*, chapter 4 and 'On Economic Development and Social Mobility', pp. 558, 562–63.
4. Hope, 'Trends in the Openness of British Society in the Present Century'. Penn, *Skilled Workers*, chapter 12.
5. In notation, the calculation for the ij^{th} cell is:

$$R_{ij} = \frac{f_{ij}\,N}{f_{i\cdot}\,f_{\cdot j}}$$

6. Goldthorpe, *Social Mobility*, pp. 74–8.
7. Ibid., p. 74.
8. See Heath, *Social Mobility*, pp. 261–2, and Goldthorpe, *Social Mobility*, pp. 78, 88 n. 17. An odds ratio is the product of a pair of disparity ratios, and for a 2×2, four cell, table the relevant calculation is:

$$\frac{f_{11}\,/\,f_{12}}{f_{21}\,/\,f_{22}}$$

where f_{11} is the frequency in the 1×1 cell, f_{12} the frequency in the 1×2 cell, and so on. For criticism of the odds ratio, see R.M. Blackburn, C. Marsh, K. Prandy and J. Silatanen, 'A New Approach to Studying Changing Inequality', paper presented to the British Sociological Association Conference, April 1990.

9. Goldthorpe, *Social Mobility*, p. 78.
10. See E.J. Hobsbawm, *Industry and Empire*, Harmondsworth, 1984, chapter 6; Crouzet, *Victorian Economy*, chapter 3.
11. Scott Lash and John Urry, *The End of Organised Capitalism*, Oxford, 1987, chapters 1, 2, 4. But see also Savage and Miles, *The Remaking*, chapter 3.

12. Crouzet, *Victorian Economy*, chapter 4. C.H. Lee, *Regional Economic Growth in the United Kingdom Since the 1880s*, Maidenhead, 1971, chapter 14. Crossick accepts the importance of the late nineteenth-century expansion of the international economy for this growth, but also points out that the bureaucratisation of the secondary sector has been neglected: 'In 1911 42 per cent of all commercial clerks were employed in manufacturing industry – 45,000 of them working for engineering and shipbuilding firms alone'. 'Emergence of the Lower Middle Class', p. 20.

13. The numbers in trade and transport increased from 1.2 to 4 million between 1841 and 1911. P. Deane and W.A. Cole, *British Economic Growth, 1688–1959*, Cambridge, 1967, p. 143.

14. There were 200,000 miners in 1841, 900,000 in 1901 and 1,200,000 in 1911. Crouzet, *Victorian Economy*, p. 68.

15. According to Crossick's calculations the number of male white-collar employees roughly doubled every 20 years from 144,035 in 1851 to 918,186 in 1911. 'Emergence of the Lower Middle Class', p. 19.

16. See F.M.L. Thompson, *Victorian England: The Horse-drawn Society*, London, 1970.

17. Szreter, *Family, Class and Gender*. R. Woods, 'The Fertility Transition in Victorian England', *Population Studies*, 41, 1987.

18. See M. Anderson, 'The Social Implications of Demographic Change', in F.M.L Thompson (ed.), *The Cambridge Social History of Britain, 1750–1950*, Vol. 2, pp. 42–3.

19. Ibid., pp. 21–2.

20. As Grusky and Fukomoto write, 'The fundamental problem of "structurally-induced" mobility was solved with the development of log-linear models'. 'Social History Update', p. 222.

21. See Goldthorpe, *Social Mobility and Class Structure*, pp. 80–1; and G. Nigel Gilbert, *Modelling Society: An Introduction to Loglinear Analysis for Social Researchers*, London, 1981. For criticism of this procedure, see Jonathan Kelley, 'The Failure of a Paradigm: Log-Linear Models of Social Mobility, in J. Clark *et al.* (eds.), *John H. Goldthorpe. Consensus and Controversy*, London 1990.

22. The no-trend model can be expressed in linear form based on natural logarithms as follows:

$$\text{Log } F_{ij} = \lambda + \lambda^o + \lambda^d + \lambda^c + \lambda^{od} + \lambda^{oc} + \lambda^{dc}$$

23. See Erikson and Goldthorpe, *Constant Flux*, pp. 90–5. My thanks to Robert Erikson who kindly sent me a copy of the unidiff macro.

24. The parameter estimates in Table 3.4 cannot be used to explore this issue because the reference categories in this case are specific to each district type. The unidiff model works by estimating an average pattern of association that comes closest to the real pattern of association in a set of tables. It then estimates the deviation of the first table from this average pattern and finally the deviations of the second and all following tables from the first. Analaysed separately, each district will have a different average association. Thus, the parameter estimates for each cohort are not directly comparable.

25. Here I am greatly indebted to Ineke Maas of the Max Planck Institute for Human Development in Berlin who developed this adaptation of the unidiff model. It is not possible to consider the two dimensions of place and time simultaneously using the standard unidiff macro. In this variation, the average association established by the unidiff model is used to create a new variable ('ass') which is then modelled in a normal glim job, while the interaction $o*d$ is added to the model to ensure that the degrees of freedom are correct.

26. With the rural district in the 1839–54 cohort as the reference category, the β parameter estimates under this model are as follows:

All district types:	1859–74	1879–94	1899–1914
	–0.05	–0.13	–0.29
All periods:	urban-rural	urban	industrial
	–0.11	–0.20	–0.24

27. Goldthorpe, *Social Mobility*, chapter 11.
28. See R.W. Fogel, *Railways and American Economic Growth. Essays in Econometric History*, Baltimore, 1964. M. Edelstein, 'Foreign Investment and Empire, 1860–1914', in R.C. Floud and D.N. McCloskey (eds.), *The Economic History of Britain since 1700*, ii, Cambridge, 1981. On the issues involved in adopting this particular heuristic device, see Peter D. McClelland, *Causal Explanation and Model Building in History, Economics, and the New Economic History*, Ithaca, 1975, chapter IV.
29. Goldthorpe, *Social Mobility*, p. 317.
30. See Frederick Mosteller, 'Association and Estimation in Contingency Tables', *Journal of the American Historical Association*, 63, 1968.
31. Kaelble, *Social Mobility*, chapter 4.
32. Goldthorpe, *Social Mobility*, chapter 11. See also, Walter Müller, 'Social Mobility in Industrial Nations', in Clark *et al.* (eds.), *John H. Goldthorpe*, pp. 315–16.
33. See Makowski, 'Social Mobility in Nineteenth-Century Poznań'.
34. On these reforms, see J.R. Hay, *The Origins of the Liberal Welfare Reforms 1906–1914*, London, 1975.
35. See Derek Fraser, *Power and Authority in the Victorian City*, Oxford, 1979, pp. 151–7; Martin Pugh, *The Making of Modern British Politics 1867–1939*, Oxford, 1982, pp. 61–62, 148; J.P.D. Dunbabin, 'Electoral Reforms and their Outcome in the United Kingdom 1865–1900', in T.R. Gourvish and Alan O'Day, *Later Victorian Britain, 1867–1900*, Basingstoke, 1988, pp. 109–10; Waller, *Town, City, and Nation*, p. 150.
36. On these reforms, see Eric J. Evans, *The Forging of the Modern State. Early Industrial Britain 1783–1870*, London, 1983, p. 287. Also Corrigan and Sayer, *The Great Arch*, pp. 159–61. Vincent argues that recruitment to the Post Office in the early years of the twentieth century created 'a real sense of a functioning meritocracy'. 'Mobility, Bureaucracy and Careers', p. 231.
37. Vincent, *Literacy*, p. 54, my brackets. Attendance was made compulsory in 1880, but the attendance officers took until the 1890s to bring the

problem of mass truancy under control. See David Wardle, *English Popular Education 1780–1970*, Cambridge, 1970, p. 70.

38. See Phil Gardner, ' "Our schools": "their schools". The case of Eliza Duckworth and John Stevenson', *History of Education*, 20, 3, 1991.

39. On the development of higher grade elementary schooling, see J.S. Hurt, *Elementary Schooling and the Working Classes, 1860–1918*, London, 1979; and O. Banks, *Parity and Prestige in English Secondary Education*, London, 1955.

40. John Benson, *The Working Class in Britain 1850–1939*, London, 1989, pp. 98–9. Also, F.B. Smith, *The People's Health 1830–1910*, London, 1979; F.M.L. Thompson, *The Rise of Respectable Society. A Social History of Victorian Britain, 1830–1900*, London, 1988, chapter 2; Diana Gittins, *Fair Sex. Family Size and Structure 1900–39*, London, 1982, chapter 2.

41. Savage and Miles, *The Remaking*, pp. 25–20. Benson, *The Working Class*, 55–6. More, *Industrial Age*, p. 169.

42. Benson, *The Working Class*, pp. 119–120. See also H.R. Southall, 'Mobility, the Artisan Community, and Popular Politics in Early Nineteenth Century England', in G. Kearns and C.W. Withers (eds.), *Urbanising Britain: Class and Community in the Nineteenth Century*, Cambridge, 1991, and 'The Tramping Artisan Revisits: Labour Mobility and Economic Distress in Early Victorian England', *Economic History Review*, II, Vol. 44, 1991.

43. On the efficacy of supportive networks see, classically, Anderson, *Family Structure*. Also Pooley and Doherty, 'Longitudinal Study', pp. 168–9.

44. On the rise of the working-class neighbourhood, see Savage and Miles, *The Remaking*, chapter 4. On the migration of the poor, see David Vincent, *Poor Citizens. The State and the Poor in Twentieth-Century Britain*, London, 1991, p. 15. Waller writes that while the proportion of migrants in London's population declined throughout the nineteenth century, 'within the city movement was ceaseless' (*Town, City, and Nation*, pp. 27–8).

45. Waller, *Town, City and Nation*, p. 12.

46. Goldthorpe, 'Economic Development and Social Mobility', p. 563.

CHAPTER 4

1. W.G. Runciman, *Relative Deprivation and Social Justice*, London, 1965, p. 55.

2. See, for example, Patrick Joyce, 'Work', in Thompson (ed.), *Cambridge Social History*, Vol. 2. Also Rosemary Crompton, *Class and Stratification: An Introduction to Current Debates*, Oxford 1993, chapters 4 and 5.

3. Geoff Payne, *Mobility and Change*, Basingstoke, 1987, p. 14; also 'Social Mobility in Britain: A Contrary View', in Clark *et al.* (eds.), *John H. Goldthorpe*.

4. Payne chooses to ignore the conceptual and organisational rationale underpinning the distinction between absolute and relative perspectives

on mobility. See *Mobility and Change* pp. 118–121. For criticism of his argument, see both Westergard's and Goldthorpe's comments in Clark *et al.*, *John H. Goldthorpe*, pp. 299–300, 413–14, 421–2.

5. Kocka, 'The Study of Social Mobility', pp. 105–106. See especially Alastair Reid's critique of the assumptions underlying the labour aristocracy theory: for example, 'Intelligent Artisans and Aristocrats of Labour. The essays of Thomas Wright', in Jay Winter (ed.), *The Working Class in Modern British History. Essay in Honour of Henry Pelling*, Cambridge, 1983; and 'The Division of Labour and Politics', in H. Husung and H. Mommsen (eds.), *The Development of Trade Unionism and Politics in Great Britain and Germany*, Brighton, 1988.

6. Thomas McLauchlan, *The Life of an Ordinary Man*, privately printed, Brunel University Library, 1979, p. 71.

7. James Scott, *Autobiography of James Scott, Stotfield*, no place or date of publication, preface dated 1883, p. 7.

8. See George Mitchell, 'Autobiography and Reminiscences of George Mitchell, "One from the Plough"', in Stephen Price (ed.), *The Skeleton and the Plough, or the Poor Farm Labourers of the West; with the Autobiography and Reminiscences of George Mitchell, 'One from the Plough'*, London, 1875, pp. 106–7.

9. See Vincent, *Literacy*, pp. 119–22.

10. See Andrew Miles, 'Occupational and Social Mobility in England 1839–1914', University of Keele PhD thesis, 1992, pp. 252–6.

11. See p. 17 above.

12. See, for example, R.M. Hartwell, *The Industrial Revolution in England*, Historical Association Pamphlet, no. 58, 1965; and P. Mantoux, *The Industrial Revolution in the Eighteenth Century: an Outline of the Beginnings of the Modern Factory System in England*, London, 1955.

13. See especially Samuel, 'Workshop of the World'.

14. Together with the 1.5 million people still working in agriculture, for example, the 1911 census records that over 2 million were engaged in domestic service. See Mitchell and Deane, *Abstract*, p. 60.

15. In the first case, the classic example is the cotton spinner, in the latter, engineers. See H.E. Turner, *Trade Union Growth, Structure and Policy. A Comparative Study of the Cotton Unions*, London, 1962; More, *Skill*; Price, *Labour*, pp. 71–83; Samuel, 'The Workshop', p. 40; Hobsbawm, 'Aristocracy of Labour', pp. 234–5; M. Holbrook-Jones, *Supremacy and Subordination of Labour*, London, 1982; R. Penn, 'Trade Union Organisation and Skill in the Cotton and Engineering Industries in Britain, 1850–1960', *Social History*, 8, 1983.

16. R. Lennard, *Economic Notes on English Agricultural Wages*, 1914, pp. 57–9, quoted in A. Armstrong, *Farmworkers. A Social and Economic History*, 1770–1980, London, 1988, p. 148.

17. Cf. their portrayal as respectable and important members of the community in the work of Thompson and Roberts. See *Lark Rise*, chapter IV, and *Classic Slum*, p. 18, although Roberts does speak of a wide differentiation in status between houses (pp. 120–1), and the fact that plain beer houses were the height of a working man's ambition (p. 19). It is probable that under the generic term 'publican' lurked a fair

proportion of the latter. After the 1830 beer Act, which inaugurated a forty-year period of free trade in Beer, 'The newly created, excise-licensed, and unregulated beerhouses ... multiplied with great speed', writes F.M.L. Thompson, 'they were suspected of being run by a lower-class, more venal and disreputable, type as beersellers than the publicans who had to be sufficiently respectable and well-behaved to hold on to magistrates licenses'. *Rise of Respectable Society*, p. 311.

18. Hobsbawm, 'Aristocracy of Labour', p. 236. In Salford artisans were considered and considered themselves, 'culturally and socially superior beings'. Roberts, *Classic Slum*, pp. 19, 22. See also Laura's father's sense of position in Thompson, *Lark Rise*, pp. 232–3.

19. Engineers, masons, cabinet makers, printers and cotton spinners. See Hobsbawm, 'Labour Aristocracy', pp. 276–90.

20. Michael Hout, *Following in Father's Footsteps. Social Mobility in Ireland*, Cambridge, Mass., 1989, p. 78.

21. Anderson, *Family Structure*, p. 124.

22. Sidney and Beatrice Webb, *Industrial Democracy*, London, 1911, pp. 458–61.

23. A rate similar to that found by Crossick in mid-Victorian Kentish London. See *An Artisan Elite*, pp. 115–16.

24. Anderson, *Family Structure*, p. 121; S.J. Chapman and A. Abbott, 'The Tendency of Children to Enter Their Fathers' Trades', *Journal of the Royal Statistical Society*, Vol. LXXV, February 1912, p. 600.

25. On the attractiveness of wage levels in the Sheffield heavy industries, see Sidney Pollard, 'Wages and Earnings in the Sheffield Trades, 1851–1914', *Yorkshire Bulletin of Economic and Social Research*, 6, 1, 1954, pp. 57–8. Black Country wage rates suggest that here 'The real aristocrats of labour were to be found in the ironworks'. See G.J. Barnsby, *Social Conditions in the Black Country 1800–1900*, Wolverhampton, 1980, p. 215. In 1906, according to Whipp, the average potter's earnings were close to those found in engineering, while 'male sanitary pressers, throwers and firemen were among some of the highest-paid workers in the country'. See Richard Whipp, *Patterns of Labour. Work and Social Change in the Pottery Industry*, London, 1990, p. 62.

26. Mantoux, *Industrial Revolution*, p. 434.

27. Cited by More, *Skill*, p. 66.

28. 'The tendency of young people to follow their father's occupation', he writes, 'was marked in all Lancashire occupations, especially in cotton. There is much evidence that this tendency found expression in the same factory, and very often in terms of either direct patrimonial employment or of supervision.' Joyce, *Work, Society and Politics*, p. 112.

29. Vincent, *Literacy*, p. 121. See also, Richard Price, *Labour in British Society. An Interpretative History*, London, 1986, p. 79.

30. 'The railway worker was an industrial soldier, a man who commissioned himself to a lifetime of service', Frank McKenna, *The Railway Workers 1840–1870*, London, 1980, pp. 30, 250.

31. See Vincent, *Literacy*, pp. 122–3, although, as he points out, in both cases great importance was still attached to an individual's background.

In the Post Office, exam candidates had to be nominated, and patronage was retained in rural districts until 1892 (n. 105, p. 303). See also M.J. Daunton, *Royal Mail*, London, 1985, pp. 243–46; and C. Steedman, *Policing the Victorian Community. The Formation of the English Provincial Police Forces 1856–80*, London, 1984, p. 103.

32. McKenna, *Railway Workers*, pp. 50, 232; P.W. Kingsford, *Victorian Railwaymen*, London, 1970, pp. 5–9.
33. See Kingsford, *Victorian Railwaymen*, chapter 8; McKenna, *Railway Workers*, pp. 27, 135–6, 156; Daunton, *Royal Mail*, p. 259; Vincent, *Literacy*, p. 127.
34. See Vincent, *Literacy*, p. 123, and p. 128 below.
35. G.L. Anderson, *Victorian Clerks*, Manchester, 1976, pp. 11–15.
36. Booth, *Life and Labour*, Vol. VII, p. 274. Anderson, *Victorian Clerks*, p. 13.
37. M. Savage, J. Barlow, P. Dickens and T. Fielding, *Property, Bureaucracy and Culture. Middle-Class Formation in Contemporary Britain*, London, 1992, pp. 49–57.
38. Ibid., pp. 36–45.
39. Hout, *Following in Father's Footsteps*, p. 79. See also F. Bechhofer and B. Elliot, 'Petty Property', in Bechhofer and Elliot (eds.), *The Petite Bourgeoisie. Comparative Studies of the Uneasy Stratum*, London, 1981, p. 185 on the symbolic importance of property among the petty bourgeoisie.
40. Bechhofer and Elliot 'Petty Property', p. 185.
41. On class, resource and inheritance, see Leonore Davidoff and Catherine Hall, *Family Fortunes. Men and Women of the English Middle Class 1780–1850*, London, 1987, pp. 205–6.
42. See More, *Skill*, p. 107.
43. See Alan Howkins, 'In The Sweat of Thy Face: The Labourer and Work', in G.E. Mingay (ed.), *The Victorian Countryside*, Vol. 2, London, 1981, p. 507. This was usual in the South and the East, but the position was reversed in parts of the country where a living-in farm servant system still operated.
44. See Trollope's contributions, by letters written in his capacity as a Surveyor, to a debate about merit which took among the Post Office's senior managers in the early 1860, less than a decade after the Northcote–Trevelyan report of 1854. Post Office Archives, *Post 30/164*. A later survey of the department's practice confirms that by 1913 the Post Office was formally committed to government policy on merit, *Post 60/119*.
45. Thomas Arthur Westwater, 'The Life Story of a Nonentity', manuscript, Ruskin College Library, written in two parts, the first in the 1940s, the second in the 1960s. See part 1, pp. 34–45. McKenna, 'Victorian Railway Workers', pp. 33–34 and *Railway Workers*, p. 33. Vincent writes that 'By 1891 a London postman who entered the service at the age of twenty-one would take thirty years to reach the top of his scale, and beyond lay the rank of sorter with its own ladder', Vincent, *Literacy*, p. 127.

46.   More, *Skill*, p. 156. Also Charles Docherty, *Steel and Steelworkers. The Sons of Vulcan*, London, 1983, p. 40.
47.   More, *Skill*, pp. 125–6.
48.   According to Whipp, 'Eighty per cent of the country's pottery workers lived within a five mile radius of Stoke Town Hall where they produced nine-tenths of Britain's pottery output in 1900', *Patterns of Labour*, p. 15.
49.   Ibid., p. 12. Across the six towns, those directly employed in industry constituted 42 per cent of the workforce.
50.   Maragaret W. Dupree, *Family Structure in the Staffordshire Potteries 1840–1880*, Oxford, 1995, p. 53. Foster, *Class Struggle*, p. 78. At the same time, Dudley was the recognised national centre of the nailmaking trade (Allen, *Industrial Development*, pp. 75–7), and Sheffield 'the steelproducing centre of the world' (Doherty, *Steel*, p. 2). Warner described Macclesfield in 1920 as having 'the best claim to be regarded as the present HQ of the British silk industry' (*Silk Industry*, p. 127), and Norris writes that from a population of under 40,000, 10,000 of the town's inhabitants were directly dependent on silk manufacture, and the remainder were more or less involved ('Gender and Class', p. 234).
51.   Handicraft occupations accounted for 19.0 per cent of the division of labour in the industrial category, 29.6 per cent in the urban, 14.6 per cent in the urban-rural, and 13.1 per cent in the rural.
52.   They ranged, in fact, from 24.7 per cent in Dudley to 39.3 per cent in Wokingham. The remaining eight districts were within 6 points of the sample mean.
53.   See, for example, D. Lockwood, 'Sources of Variation in Working Class Images of Society', *Sociological Review*, 14, 1966.
54.   Norman Dennis, Fernando Henriques and Clifford Slaughter, *Coal is Our Life. An Analysis of a Yorkshire Mining Community*, London, 1969, pp. 79–80. See also, M.I.A. Bulmer, 'Sociological Models of the Mining Community', *Sociological Review* 23, 1, February 1975.
55.   See Jordan, untitled, p. 3ff.
56.   Benson, *British Coalminers*, p. 9.
57.   Ibid., p. 83.
58.   C. Baylies, *The History of the Yorkshire Miners 1881–1918*, London, 1993. A.R. Griffin, *The British Coalmining Industry: Retrospect and Prospect*, Buxton, 1977, pp. 157, 161.
59.   Mitchell, *Economic Development*, p. 113. Benson, *British Coalminers*, pp. 78, 140.
60.   B.R. Mitchell, *Economic Development of the British Coal Industry 1800–1914*, Cambridge, 1984, p. 113. M. Daunton, 'Down the Pit. Work in the Great Northern and South Wales Coalfields, 1870–1914', *Economic History Review*, 34, 1981; R. Harrison, *Independent Collier. The Coal Miner as Archetypal Proletarian Reconsidered*, Hassocks, 1978.
61.   Benson, *British Coalminers*, p. 140.

62. See R. Church, *History of the British Coal Industry*, Vol. 3, Oxford, 1986, p. 231; Mitchell, *Economic Development*, p. 113.
63. Jordan was clearly expected to respond positively to the experience, and felt constrained to do so because otherwise he feared his father would think him 'queer'. Jordan, untitled typescript, p. 4.
64. Jordan, untitled typescript, p. 5; Church, *History*, Vol. 3, pp. 611, 637.
65. Sewell, *Structure and Mobility*, p. 51.
66. Booth, *Life and Labour*, Vol. VII, p. 301.
67. See Jean Robin, *Elmdon; Continuity and Change in a North-West Essex Village, 1861–1964*, Cambridge, 1980, p. 168; Snell, *Annals*, p. 388. Also Armstrong, *Farmworkers*, p. 148. In Samford just 11 out 535 labourers' sons left the working class. Many more – 139 – improved their status within it, but only 38 became skilled men.
68. J. Burnett, *Idle Hands. The Experience of Unemployment, 1790–1990*, London, 1994, p. 140.
69. See Vincent, *Literacy*, pp. 130–31, and David F. Mitch, *The Rise of Popular Literacy in Victorian England: The Influence of Private Choice and Public Policy*, Philadelphia, 1992, pp. 22–3.
70. See Mitch's survey of the usefulness of literacy in the workplace. *The Rise*, pp. 13–22. Also Vincent, *Literacy*, pp. 132–3.
71. Crossick, 'Emergence of the Lower Middle Class', p. 37. Also Hobsbawm, 'Artisans and Labour Aristocrats?', who writes that 'the attraction of office jobs for tradesmen's sons was small', p. 264.
72. Hobsbawm, 'Artisans and Labour Aristocrats?', pp. 264–5.
73. Gray, *The Labour Aristocracy*, chapters 5 and 7.
74. See p. 23 above and p. 121 below.
75. Kingsford, *Victorian Railwaymen*, p. 2. McKenna, *Railway Workers*, p. 27.
76. Booth *Life and Labour*, Vol. II, pp. 296–300.
77. See Mitchell, *Economic Development*, p. 120.
78. Although the cultural transition might not be so straightforward. See Chester Armstrong, *Pilgrimage from Nenthead. An Autobiography*, London, 1938, pp. 35–6, 51–7.
79. Crossick writes that, 'The ambition of the salaried employees was being undermined both by changes in the composition of their labour market and in the structure of their firms. Easier entry at the bottom end of the white collar world possibly followed the extension of elementary education ... [although] ... The improvement in the quality of education with progressive urban school boards was probably more important', Crossick, 'Emergence of the Lower Middle Class', p. 22.
80. More, *Skill*, p. 234.
81. See Musson, *The Growth*, pp. 228–30, 232–3. Also Robert Tressell, *The Ragged Trousered Philanthropists*, London, 1955.
82. According to More, 'The blurring of distinctions arose ... because as old trades declined they were replaced by industries in which the customary method of acquiring skill was by migration or following up ... the growing identification between the labour aristocracy and

the rest of the working class, in so far as this was caused by changes at work, was not due so much to a reduction of the aristocrats' skill as to changes in the methods of recruitment to skilled work'. More, *Skill*, pp. 231, 234. Henry Pelling reaches a similar conclusion in his *Popular Politics and Society in Late Victorian Britain*, London, 1968, pp. 45–6.

83. See Keith Burgess, *The Challenge of Labour. Shaping British Society, 1850–1930*, London, 1980, chapter 3; Hobsbawm, 'Artisans and Labour Aristocrats?', p. 267; Gray, *Labour Aristocracy*, pp. 167–73; Crossick, *Artisan Elite*, pp. 248–9; Meacham, 'English Working-Class Unrest'.

84. More, *Skill*, pp. 233–4.

85. Although see Crossick, *Artisan Elite*, p. 248.

86. See Benson, *British Coalminers*, p. 13; and Musson, *The Growth*, p. 176. Also Perkin, *The Rise*, p. 18.

87. Benson, *British Coalminers*, chapter 2. Church, *History*, Vol. 3, pp. 612, 637.

88. Crossick, 'Emergence of the Lower Middle Class', p. 19.

89. H. Llewellyn Smith, 'Influx of Population', in Booth, *Life and Labour*, Vol. III, p. 120. Cf. Mingay's contention that the farm labourer at the end of the nineteenth century was 'still too poorly educated, too ignorant, too apathetic ... to enter the new, semi-urbanised existence'. Mingay, *Rural Life*, p. 196.

90. Sewell, *Structure and Mobility*, pp. 257–66.

91. Llewellyn-Smith further noted that countrymen in London were especially likely to be found in 'outdoor trades which have some affinity with those to which they had been accustomed in the country'. 'Influx of Population', p. 120.

92. Winstanley, *Shopkeeper's World*, p. 34.

93. According to Winstanley, the retail trades 'could be increasingly "picked up" ... intruders ... colonised every working-class street and apparently cornered the local markets ... They brought shopkeeping itself into disrepute, denying wealthier brethren the social esteem and respect they felt their capital, skill and position ought to command', ibid., pp. 40, 44–5. On the challenge of the multiples and Co-ops, see chapters 3 and 4. Also J.B. Jeffreys, *Retail Trading in Britain 1850–1914*, Cambridge, 1954; Gareth Shaw, 'Retail Patterns', in J. Langton and R.J. Morris (eds.), *Atlas of Industrialising Britain, 1780–1914*, London, 1986; Crossick, 'Emergence of the Lower Middle Class' p. 16.

94. Crossick, 'Emergence of the Lower Middle Class', p. 22.

95. See Hobsbawm, 'Aristocracy of Labour', pp. 227, 229, 233, 242, 246, and 'Artisans and Labour Aristocrats?', pp. 265–6.

96. On the question of the chronological trajectory of the labour aristocracy, see Penn, *Skilled Workers*, pp. 31–3. Amongst Hobsbawm's super aristocracy (see n. 19 above), rates of mobility into and recruitment from classes IV and V rose from under 10 per cent to almost 25 per cent between the 1839–1854 and 1879–1894 cohorts. Thereafter, there was some improvement but the figures remained high at 20 per cent and 17 per cent respectively.

CHAPTER 5

1. Charles Booth and Ernest Aves, 'The Choice of Employment', in Booth, *Life and Labour*, Vol. IX, p. 393.
2. See Sørensen, 'Theory and Methodology', p. 78. Erikson and Goldthorpe argue that the standard mobility table retains its relevance and power as a provider of information 'on mobility rates and patterns understood as societal attributes', *Constant Flux*, pp. 281–3, 306–7.
3. See R. Brown, 'Work Histories, Career Strategies and the Class Structure', in A. Giddens and G. Mackenzie (eds.), *Social Class and the Division of Labour*, Cambridge, 1982, who notes that 'the failure to respond to the pleas made for more than 30 years may be partly explained by the very considerable practical difficulty of securing adequate work history information', p. 122.
4. Employment and career progress in banking, for example, were dependent on age, marital status and class background. See Katherine W. Stovel, Michael Savage, and Peter Bearman, 'Ascription into Achievement: Models of Career Systems at Lloyds Bank, 1890–1970', *American Journal of Sociology*, 102, 2, 1996, pp. 362–3.
5. See above, p. 23.
6. Thernstrom came to the same conclusion on the basis of his census and city directory data which disclosed, 'a marked slowing of occupational mobility after age 30'. *Other Bostonians*, p. 62.
7. Goldthorpe, *Social Mobility*, pp. 78–85.
8. Erikson and Goldthorpe, *Constant Flux*, p. 94.
9. Running the CnSF and unidiff models for the three skill sectors of the working class only across three marriage cohorts, the results were as follows:

	G^2	BIC	df	p	Δ
under 30s					
CnSF	38.1	−27.9	8	0.00	4.1
Unidiff	1.1	−48.4	6	0.98	0.4
over 30s					
CnSF	9.2	−45.6	8	0.33	3.1
Unidiff	4.5	−36.5	6	0.61	1.9

β parameters:	1859–1874	1879–1894	1899–1914
under 30s	set at zero	−0.31	−0.62
over 30s	set at zero	−0.17	−0.31

10. See, for example, D. Featherman and K. Selbee, 'Class Formation and Class Mobility. A New Approach with Counts from Life History Data', in M. Riley and B. Huber (eds.), *Social Structure and Human Lives*, Newbury Park, 1988; Brendan Halpin, 'Work-Life Mobility in the Republic of Ireland', unpublished paper presented to the Conference on the Development of Industrial Society in Ireland, Nuffield College, December 1990; Dex (ed.), *Life and Work History Analyses*; Andrew

Abbott and Alexandra Hrycak, 'Measuring Resemblance in Sequence Data: An Optimal Matching Analysis of Musicians' Careers', *American Journal of Sociology*, 96, 1990.

11. Vincent, 'Mobility, Bureaucracy and Careers', p. 219. See also Kaelble, *Social Mobility*, pp. 15, 22.
12. See Thernstrom, *Other Bostonians*, chapter 4.
13. Vincent used the unexploited work-history material from the 'Family, Life and Work before 1918' oral history project undertaken by Paul Thompson and various collaborators at the University of Essex in 1969 and 1970. See P. Thompson, *The Edwardians*, London, 1975, pp. 7–8. This material has also been used, as an adjunct to employment records from the Post Office, the Great Western Railway, Cadburys and Lloyds Bank, for an ESRC-funded project entitled, 'Pathways and Prospects: the Emergence of the Modern Bureaucratic Career in Britain, 1840–1940' [directed by Andrew Miles, Mike Savage and David Vincent]. Genealogical material is the subject of another ESRC-supported project – on the family and social mobility – which is directed by Ken Prandy at the University of Cambridge.
14. See Crouzet, *Victorian Economy*, chapter 3.
15. See Francis Alfred Peet, 'Recollections', typescript, Brunel University Library, written in 1954.
16. See George Healey, *Life and Remarkable Career of George Healey, Birmingham*, Birmingham, c.1880.
17. These have been adapted from the discussion in R. Kanter, 'Careers and the Wealth of Nations: a Macro-Perspective on the Structure and Implications of Career Forms', in M.B. Arthur, D.T. Hall and B.S. Lawrence (eds.), *Handbook of Career Theory*, Cambridge, 1989, pp. 508–18.
18. *The Autobiography of the Working Class*, Abstract 213.
19. Ibid., Abstract 518.
20. See, for example, John Tough, *A Short Narrative of the Life, and some Incidents in the Recollection, of an Aberdonian, nearly Eighty Years of Age, including his Evidence on 'The Wood Case'. To which is added, an Account of the Hadden Family, for upwards of one hundred years back*, Aberdeen, 1848. Also William Johnston, *The Life and Times of William Johnston, Horticultural Chemist, Gardener, and Cartwright, Peterhead; written by himself, and edited from the original M.S.S. by Reginald Alenarley, Esq., member of the Archaeological Society, Edinburgh*, Peterhead, 1859.
21. *The Autobiography of the Working Class*, Abstract 380.
22. Ibid., Abstract 630.
23. J.A. Holt, *Looking Backwards*, Bolton, 1949.
24. For an example of the former, see James Scott, *Autobiography*, a fisherman turned evangelist preacher. Ben Brierley was a cotton- and silk-mill worker before turning to the pen, initially as a sub-editor on the *Oldham Times*, then as the writer and editor of his own journal. See his, *Home Memories, and Recollections of a Life*, Manchester, 1886. The Cornish poet John Harris, who began his working life as copper miner,

combined both, composing his verse whilst working as a scripture reader in Falmouth. Harris, *My Autobiography*, London, 1882.

25. *The Autobiography of the Working Class*, Abstract 614.
26. See Vincent, 'Mobility, Bureaucracy and Careers', p. 218. Also Müller, 'Social Mobility in Industrial Nations', p. 309.

CHAPTER 6

1. See, for example, John Wood, *Autobiography of John Wood, An Old and Well Known Bradfordian, Written in the 75th Year of his Age*, Bradford, 1877. Wood went straight into a cotton mill at the age of six [p. 4]. George Mallard became a farm boy at nine. See his, 'Memories', manuscript, written in 1918, Northampton Record Office pp. 1–2. Emanuel Lovekin was a trapper in a coal mine at seven and a half. See 'Some notes of my life', manuscript, written 1895–1904, Brunel University Library, p. 2.
2. George Mitchell, for example, began work as a bird scarer at this age in 1832, and Moses Heap as a cotton-mill worker in 1829. See Mitchell, 'One from the Plough', p. 96, and Heap, 'My Life and Times, or An Old Man's Memories, illustrated with numerous anecdotes and quaint sayings', manuscript and typescript, with an introduction by J. Elliot, District Central Library, Rawtenstall, written in 1904, p. 4.
3. For discussion of the half-time system, which began in textile factories in 1844, before being extended to other workshops, mines and mills more generally, see M. Cruickshank, *Children and Industry*, Manchester, 1981, pp. 85–7, 94–8. The system was abolished in 1918.
4. *The Autobiography of the Working Class*, Abstract 124.
5. See, for example, Ebenezer Elliot, 'Autobiography', in J. Watkins (ed.), *Life, Poetry and Letters of Ebenezer Elliot*, London, 1850, pp. 16, 25–6, who worked at his father's foundry at Masborough near Rotherham until he was 23. Like many others, Arthur Gill ran errands for his shoe-maker father before starting work sieving the floor sweepings for a goldbeater in 1900 at age 13. Gill, 'I Remember! Reminiscences of a Cobbler's Son', manuscript, Brunel University Library, written in 1969 pp. 9–10, 40.
6. As did Campion, for example. See also Jordan, untitled typescript, p. 4.
7. On pupil teachers and the development of teacher-training, see A. Tropp, *The School Teachers*, London, 1957. See also Vincent *Literacy*, p. 127.
8. The numbers in the table do not sum to 100 because not all of the texts give information about this aspect of the work course.
9. Brierley, *Home Memories*, p. 2.
10. See, for example, Thomas Wilkinson Wallis, *Autobiography of Thomas Wilkinson Wallis, Sculptor in Wood, and Extracts from his Sixty Years' Journal, with twenty-four illustrations and four diagrams*, Louth, 1899, pp. 9–10. In 1830, at the age of nine, Wallis was forced out to work in

a whalebone factory in Hull following the failure of his father's cabinet-making business.

11. See, for example, Scott, *Autobiography*, p. 7; also Edward Allen Rymer, *The Martyrdom of the Mine, or, A 60 Years' Struggle for Life*, Middlesbrough, 1898, p. 3.

12. Cecil George Harwood, 'Down Memory Lane', typescript, Brunel University Library p. 8. By the 1890s, elementary education was compulsory until age 13 or 14, according to local bye laws. However, earlier exemption could be obtained subject to the reaching of a certain standard of proficiency, or a certain number of attendances over a five-year period, as laid down by the local authority.

13. Tough, *Short Narrative*, p. 17; David Barr, *Climbing the Ladder: the Struggles and Successes of a Village Lad*, London, 1910, pp. 23–5; James Cruickshank, *Nearing the Ferry: the Memoirs of a Wayfaring Man*, stencilled copy, 1939, p. 4.

14. McLauchlan, *The Life*, p. 63.

15. Arthur Frederick Goffin, 'A Grey Life', with a preface and appendices by J.R. Goffin, typescript, Brunel University Library, chapter 5.

16. Anthony Errington, 'Coals and Rails: the Autobiography of Anthony Errington, Tyneside Colliery Waggonway-wright, 1776–c.1825', transcribed and edited by P.E.H. Hair, typescript, Keele University Library p. 17.

17. Cruickshank, *Nearing the Ferry*, p. 5.

18. Goffin, 'A Grey Life', chapter 5.

19. See, for example, John Taylor, *Autobiography of John Taylor*, Bath, 1893, pp. 7–8. Taylor's father was a butcher, but nevertheless apprenticed him to an ornamental painter and glazier.

20. Barr, *Climbing the Ladder*, pp. 34, 37.

21. Johnston, *Life and Times* p. 12.

22. Thomas Hardy, *Memoir of Thomas Hardy, Founder of, and Secretary to, the London Corresponding Society, for Diffusing Useful Political Knowledge among the People of Great Britain and Ireland, and for Promoting Parliamentary Reform, From its Establishment, in Jan 1792, until his Arrest on a False Charge of High Treason, On the 12th of May, 1794. Written By Himself*, London, 1832, pp. 2–3.

23. John Brown, *Sixty Years' Gleanings From Life's Harvest. A Genuine Autobiography*, Cambridge, 1858, pp. 2–3.

24. J. Wardle, *The Story of My Life*, London, 1924, p. 12.

25. Jack Lanigan, 'Thy Kingdom *Did* Come', p. 8.

26. T. Lloyd Roberts, *Life Was Like That*, with a foreword by Sidney Walton, Bala, no date of publication, pp. 14–16; William Bowyer [pseudonym of William Bowyer Honey], *Brought out in Evidence: An Autobiographical Summing-Up*, London 1941, pp. 95, 118; Thomas Raymont, 'Memories of an Octogenarian, 1864–1849', typescript, Brunel University Library, p. 11.

27. Gair writes that 'Obtaining a place with the Hetton Engine Works as an Engineer Apprentice was a great privilege and opportunity. At that time all the Apprentices were the sons of colliery officials and as my father was an ordinary workman on the Hetton Railway I could hardly believe my good luck. I think my uncle was responsible,

as at that time he was Engineer at Elemare Colliery, one of the collieries of the group. Previously, he had been Chief Draughtsman for the Coal Company, and in that position had been in daily contact with the Chief Engineer, a Mr Simpson, to whom he must have spoken about myself'. Gair's father, 'himself an engineer at heart', who had never had the same opportunity but had attended engineering classes 'just for the sheer delight of doing so', was '"extremely delighted"', telling his son, '"Now you have got your opportunity, it is up to you to make the most of it"'. Arthur Gair, *Copt Hill to Ryhope. A Colliery Engineer's Life*, with a foreword by Frank Atkinson, Chester-le-Street, 1982, p. 26. Gair's experience bears out the argument that the decline of apprenticeship was a piecemeal and incomplete process. See More *Skill*.

28. Roberts, *Life*, p. 13.
29. Bowyer, *Brought out in Evidence*, p. 95.
30. Charles Bacon, 'The Life Story of Charles Bacon (as told by himself)', typescript, Leicestershire Record Office, pp. 18–19, 23.
31. Jordan, untitled typescript, p. 4.
32. John A. Leatherland, 'Autobiographical Memoir', in *Essays and Poems with a Brief Autobiographical Memoir*, London, 1862, pp. 7–9.
33. James Murdoch, 'Autobiography', in his *The Autobiography of James Murdoch, known as 'Cutler Jamie'*, Elgin, 1863, p. 2.
34. Bowyer, *Brought out in Evidence*, p. 118–20.
35. Barr, *Climbing the Ladder*, p. 37.
36. Wood, *Autobiography*, pp. 18–19.
37. Goffin, 'Grey Life', chapter 17.
38. Healey, *Life and Remarkable Career*, p. 38.
39. Jonathan Saville, 'Autobiography', in Francis A. West, *Memoirs of Jonathan Saville of Halifax; Including his Autobiography*, London, 1848, pp. 6–9.
40. Harwood, 'Down Memory Lane', p. 61.
41. John Hodge, *Workman's Cottage to Windsor Castle*, London, 1931. pp. 16–17.
42. Wardle, for example, left his position as waggon conductor with the London and North Western Railway because he was obliged to associate with the 'wicked, drinking' navvies. See, Wardle, *The Story of My Life*, p. 18.
43. Murdoch, *Autobiography*, p. 12. Thomas Jackson, *Narrative of the eventful life of Thomas Jackson, Late Sergeant of the Coldstream Guards, Detailing His Military Career during Twelve Years of the French War. Describing also his Perils by Sea and Land; his many Hair-breadth Escapes from Death; the Hardship, Privation, and Barbarity he endured from the Enemy, while a Prisoner and Wounded, in Bergen-op-Zoom. His Subsequent Life; in which he meets with many opposing Events and Sharp Adversities all of which he ultimately gets through, by the Help of God, and lives in Peace. Written by Himself*, Birmingham, 1847, pp. 152–3.
44. See, Mallard, 'Memories', p. 43. Jordan, untitled typescript, p. 17.
45. Roberts, *Life* pp. 42–5; Edward Balne, 'Autobiography of an ex-Workhouse and Poor Law School Boy', manuscript, Brunel University Library, p. 159.

46. See Allan McEwen, *This is a Short Account of the Life of Allan McEwen, late Sergeant 72nd Highlanders. Written by Himself for the benefit of his children*, Dumbarton, 1860.
47. Westwater, 'Life Story'.
48. William Farish wrote in 1835 of his wish to see the world beyond his native Carlisle thus: 'Like most lads of eighteen I had indulged a love for some sort of adventure, and a variety of hopes possessed me that had never been realised, but a longing desire to see some places of note just then was strongest upon me', 'Reminiscences of an Old Teetotaller', p. xi, in William Farish, *The Autobiography of William Farish. The Struggles of a Hand Loom Weaver. With Some of his Writings*, privately printed, 1889. He subsequently set off on a tramping tour of Scotland, which lasted until homesickness got the better of him and his companions at Christmas in 1836.
49. See Hardy *Memoir*, p. 4; Mallard 'Memories', p. 9.
50. Bacon, 'Life Story', p. 9.
51. Barr, *Climbing the Ladder*, pp. 52, 58.
52. Mitchell, 'Autobiography and Reminiscences', pp. 108–14; Bowyer, *Brought out in Evidence*, pp. 249–50.
53. Edward Cain, 'Reminiscences from the Life Story of Mr E. Cain MBE (Deceased)', typescript, Brunel University Library, p. 4.
54. Bowyer, *Brought out in Evidence*, p. 118.
55. Hodge, *Workman's Cottage*, p. 20.
56. Westwater, 'Life Story', part 1, pp. 104–5.
57 Spurr, 'Autobiography', p. 285.
58. Ibid., p. 282.
59. William Fairbairn, *The Life of Sir William Fairbairn, Bart., FRS., LL.D., DCL, Corresponding Member of the National Institute of France, Member of the Institution of Civil Engineers, Honorary Associate of the Institution of Naval Architects, Corresponding Associate of the Royal Academy of Sciences, Turin, etc., Partly Written by Himself*, edited and completed by William Pole, London, 1877, p. 104.
60. Edward Brown, untitled typescript, Brunel University Library, p. 47.
61. Goffin, 'Grey Life', chapter 14.
62. Langdon, *The Life*, p. 64; Harwood, 'Down Memory Lane' p. 51.
63. Thompson, *The Rise*, p. 125.
64. McLauchlan, *The Life*, p. 8.
65. Gill, 'I Remember!', p. 98.
66. Barr, *Climbing the Ladder*, p. 37.
67. Jackson, *Narrative*, p. 126.
68. Harwood, 'Down Memory Lane', p. 51.
69. Farish, *The Autobiography*, p. 70.
70. Rymer, *Martyrdom* p. 23.
71. Barr, *Climbing the Ladder*, pp. 55–6.
72. William Hart, 'The Autobiography of William Hart, Cooper, 1776: A Respectable Artisan in the Industrial Revolution', edited with an introduction and notes by Pat Hudson and Lynette Hunter, *London Journal*, Vol. 7, No. 2, Winter 1981 and Vol. 8, No. 1, Summer 1982 (2 parts), part 1, p. 157; Lovekin, 'Some notes', p. 4ff.; William Miles, *An Autobiography. From Pit Bank to Balliol College. A Mineworker*

became a Labour Election Agent for 20 Years, with a foreword by Christopher Hill, privately published, 1972, pp. 39, 103.

73. Harwood, 'Down Memory Lane', p. 47..
74. Gill, 'I Remember!' pp. 49, 51; Ralph Rooney, *The Story of My Life*, with a preface by J. H. Bury, 1947, p. 5; Lanigan, 'Thy Kingdom *Did Come*', p. 9; Edward Brown, untitled typescript, p. 56.
75. George Herbert, *Shoemaker's Window. Recollections of a Midland Town Before the Railway Age*, edited by C.S. Cheney, with an introduction by C.R. Cheney, Oxford, 1948, pp. 16–17; William Smith, 'The Memoir of William Smith', edited by Barry S. Trinder, *Transactions of the Shropshire Archaeological Society*, LVIII, Part 2, 1965–8, p. 184.
76. Johnston, *Life and Times*, pp. 16–17.
77. Ernest Richard Shotton, *The Personal History and Memoirs of Ernest Richard Shotton*, privately printed, 1978, np.
78. McAdam, 'Autobiography', p. 15.
79. Farish, *The Autobiography*, pp. 110–11. Brierley, *Home Memories*, p. 77.
80. John Bedford Leno, *The Aftermath: with Autobiography of the Author*, London, 1892, p. 41.
81. Samuel Marshall, *The Life of a Successful Farmer in Surrey*, Farnham, 1942, p. 10.
82. Davis, *Some Passages From My Life*, p. 13.
83. Barr, *Climbing the Ladder*, pp. 54–5.
84. See J. Benson, 'Work', in J. Benson (ed.), *The Working Class in England 1875–1914*, London, 1985.
85. Smith, 'The Memoir', p. 184
86. Harwood, 'Down Memory Lane', p. 50.
87. George Marsh, 'A Sketch of the Life of George Marsh, a Yorkshire Collier. 1834–1921', Barnsley Reference Library, pp. 13–14.
88. John Shinn, 'A Sketch of My Life and Times', manuscript, Brunel University Library, p. 36.
89. Joseph Livesey, *Autobiography of Joseph Livesey*, Preston, 1881, p. 15.
90. Wallis, *Autobiography*, pp. 60–3.
91. Hart, 'The Autobiography', part 2 pp. 72–73.
92. Leatherland, 'Autobiographical Memoir', p. 33.
93. Smith, 'The Memoir', p. 184.
94. Leatherland, for example, turned to journalism when an injury from an omnibus accident in 1849 forced him to give up manufacturing vests. 'Autobiographical Memoir', pp. 34–6.
95. After the death of his father, Hardy's mother intended he should join 'the clerical profession', but financial difficulties meant he had to settle for being taught shoemaking by his grandfather. *Memoir*, p. 114. Brown comments on his acquaintance with two men whom he terms 'the better sort of Irish' because they held responsible jobs as clerks. *Sixty Years' Gleanings*, pp. 305–6. Hodge's iron-puddler father's first choice for him was some sort of pen-oriented position. *Workman's Cottage*, p. 14.
96. Farish, *The Autobiography*, p. 98.
97. Balne, 'Autobiography', pp. 98–9.
98. Brown, untitled typescript, pp. 31–2.
99. Confirming Anderson's observations on 'age of retirement' as a virtually unknown concept in the mid-nineteenth century. See Michael Anderson,

'The Emergence of the Modern Life Cycle in Britain', *Social History*, 10, 1, 1985, p. 85.

100. See Thomas Dunning, 'The Reminiscences of Thomas Dunning (1813–1894) and the Nantwich Shoemakers' Case of 1834', edited with an introduction and notes by W.H. Chaloner, *Transactions of the Lancashire and Cheshire Antiquarian Society*, LIX, 1947.

101. Marsh, 'A Sketch', p. 21.

102. Shinn, 'A Sketch', p. 43.

103. William Chadwick, *Reminiscences of a Chief Constable*, with a preface by Colonel Sir Howard Vincent and illustrations by R. Wallace Coop, Manchester, 1900 p. 10.

104. William Sutton, *Multum in Parvo; or the Ups and Downs of a Villager Gardener*, Kenilworth, 1903, p. 17.

105. Joseph Wilson, *Joseph Wilson, His Life and Work*, London, nd, p. 10.

106. Tough, *Short Narrative*, p. 7.

107. Rymer, *Martyrdom*, p. 28.

108. Edward Purkiss, *Memories of a London Orphan Boy*, with a foreword by Rev. A.E. Ramsbottom, privately published, Bexley, 1957, p. ••; E.G. Robinson, 'I Remember', manuscript, Brunel University Library, p. 91; Westwater, 'The Life Story', part 2; Miles, *Autobiography*, p. ••.

109. Cruickshank, *Nearing the Ferry*, p. 73.

110. Balne, 'Autobiography', p. 158.

111. Cruickshank, *Nearing the Ferry*, p. 74.

112. Roberts, *Life*, p. 44.

113. Westwater, 'Life Story', part 2, p. 15.

114. Harry Alfred West, 'The Autobiography of Harry Alfred West. Facts and Comments', typescript, Brunel University Library, pp. 39–40.

115. Roberts, *Life*, p. 48.

116. Westwater, 'The Life Story', part 2, pp. 16–26.

117. Robinson, 'I Remember', p. 92,

118. Gair, *Copt Hill to Ryhope* pp. 96–8.

119. Balne was so shocked at his shabby treatment as a part-time office 'small fry' that he felt the conditions of retirees in temporary employment warranted an investigation by the press. 'Autobiography', pp. 159–60.

120. See Goldthorpe, *Social Mobility*, chapter 8.

121. See the reference to James Ashley and his professor son below, for example.

122. Brown, *Sixty Years' Gleanings*, p. 420.

123. Farish, *The Autobiography*, pp. 112–13.

124. Robert Loisan, *Confession of Robert Loisan, alias, Rambling Bob*, Beverley, 1870, p. 28.

125. See William Thom, 'Recollections', in *Rhymes and Recollections of a Hand-Loom Weaver*, London, 1844.

126. Mallard, 'Memories', p. 12.

127. Ashley, untitled typescript pp. 1, 3–8, 39; Henry Edward Price, 'My Diary', manuscript, Islington Public Library, written in 1904, pp. 58–9, 67–9, 73–7.

128. Farish, *The Autobiography*, p. 2. See also Barr, *Climbing the Ladder*, p. 58, and Livesey, *Autobiography*, pp. 26–7.
129. Brown, *Sixty Years' Gleanings* , p. 458.
130. James Watson, 'Autobiographical Speech', *The Reasoner* (supplement), Vol. 16, 5, February 1854, p. 108.
131. Harrison, 'Victorian Gospel', p. 163.
132. Isaac Anderson, *The Life History of Isaac Anderson. A Member of the Peculiar People*, published after 1882, p. 10; Healey, *Life and Remarkable Career*, p. 38.
133. In order to avoid the fate of unqualified boy copyists in the Civil Service, who were obliged to resign their positions at 20, Roberts prepared for the necessary examinations for the permanent service by attending a class at King's College from 6 to 9 pm every evening after work. Roberts, *Life Was Like That*, p. 21.
134. Lanigan, 'Thy Kingdom *Did* Come', pp. 22–3.
135. Ibid., pp. 23–4.
136. Hanson, *Life of William Hanson* , p. 34.
137. John Plummer, 'An Autobiographical Sketch of the Author's Life', in his *Songs of Labour. Northamptonshire Rambles and other Poems*, London, 1860, pp. xxiii, xxvii–xxxi.
138. Westwater, 'Life Story', part 1, pp. 382–5, part 2, pp. 1, 57–8. 139.
139. Ashley, untitled typescript, pp. 29–30.
140. See, for example, Shotton's pride in his son's academic achievement, *Personal History*.
141. Cruickshank, *Nearing the Ferry*, p. 58.
142. Livesey, *Autobiography*, chapter 4; Barr, *Climbing the Ladder*, p. 66.
143. Brown, untitled typescript, pp. 53–4.
144. See Roberts, *Life*, p. 43.
145. Farish, *The Autobiography*, p. 126; Leno, *The Aftermath*, pp. 42–3.
146. Chadwick, *Reminiscences*, pp. 143–4; Raymont, 'Memories', pp. 11–12; Roberts, *Life*, p. 21.
147. Cruickshank, *Nearing the Ferry*, p. 70.
148. Albert Charles Adams, *The History of a Village Shopkeeper: An Autobiography*, Dundee, 1876, p. 177.
149. Purkiss, *Memories*, p. 20.
150. See Goldthorpe, 'On Economic Development and Social Mobility', p. 558. Also Hout, *Following in Father's Footsteps*, pp. 321–3. Kaelble, *Social Mobility*, p. 124.
151. Vincent, 'Mobility, Bureaucracy and Careers'.

CHAPTER 7

1. See Penn, *Skilled Workers*, pp. 154–7, for a brief summary.
2. Thompson, *The Rise*, p. 93. See also Schüren, 'Intergenerational Occupational and Marriage Mobility'; Mitch, '"Inequalities"'; Penn and Dawkins, 'Structural Transformations'.

3. See Lawrence Stone, *Family, Sex and Marriage in England 1500–1800*, London, 1977.
4. For example, Peter Laslett, *Household and Family in Past Time*, Cambridge, 1972.
5. Foster, *Class Struggle*, pp. 125–31, 162–66, 260–69. Crossick, *An Artisan Elite*, chapter 6. Gray, *The Labour Aristocracy*, pp. 111–20. Penn, *Skilled Workers*, pp. 158–82. Mitch '"Inequalities"'. T.H. Hollingsworth 'The Demography of the British Peerage, *Population Studies*, supplement to 18, 2, 1964. D. Thomas, 'The Social Origins of Marriage Partners of the British Peerage in the Eighteenth and Nineteenth Centuries', *Population Studies*, 26, 1972.
6. Thompson, *The Rise*, p. 105.
7. Marshall *et al.*, *Social Class*, p. 83.
8. See especially, John H. Goldthorpe, 'Women and Class Analysis: In Defence of the Conventional View', *Sociology*, 17, 4, 1983 and *Social Mobility*, chapter 10.
9. See, for, example the debate in *Sociology*, vol. 18, 1984, including Michelle Stanworth, 'Women and Class Analysis: a Reply to John Goldthorpe', and Anthony Heath and Nick Britten, 'Women's Jobs do Make a Difference: a Reply to Goldthorpe'. Also the contributions by Walby, and Delphi and Leonard to Rosemary Crompton and Michael Mann (eds.), *Gender and Stratification*, Cambridge 1996, and the essays by McRae and Dex in Clark *et al.* (eds.), *John Goldthorpe*. More recent empirical contributions to the debate include Colin Mills, 'Who 'dominates whom? Social Class, Conjugal Household and Political Identification', *Sociological Review*, 42, 1994, and Richard Lampard, 'Research Note. Parents' Occupations and their Children's Occupational Attainment: A Contribution to the Debate on the Class Assignment of Families', *Sociology*, 29, 4, 1995.
10. Goldthorpe, 'Women and Class Analysis', p. 469.
11. Erikson and Goldthorpe, *Constant Flux*, p. 276.
12. Goldthorpe, *Social Mobility*, p. 281.
13. Sewell, *Structure and Mobility*, p. 271.
14. 'Family Life and Work', Interview 125. See also John Burnett, *Destiny Obscure. Autobiographies of Childhood, Education and Family from the 1820s to the 1920s*, London, 1984, pp, 120, 219; Davidoff and Hall, *Family Fortunes*, p. 272; Dorothy Crozier, 'Kinship and Occupational Succession', *Sociological Review*, 13, 1965, p. 40.
15. Michael Anderson, 'The Social Implications of Demographic Change', in F.M.L. Thompson (ed.), *The Cambridge Social History of Britain 1750–1950*, Vol. 2, pp. 28–31.
16. See E.H. Hunt, *British Labour History, 1815–1914*, London, 1981, p. 18.
17. On married women's work, see Eric Richards, 'Women in the British Economy since about 1700: An Interpretation', *History*, 59, 1974; Benson, 'Work', p. 72.
18. Kocka notes that 'The lack of an occupational listing beside the bride's name in the marriage registers indicates, indeed, not only a source problem, but points to a predominant reality of that time'. 'Family and Class Formation', p. 420. Authors such as Chinn and Roberts have

argued for the importance of matriarchal power in working-class communities, and it is clear that women's networks played an important role in the economies of poor neighbourhoods. Carl Chinn, *They Worked All Their Lives. Women of the Urban Poor in England, 1880–1939*, Manchester, 1988; Elizabeth Roberts, *A Woman's Place. An Oral History of Working-Class Women, 1890–1940*, Oxford, 1984. See also Ellen Ross, 'Survival Networks. Women's Neighbourhood Sharing in London Before World War I', *History Workshop*, 15, Spring 1983. However, as Bourke writes, 'Clearly, the ability of working-class housewives to make the most of their domestic power depended on factors such as the chief wage-earner's income, and the stability of that income'. Joanna Bourke, *Working-Class Cultures in Britain 1890–1960. Class, Class, and Ethnicity*, London, 1994, p. 96.

19. Vincent, 'Mobility, Bureaucracy and Careers'.
20. Ibid., pp. 228–30.
21. Penn, *Skilled Workers*, p. 158.
22. J. Liddington and J. Norris, *One Hand Tied Behind Us: the Rise of the Women's Suffrage Movement*, London, 1978, p. 87. In her work on Macclesfield Norris writes that women were 'fundamental to the silk industry' but 'largely without power or status' and this 'conformed to the mainstream of British industrial practice', 'Gender and Class', p. 24.
23. Davidoff and Hall, *Family Fortunes*, pp. 30, 33.
24. Savage *et al.*, *Property, Bureaucracy and Culture*, chapters 2 and 3.
25. See Brown, *Sixty Years*, *Gleanings*, pp. 373–80. For another example, see Thomas Jackson's account of the importance of his wife's practical support when setting up in the plating trade in Walsall in the same decade. Jackson, *Narrative*, p. 147.
26. Davis, *Some Passages*, pp. 12–13
27. Bacon, 'Life Story', p. 68.
28. Livesey, *Autobiography*, pp. 13–16.
29. Janet Finch, *Married to the Job: Wives' Incorporation in Men's Work*, London, 1983, p. 131.
30. Ibid., pp. 117, 131.
31. Davidoff and Hall, *Family Fortunes*, p. 33.
32. Livesey, *Autobiography*, pp. 16
33. Adams, *History*, pp. 138, 164, 167–8.
34. Farish, *Autobiography*, p. 70.
35. Livesey, *Autobiography*, p. 16; Bacon 'Life Story', p. 68.
36. Lanigan, 'Thy Kingdom *Did* come', pp. 27–9.
37. Raymont, 'Memories', p. 15.
38. Anne Witz, 'Gender and Service-class Formation', in Tim Butler and Mike Savage (eds.), *Social Change and the Middle Classes*, London 1995.
39. Rymer, *Martyrdom*, p. 13; Brierley, *Home Memories*, p. 54.
40. Leatherland, 'Autobiographical Memoir', pp. 3–5
41. Adams, *History*, p. 16; Shinn, 'A Sketch', pp. 17–18; Leno, *The Aftermath*, p. 4; Brierley, *Home Memories*, p. 26. Shotton, *Personal History*; Goffin, 'A Grey Life', chapter 6.

42. See, for example, Schüren, 'Intergenerational Occupational and Marriage Mobility'. Also H. van Dijk, J. Visser and E. Wolst, 'Regional Differences in Mobility in the Netherlands between 1830 and 1940', *Journal of Social History*, 17, 1984. In Marseilles, 'Women were considerably less likely than men to remain socially stationary'. Sewell, *Structure and Mobility*, pp. 274.

43. Mitch, ' "Inequalities" ', pp. 157–60.

44. Goldthorpe, *Social Mobility and Class Structure*, chapter 10. See also, Lucienne Portocarero, 'Social Mobility in France and Sweden: Women, Marriage and Work', *Acta Sociologica*, XXVIII, 1985, p. 154; N.D. Glenn, A. Ross and J. Tully, 'Patterns of Intergenerational Mobility of Females through Marriage', *American Sociological Review*, 39, 1974, p. 698; Ivan D. Chase, 'A Comparison of Men's and Women's Intergenerational Mobility in the United States', *American Sociological Review*, 40, 1975, p. 490.

45. Thompson, *The Rise*, pp. 94–5. Here he is synthesising the findings of Foster, Crossick and Gray.

46. Davidoff and Hall, *Family Fortunes*, p. 327.

47. Sewell reached the same conclusion in the case of the overall pattern of men and women's mobility in Marseille. *Structure and Mobility*, p. 281.

48. Burnett confirms that working-class courtship 'seems generally to have been limited by geography and, to a degree, by social status. Boys and girls, men and women, generally met and ultimately married near neighbours who lived in walking distance and whose parents followed a broadly similar occupation and standard of living'. *Destiny Obscure*, p. 255.

49. Using men as the baseline, a comparison of the fluidity patterns by gender produces the following result:

	G^2	BIC	df	p	Δ
CnSF	303.1	144.3	16	0.00	5.53
Unidiff	89.6	−59.2	15	0.00	1.99

β Parameters	men	women
	set at zero	−0.33

50. Thompson, *The Rise*, p. 105.

51. See Newby, *Country Life*, pp. 155–6.

52. See W.D. Rubinstein, *Elites and the Wealthy in Modern British History*, Brighton, 1987, p. 70.

53. Sewell, *Structure and Mobility*, p. 281. See also Mitch, ' "Inequalities" ', p. 145.

54. See Goldthorpe, *Social Mobility*, p. 282.

55. Sewell, *Structure and Mobility*, p. 281.

56. See M. Savage and A. Miles, *The Remaking*, chapter 2. Thompson suggests that the young middle-class males' increasing exposure to women from such different social backgrounds made little impression on 'the class and group defences which the middle classes had erected around their daughters and sons' (*The Rise*, p. 125), but see pp. 163–4 below.

57. Vincent *Bread, Knowledge and Freedom*, p. 51.
58. Working-class men's rate of mobility into sectors associated with property (the independent, business and farming categories) was 3.7 per cent, while 4.1 per cent of women married into these categories. Both were substantially under-represented in these categories according to perfect mobility expectations but women were less so (at a ratio of 0.45 compared to 0.38 for men). 12.4 per cent of the daughters of white-collar employees married men from the same category, while 14.8 per cent married into the business sector.
59. See Dex, 'Goldthorpe on Class and Gender', p. 145.
60. Thompson, *The Rise*, p. 92. See also Mitch, '"Inequalities"', pp. 148–9. The proportion of men in the workshop category who married the daughter of a craftsmen fell from almost a third in the 1840s to less than a quarter by the 1880s.
61. Hout, *Following in Father's Footsteps*, p. 79.
62. See chapter 6, p. 131.
63. Vincent, *Bread, Knowledge and Freedom*, p. 49.
64. Wilson, *Joseph Wilson*, p. 10.
65. See Mitch, 'Inequalities', pp. 155–6, whose findings are very similar.
66. See Goldthorpe, *Social Mobility*, chapters 6 and 7.
67. See p. 160 above.
68. See Thompson, *The Rise*, p. 111.
69. See Davidoff and Hall, *Family Fortunes*, pp. 219–21; and Burnett, *Destiny Obscure*, p. 255.
70. Vincent, *Bread, Knowledge and Freedom*, p. 50.
71. Burnett, *Destiny Obscure*, p. 255.
72. Wilson, *Joseph Wilson*, p. 10.
73. Joseph Gutteridge, *Lights and Shadows in the Life of an Artisan, by Joseph Gutteridge, ribbon weaver*, with a preface by William Jolly, Coventry, 1893, chapter 3; Vincent, *Bread, Knowledge and Freedom*, p. 50; Burnett, *Destiny Obscure*, p. 255.
74. In a comparison of men's labour market mobility (groom's father's class by groom's class) with family mobility (groom's father's class by bride's father's class) the Unidiff model achieves a reduction of 402.6 in G^2 over the CmSF model for the loss of 1 degree of freedom. With labour market mobility as the reference category, the β parameter estimate under the model is –0.51 confirming that the family marriage market was considerably more fluid.
75. Penn, *Skilled Workers*, Tables 12.1 and 12.2., pp. 173–4. Although his numbers were dangerously small. There were only 15 cases of bourgeois fathers in the 1856–65 cohort, seven in the 1875–84 cohort, and none at all in the 1900–09 sample.
76. As the division of labour among grooms' and brides' fathers was largely similar, so too is the pattern of intermarriage when viewed from either the sons' or daughters' perspective. Craftsmen's daughters were slightly more upwardly mobile than their sons, but there is nothing like the disjunction – either between the sexes or over time – suggested by Thompson from his reworking of Crossick's figures for mid-Victorian London, and therefore no indication that men policed class boundaries more vigorously than

women. See Thompson, *The Rise*, p. 95. Moreover, while there would seem to be a disparity between men and women in Crossick's data, Thompson's does not in fact compare men and women in the same terms, and at one point confuses skilled workers with sons of the same.

77. The rate of working-class endogamy is very similar to that found elswhere. In Rochdale, in the three pre-1914 cohorts, 85.3 per cent of working-class children married into working-class families. Across the two sample periods (1851–3 and 1873–5) in Crossick's London, the figure is 84.7 per cent. Calculated from Penn, *Skilled Workers*, Table 12.6, p. 180, and Crossick, *An Artisan Elite*, Table 6.8, p. 124.

78. Thompson, *The Rise*, p. 105.

79. See Sorokin, *Social and Cultural Mobility*, chapter 8.

80. On women schoolteachers, see F. Widdowson, *Going Up into the Next Class. Women and Elementary Teacher Training 1840–1914*, London 1980. More generally on opportunities for women in white-collar work, see G. Anderson (ed.), *The White Blouse Revolution: Female Office Workers since 1870*, Manchester, 1988.

CHAPTER 8

1. See, generally, the collection of essays in Miles and Vincent (eds.) *Building European Society*, but especially, the essays by Fukomoto and Grusky, Schüren, Makowski, and Pinol.

2. See Schüren, 'Intergenerational Occupational and Marital Mobility'.

3. See chapter 1, pp. 6–8.

4. See chapter 5, n. 7.

5. This is an argument that is supported by the work of demographers and economic historians using the census. See Anderson, 'The Emergence', pp. 85–6, and Paul Johnson, 'The Employment and Retirement of Older Men in England and Wales, 1881–1981, *Economic History Review*, 47, I, 1994.

6. See chapter 1, n. 64.

7. See Hobsbawm, 'Labour Aristocracy', pp. 280–8.

8. R. Trainor, *Black Country Elites. The Exercise of Authority in an Industrialized Area*, Oxford 1993, p. 167.

9. See Daunton, *Royal Mail*, chapter 6.

10. Booth, *Life and Labour*, Vol. VII, p. 278, where he writes that 'the profession of clerk does seem to lead to a genuine rise in the social standard of living'. See also Michael Mann, *The Sources of Social Power*, Vol. II, Cambridge, 1993, pp. 561–2.

11. See D.V. Glass and J.R. Hall, 'A Description of a Sample Enquiry into Social Mobility in Great Britain', in Glass (ed.), *Social Mobility*.

12. See Glass and Hall, 'Social Mobility in Britain', ibid., pp. 184–8, and, for example, the scathing comments of Frank Musgrove, *School and the Social Order*, Chichester, 1979, pp. 123–4.

13. Heath, *Social Mobility*, pp. 84–6.

14. Glass and Hall, 'Social Mobility', pp. 201–4; Hope, 'Trends', p. 161.
15. Leaving out the last of Glass's five birth cohorts, the CnSF and Unidiff models compare as follows:

	G^2	BIC	df	Δ	p
CnSF	29.2	–351.1	48	3.2	0.99
Unidiff	27.1	–328.5	45	3.3	0.98

The β parameters by cohort are:

pre-1890	1890–9	1900–9	1910–19
set at zero	0.07	–0.02	0.09

16. J.M. Ridge, 'Fathers and Sons', in his (ed.), *Mobility in Britain Reconsidered*, Oxford, 1974.
17. See Pinol, 'Occupational and Social Mobility in Lyon', p. 133.
18. Perkin, *The Rise*, p. 248
19. Jean Floud, 'The Educational Experience of the Adult Population of England and Wales as at July 1949', in Glass (ed.), *Social Mobility*, pp. 120–1. See also Alan Little and John Westergaard, 'The Trend of Class Differentials in Educational Opportunity in England and Wales', *British Journal of Sociology*, 15, 1964.
20. On hierarchies in the emerging secondary school system, see Hilary Steedman, 'Defining Institutions: the endowed grammar schools and the systematisation of English secondary education', in Detlev K. Müller, Fritz Ringer and Brian Simon (eds.), *The Rise of the Modern Educational System. Structural Change and Social Reproduction 1870–1920*, Cambridge, 1989.
21. David Reeder, 'The Reconstruction of Secondary Education in England', ibid., pp. 143, 149.
22. According to the figures in Table 2 of Floud's analysis, just 14 per cent of those born before 1930 attended Grammar or Public Schools, while 1.8 per cent attended University. See Floud, 'The Educational Experience', pp. 120–1.
23. John Westergaard and Henrietta Resler, *Class in a Capitalist Society. A Study of Contemporary* Britain, Harmondsworth, 1976, p. 327, n. 5.
24. Little and Westergaard, 'Trend of Class Differentials', p. 314.
25. Goldthorpe, *Social Mobility*, pp. 55–8.
26. See p. 222, n. 13.
27. See Witz, 'Gender and Service-Class Formation', pp. 49–54. Also, Savage and Miles, *The Remaking*, chapter 3.
28. Witz, ibid.
29. Hobsbawm, 'The Making of the Working Class 1870–1914', in his *Worlds of Labour*. See also, Gareth Stedman Jones, 'Working-Class Culture and Working-Class Politics in London. Notes on the Remaking of the Working Class', in his *Languages of Class*, and Ross McKibbin, 'Why Was There No Marxism in Great Britain?', in his *The Ideologies of Class. Social Relations in Britain, 1850–1950*, Oxford, 1990.
30. See Savage and Miles, *Remaking*, chapters 3 and 4.
31. See Figure 2.2, p. 33.

32. See B. Waites, *A Class Society at War. England 1914–18*, Leamington Spa, 1987, Chapter 2, McKibbin, pp. 81–5; *Ideologies of Class*, pp. 270–5.
33. For example, Waites, ibid., chapters, 4 and 5; James E. Cronin, *Labour and Society in Britain 1918–1979*, London 1984, chapters 1 and 2; James Hinton, *Labour and Socialism. A History of the British Labour Movement, 1867–1974*, Brighton, 1983, pp. 96–7.
34. Savage and Miles, *The Remaking*, chapter 5.
35. McKibbin, *Ideologies*, pp. 298–300.
36. Goldthorpe, *Social Mobility*, p. 247.
37. Vincent, 'Mobility, Bureaucracy and Careers', pp. 226–32.
38. David Vincent, 'Shadow and Reality in Occupational History. Britain in the First Half of the Twentieth Century', in D. Bertaux and P. Thompson (eds.), *Pathways to Social Class. A Qualitative Approach to Social Mobility*, Oxford, 1997.

APPENDIX I

1. As Morris argues, this term is clearly problematic. It seems to reasonably safe to assume, however, that most of those using the title had means enough to justify their inclusion in the fairly broad-based 'elite' category being used here. See Morris, 'Fuller Values'. Also Simon Raven, *The Decline of the Gentleman*, New York, 1962, and F.M.L Thompson, *English Landed Society in the Nineteenth Century*, London, 1963, pp. 16–17, 131.

2. For example, 'opticians' are coded as retailers (spectacle vendors, class II) until they acquire professional status through the establishment of an association and an entrance examination between 1895 and 1898, and 'accountants' are placed in the same category as book-keepers (class II) until the establishment of the Institute of Chartered Accountants in 1880. Movement towards professionalisation amongst the latter in England can be dated from the Companies Act of 1862. But despite the spread of associations after 1870, 'we hear at this time of many persons styling themselves accountants who carried on a practice of a very dubious character'. A.M. Carr-Saunders and P.A. Wilson, *The Professions*, Oxford, 1933, p. 210. For opticians, see pp. 141–144. See also W.J. Reader, *Professional Men. The Rise of the Professional Classes in Nineteenth Century England*, London, 1966. As to the 'newness' of law and medicine, it is, of course, true that each have very long histories of organisational development. However, from the beginning of the nineteenth century both became exposed to concerted pressures for 'professional improvement', which resulted in the series of institutional reforms that underpin their contemporary forms. The parallel process of reform amongst the clergy, for example, tended to be more piecemeal and to lag behind developments in other areas.

3. Merchants, for example, would seem to be very much on the borderline between class I and II. Their mobility profile (see Appendix 2) also suggests this. See Winstanley, *Shopkeeper's World*, p. 13. On the problem more generally, see Gray, *The Labour Aristocracy*, Appendix 2.

4. Clerks were coded to class II in the 1911 classification. See also Crossick, 'Emergence of the Lower Middle Class', esp. p. 35. Lockwood writes, 'If economically clerks were sometimes on the margin, socially they were definitely a part of the middle class. They were so regarded by the outside world, and they regarded themselves as such' (*The Blackcoated Worker. A Study in Class Consciousness*, Oxford, 1989, p. 35).

5. See More, *Skill*, London, 1980. Also Penn, *Skilled Workers*, chapter 8.

6. See G.D.H. Cole, *Studies in Class Structure*, London, 1955, pp. 45–46, who writes of class III in the 1951 census classification: 'This grouping is evidently too wide to be of much use ... the Census figures put too many occupations in the skilled category, and thus tend to swell the size of class III as against class IV'.

7. For example, hammermen in metal manufacturing and piecers in cotton manufacture are both coded to class III in the 1951 classification. See More, *Skill*, pp. 125–6, and Penn, *Skilled Workers*, p. 128, who point out that technical expertise in itself is by no means always the basis of the skilled/semi-skilled divide.

8. See More, ibid., p. 57.

9. See, for example, K. Marx, *Capital: A Critique of Political Economy*, Vol. I, Harmondsworth, 1976, p. 545.

10. Whilst it is recognised that 'Rural workers were not an undifferentiated mass of hired men, any more than factory workers were an undifferentiated mass of proletarians' (Alun Howkins, *Poor Labouring Men: Rural Radicalism in Norfolk 1870–1923*, London, 1985, p. 19), it seems that, for the most part, agricultural workers entered themselves in the register simply as 'labourer'. Where there is greater definition they have, as noted, been coded accordingly.

11. Regional factors have been taken into account here. The Registrar General includes shepherds in class IV, but fails to distinguish other farm-working specialists. On the division of labour and skill in farm work see, together with *Poor Labouring Men*, pp. 18–21; Howkins, 'In the Sweat of Thy Face', pp. 516–20; G.E. Mingay, *Rural Life in Victorian England*, London, 1977, p. 77; Pamela Horn, *Labouring Life in the Victorian Countryside*, Dublin, 1976, p. 63; Raphael Samuel (ed.), *Village Life and Labour*, London, 1985; David Morgan, *Harvesters and Harvesting 1840–1900*, London, 1982; Thompson, *Lark Rise*, p. 173.

12. See Mayhew, for example, who quotes John Stuart Mill in stressing the differentiation between itinerant or street traders and those with 'fixed abodes', and the fact that the former were often the victims of the latters' usury; 'The costermongers', he writes, 'though living by buying and selling, are seldom or never capitalists'. And his qualified characterisation of them as 'much more honest than their wandering habits, their want of education and "principle" would lead even the

most charitable to suppose', still denotes lowly status (Henry Mayhew, *London Labour and the London Poor*, Vol. 1, London, 1865, pp. 10–11, 31–6, cited in the collection edited by Victor Neuberg and published by Penguin Books, Harmondsworth, 1985, pp. 11–33). See also Andrew Halliday 'Beggars and Swindlers', in Mayhew, Vol. 4, pp. 438–40, who writes that 'The police are obliged to respect the trader, though they know very well that under the disguise of the merchant there lurks a beggar', in Neuberg (ed.), p. 500.

Bibliography

ARCHIVES

Berkshire Record Office
Bodleian Library, Oxford
British Library
Brunel University Library
Derbyshire County Library
Dudley Public Library
Family, Life and Work Collection, University of Essex
Institute of Agricultural Research, University of Reading
Keele University Library
Lancashire Record Office
Leicester Local Studies Library
London School of Economics Library
Modern Records Office, Warwick University
Newcastle-Under-Lyme Public Library
Northampton Central Library
Northampton Record Office
Northumberland County Library
Nuneaton Public Library
Post Office Archive, London
Reading Central Library
Ruskin College Library
Shropshire Record Office
William Salt Library

UNPUBLISHED SOURCES

Ashley, James, untitled typescript, Brunel University Library
Bacon, Charles, 'The Life Story of Charles Bacon (as told by himself)', typescript, Leicestershire Record Office
Balne, Edward, 'Autobiography of an ex-Workhouse and Poor Law Schoolboy', manuscript, Brunel University Library
Brown, Edward, untitled typescript, Brunel University Library
Cain, Edward, 'Memories', typed transcript of a tape recording entitled 'Reminiscences from the Life Story of Mr E. Cain MBE (Deceased)', Brunel University Library
Davies, V.L. and Hyde, H., *Dudley and the Black Country, 1760–1860*, Dudley Public Libraries, Transcript No. 16
de Sève, M. and Bouchard, G., 'Long-term Social Mobility in Quebec: the Case of the Saguenay/Lac St Jean 1851–1951', paper to the ISA Committee on Social Stratification, Bielefeld, 1994

240 *Bibliography*

Errington, Anthony, 'Coals and Rails: the Autobiography of Anthony Errington, Tyneside Colliery Waggonway-wright, 1776–*c.* 1825', transcribed and edited by P.E.H. Hair, typescript, Keele University Library
Gill, Arthur, 'I Remember! Reminiscences of a Cobbler's Son', manuscript, Brunel University Library
Goffin, Arthur Frederick, 'A Grey Life' (originally entitled 'Aspidistra'), with a preface and appendices by J.R. Goffin, typescript, Brunel University Library
Halpin, B., 'Work-Life Mobility in the Republic of Ireland', unpublished paper presented to the Conference on the Development of Industrial Society in Ireland, Nuffield College, December 1990
Harwood, Cecil George, 'Down Memory Lane', typescript, Brunel University Library
Heap, Moses, 'My Life and Times, or An Old Man's Memories, illustrated with numerous anecdotes and quaint sayings', manuscript and typescript with an introduction by J. Elliott, District Central Library, Rawtensall
Jordan, Thomas, untitled typescript, from an interview conducted on 22 November 1976, Brunel University Library
Lanigan, Jack, 'Thy Kingdom *Did* Come', typescript, Brunel University Library
Lovekin, Emanuel, 'Some Notes of My Life', manuscript, Brunel University Library
Mallard, George, 'Memories', manuscript, Northampton Record Office
Marsh, George, 'A Sketch of the Life of George Marsh, a Yorkshire Collier. 1834–1921', typescript, Barnsley Reference Library
Milburn, D., 'Nuneaton: The Growth of a Town', Nuneaton Corporation Library and Museum Committee, 1963
Peet, Francis Alfred, 'Recollections', typescript, Brunel University Library
Price, Henry Edward, 'My Diary', typescript, Islington Public Library
Raymont, Thomas, 'Memories of an Octogenarian, 1864–1949', typescript, Brunel University Library
Robinson, E.G., 'I Remember', manuscript, Brunel University Library
Shinn, John, 'A Sketch of My Life and Times', manuscript, Brunel University Library
Van Leeuwen, M.H.D. and Maas, I., 'Long-term Mobility in a European City: Berlin 1835–1957', paper to the ISA Committee on Social Stratification, University of Trento, 1992
West, Harry Alfred, 'The Autobiography of Harry Alfred West. Facts and Comments', typescript, Brunel University Library
Westwater, Thomas Arthur, 'The Life Story of a Nonentity', manuscript, Ruskin College Library

PRE–1914 PRINTED SOURCES

[Adams, Albert Charles], *The History of a Village Shopkeeper: An Autobiography*, Dundee, 1876
Anderson, Isaac, *The Life History of Isaac Anderson. A Member of the Peculiar People*, published after 1882

Barr, David, *Climbing the Ladder: the Struggles and Successes of a Village Lad*, London, 1910

Biddell, H., 'Agriculture' in W. Page (ed.), *A History of Suffolk*, Vol. II, *Victoria History of the Counties of England*, London, 1907

Booth, C. (ed.), *Life and Labour of the People of London*, 2nd Series, Vols. II, III, IV, V, VI, VII, VIII, IX, London, 1892–7

Brierley, Benjamin, *Home Memories, and Recollections of a Life*, Manchester, 1886

Brown, John, *Sixty Years' Gleanings From Life's Harvest. A Genuine Autobiography*, Cambridge, 1858

Burstow, Henry, *Reminiscences of Horsham, being Recollections of Henry Burstow, the celebrated Bellringer and Songsinger, with some account of the Old Bell Foundry, of Horsham Parish Church Bells, and of Famous Peals rung by Horsham Ringers. Together with a list of 400 and odd songs he sings from memory*, Horsham, 1911

Chadwick, William, *Reminiscences of a Chief Constable*, with a preface by Colonel Sir Howard Vincent and illustrations by R. Wallace Coop, Manchester, 1900

Chapman, S.J. and Abbott, A., 'The Tendency of Children to Enter Their Fathers' Trades', *Journal of the Royal Statistical Society*, 76, 1912–13

Davis, Edward G., *Some Passages From My Life*, Birmingham, 1898

Elliott, Ebenezer, 'Autobiography', *The Athenaeum*, Vol. 1, No. 1159, 12 January 1850, reprinted in J. Watkins (ed.), *Life, Poetry and Letters of Ebenezer Elliot*, London, 1850

Fairbairn, William, *The Life of Sir William Fairbairn, Bart., FRS., LL.D., DCL, Corresponding Member of the National Institute of France, Member of the Institution of Civil Engineers, Honorary Associate of the Institution of Naval Architects, Corresponding Associate of the Royal Academy of Sciences, Turin, etc. Partly written by Himself*, edited and completed by William Pole, London, 1877

Farish, William, *The Autobiography of William Farish. The Struggles of a Hand Loom Weaver. With Some of his Writings*, privately printed, 1889

Gutteridge, Joseph, *Lights and Shadows in the Life of an Artisan, by Joseph Gutteridge, ribbon weaver*, with a preface by William Jolly, Coventry, 1893

Hanson, William, *The Life of William Hanson, Written by Himself (in his 80th year), and Revised by a Friend*, Halifax, 1883

Hardy, Thomas, *Memoir of Thomas Hardy, Founder of, and Secretary to, the London Corresponding Society, for Diffusing Useful Political Knowledge among the People of Great Britain and Ireland, and for Promoting Parliamentary Reform, From its Establishment, in Jan. 1792, until his Arrest, on a False Charge of High Treason, On the 12th of May, 1794. Written by Himself*, London, 1832

Hardy, T., *The Mayor of Casterbridge*, 1886

Harris, John, *My Autobiography*, London, 1882

Healey, George, *Life and Remarkable Career of George Healey*, Birmingham, c. 1880

Herbert, Henry, *Autobiography of Henry Herbert, a Gloucestershire Shoemaker and Native of Fairford*, Gloucester, 1866

Jackson, Thomas, *Narrative of the eventful life of Thomas Jackson, Late Sergeant of the Coldstream Guards, Detailing His Military Career during Twelve Years of the French War. Describing also his Perils by Sea and Land; his many Hair-breadth Escapes from Death; the Hardship, Privation, and Barbarity he endured from the Enemy, while a Prisoner and Wounded, in Bergen-op-Zoom. His Subsequent Life; in which he meets with many opposing Events and Sharp Adversities all of which he ultimately gets through, by the Help of God, and lives in Peace. Written by himself,* Birmingham, 1847

Johnston, William, *The Life and Times of William Johnston, Horticultural Chemist, Gardener, and Cartwright, Peterhead; written by himself, and edited from the original M.S.S. by Reginald Alenarley, Esq., member of the Archaeological Society, Edinburgh,* with a preface by the editor, Peterhead, 1859

Jones, D., 'The Forest of Wyre Coalfield', *The Mining Journal,* December 1870

Leatherland, John A., 'Autobiographical Memoir', in *Essays and Poems with a brief Autobiographical Memoir,* London, 1862

Leno, John Bedford, *The Aftermath: with Autobiography of the Author,* London, 1892

Livesey, Joseph, *Autobiography of Joseph Livesey,* London, 1881

Loisan, Robert, *Confession of Robert Loisan, alias, Rambling Bob,* Beverley, 1870

McEwan, Allan, *This is a Short Account of the Life of Allan M'Ewan, late Sergeant 72nd Highlanders. Written by Himself for the benefit of his children,* Dumbarton, 1890

Mill, J.S., *Principles of Political Economy,* (Sir William Ashley ed.), London, 1909

Mitchell, George, 'Autobiography and Reminiscences of George Mitchell, "One from the Plough"', in S. Price (ed.), *The Skeleton at the Plough, or the Poor Farm Labourers of the West; with the Autobiography and Reminiscences of George Mitchell, 'One from the Plough',* London, 1875

Murdoch, James, 'Autobiography', in his *The Autobiography and Poems of James Murdoch, known as 'Cutler Jamie',* Elgin, 1863

Orr, J., *Agriculture in Berkshire. A survey made on behalf of the Institute for Research in Agricultural Economics, University of Oxford,* Oxford, 1914

Page, W. (ed.), *The Victoria History of the County of Warwick,* Vol. II., *Victoria History of the Counties of England,* London, 1908

Plummer, John, 'An Autobiographical Sketch of the Author's Life', in his *Songs of Labour. Northamptonshire Rambles and other Poems,* London, 1860

Rymer, Edward Allen, *The Martyrdom of the Mine, or, A 60 Years' Struggle for Life,* Middlesbrough, 1893

Saville, Jonathan, *Autobiography,* in Francis A. West, *Memoirs of Jonathan Saville of Halifax, Including his Autobiography,* London, 1848

Scott, James, *Autobiography of James Scott, Stotfield,* no place or date of publication, preface dated 1883

Smiles, S., *Self Help,* London, 1859

Smiles, S., *Lives of Engineers,* 3 vols, London, 1861–62

Taylor, John, *Autobiography of John Taylor,* Bath, 1893

Thom, William, 'Recollections', in *Rhymes and Recollections of a Hand-Loom Weaver,* London, 1844

Tough, John, *A Short Narrative of the Life, and Some Incidents in the Recollection, of an Aberdonian, nearly Eighty Years of Age, including his Evidence on "The Wood Case". To which is added, an Account of the Hadden Family, for upwards of one hundred years back*, Aberdeen, 1848

Wallis, Thomas Wilkinson, *Autobiography of Thomas Wilkinson Wallis, Sculptor in Wood, and Extracts from his Sixty Years' Journal, with twenty-four illustrations and four diagrams*, Louth, 1899

Watson, James, 'Autobiographical Speech', *The Reasoner* (supplement), Vol. 16, 5, February 1854

Webb, S. and Webb, B., *Industrial Democracy*, London, 1911

Wilson, Joseph, *Joseph Wilson, His Life and Work*, with a foreword by the Rev. H.J. Taylor and a prefatory note by the Rev. George Bennett, London, no date of publication

Wood, John, *Autobiography of John Wood, An Old and Well Known Bradfordian, Written in the 75th Year of his Age*, Bradford, 1877

POST–1914 PRINTED SOURCES

Abbot, A. and Hrycak, A., 'Measuring Resemblance in Sequence Data: an Optimal Matching Analysis of Musicians' Careers', *American Journal of Sociology*, 96,1990

Allen, G.C., *The Industrial Development of Birmingham and the Black Country, 1860–1927*, London, 1929

Ambrose, E., *Melford Memories. Recollections of 94 years*, Long Melford Historical and Archaeological Society, 1972

Anderson, G.L., *Victorian Clerks*, Manchester, 1976

Anderson, G.L. (ed.), *The White Blouse Revolution; Female Office Workers since 1870*, Manchester, 1988

Anderson, M., *Family Structure in Nineteenth Century Lancashire*, Cambridge, 1971

Anderson, M., 'The Emergence of the Modern Life Cycle in Britain', *Social History*, 10, 1, 1985

Anderson, M., 'The Social Implications of Demographic Change', in Thompson (ed.), *Cambridge Social History*, Vol. 2

Anderson, O., 'The Incidence of Civil Marriage in Victorian England and Wales', *Past and Present*, 69, November 1975

Anderson, P, 'Origins of the Present Crisis', in P. Anderson and R. Blackburn (eds.), *Towards Socialism*, London, 1965

Armstrong, A., *Farmworkers. A Social and Economic History, 1770–1980*, London, 1988

Armstrong, Chester, *Pilgrimage from Nenthead. An Autobiography*, London, 1938

Armstrong, W.A., 'The Use of Information about Occupation', in E.A. Wrigley (ed.), *Nineteenth-Century Society*, Cambridge, 1972

Bagehot, W., 'Sterne and Thackeray', *The Collected Works of Walter Bagehot. Vol 2. The Literary Essays* (Norman St John-Stevas ed.), London, 1965

Banks, O., *Parity and Prestige in English Secondary Education*, London, 1955

Barnsby, G., *Social Conditions in the Black Country 1800–1900*, Wolverhampton, 1980

Baylies, C., *The History of the Yorkshire Miners 1881–1918*, London, 1993

Bearman, P. and Deane, G., 'The Structure of Opportunity: Middle Class Mobility in England, 1548–1689', *American Journal of Sociology*, 98, 1, 1992

Bechhofer, F. and Elliot, B., 'Petty Property' in Bechhofer and Elliot (eds.) *The Petite Bourgeoisie: Comparative Studies of the Uneasy Stratum*, London, 1981

Benson, J., *British Coalminers in the Nineteenth Century. A Social History*, Dublin, 1980

Benson, J., 'Work', in J. Benson (ed.), *The Working Class in England, 1875–1914*, London, 1985

Benson, J., *The Working Class in Britain 1850–1939*, London, 1989

Berg, M., *The Age of Manufacturers: Industry, Innovation and Work in Britain, 1700–1820*, London, 1985

Best, G., *Mid-Victorian Britain*, London, 1971

Birch, A., 'Iron and Steel', in M.W. Greenslade and J.G. Jenkins (eds.), *A History of the County of Stafford*

Blau, P.M. and Duncan, O.D., *The American Occupational Structure*, New York, 1967

Bourke, J., *Working-Class Cultures in Britain 1890–1960. Gender, Class and Ethnicity*, London, 1994

Bowd, James, 'The Life of a Farm Worker', *The Countryman*, Vol. 51, Part 2, 1955

Bowyer, William, [pseudonym of William Bowyer Honey], *Brought Out in Evidence: An Autobiographical Summing-Up*, London, 1941

Briggs, A., *Victorian Cities*, London, 1961

Brown, R., 'Work Histories, Career Strategies and the Class Structure', in A. Giddens and G. Mackenzie (eds.), *Social Class and the Division of Labour*, Cambridge, 1982

Bulmer, M.I.A., 'Sociological Models of the Mining Community', *Sociological Review*, 23, 1, February 1973

Burnett, J. (ed.), *Useful Toil. Autobiographies of Working People from the 1820s to the 1920s*, Harmondsworth, 1977

Burnett, J., *Destiny Obscure. Autobiographies of Childhood, Education and Family from the 1820s to the 1920s*, Harmondsworth, 1984

Burnett, J., Vincent, D., Mayall, D. (eds.), *The Autobiography of the Working Class. An Annotated, Critical Bibliography, Volume I: 1790–1900*, London, 1984

Burnett, J., *Idle Hands. The Experience of Unemployment, 1790–1900*, London, 1994

Carlsson, G., *Social Mobility and Class Structure*, Lund, 1958

Cassis, Y., 'Bankers in English Society in the Late Nineteenth Century', *Economic History Review*, 38, 1985

Census 1911. Classification of Occupations

Census 1921. Classification of Occupations

Census 1951. Classification of Occupations

Chase, I.D., 'A Comparison of Men's and Women's Inter-generational Mobility in the United States', *American Sociological Review*, Vol. 40, 1975

Chinn, C., *They Worked All Their Lives. Women of the Urban Poor in England 1880–1939*, Manchester, 1988

Church, R.A., *The Great Victorian Boom, 1850–1873*, London, 1972

Church, R.A., *History of the British Coal Industry*, Vol. 3, Oxford, 1986

Clark, J., Modgil, J. and Modgil, S. (eds.), *John H. Goldthorpe. Consensus and Controversy*, London, 1990

Corrigan, P. and Sayer, A., *The Great Arch. English State Formation as Cultural Revolution*, Oxford, 1991

Crafts, N.F.R., *British Economic Growth during the Industrial Revolution*, Oxford, 1985

Crompton, R., *Class and Stratification: An Introduction to Current Debates*, Oxford, 1993

Cronin, J., *Labour and Society in Britain 1918–1979*, London, 1984

Crossick, G., 'The Emergence of the Lower Middle Class in Britain', in G. Crossick (ed.), *The Lower Middle Class in Britain*

Crossick, G. (ed.), *The Lower Middle Class in Britain 1870–1914*, London, 1977

Crossick, G., *An Artisan Elite in Victorian Society*, London, 1978

Crossick, G. and Haupt, H.G. (eds.), *Shopkeepers and Master Artisans in Nineteenth-Century Europe*, London, 1984

Crouzet, F., *The Victorian Economy*, London, 1982

Crozier, D., 'Kinship and Occupational Succession', *Sociological Review*, new series, XIII, 1965

Cruickshank, J., *Nearing the Ferry: the Memoirs of a Wayfaring Man*, Stencilled copy, 1939

Cruickshank, M., *Children and Industry*, Manchester, 1981

Daunton, M., 'Down the Pit. Work in the Great Northern and South Wales Coalfields, 1870–1914', *Economic History Review*, 34, 1981

Daunton, M.J., *Royal Mail. The Post Office since 1840*, London, 1985

Davidoff, L. and Hall, C., *Family Fortunes. Men and Women of the English Middle Class, 1780–1850*, London, 1987

Davies, C.S. (ed.), *A History of Macclesfield*, Manchester, 1961

Davies, S., 'Rural Colliers of Wyre', *Folk Life*, Vol. 22, 1983–4

Deane, P. and Cole, W.A., *British Economic Growth, 1688–1959*, Cambridge, 1967

Delphy, C. and Leonard, D., 'Class Analysis, Gender Analysis, and the Family', in R. Crompton and M. Mann (eds.), *Gender and Stratification*, Cambridge, 1996

Dennis, N., Henriques, F., Slaughter, C., *Coal is Our Life. An Analysis of a Yorkshire Mining Community*, London, 1969

Denzin, N.K., *Interpretive Biography*, London, 1989

Dex, S., 'Goldthorpe on Class and Gender: the Case Against', in J. Clark *et al.* (eds.), *John H. Goldthorpe*

Dils, J.A., *et al.*, *An Account of Early Victorian Wokingham. Town and Parish*, Oxford University Department for External Studies, 1985

Docherty, C., *Steel and Steelworkers. The Sons of Vulcan*, London, 1983

Dunabin, J.P.D., 'Electoral Reforms and their Outcome in the United Kingdom 1865–1900', in T.R. Gourvish and A.O'Day, *Later Victorian Britain 1867–1900*, Basingstoke, 1988

Dunning, Thomas, 'The Reminiscences of Thomas Dunning (1813–1894) and the Nantwich Shoemakers' Case of 1834', edited with an introduction and notes by W.H. Chaloner, *Transactions of the Lancashire and Cheshire Antiquarian Society*, LIX, 1947

Dupree, M.W., *Family Structure in the Staffordshire Potteries 1840–1880*, Oxford, 1995.

Edelstein, M., 'Foreign Investment and Empire, 1860–1914', in R.C. Floud and D.N. McCloskey (eds.), *The Economic History of Britain since 1700*, ii, Cambridge, 1981

Engels, F., 'England in 1845 and 1885', in K. Marx and F. Engels, *On Britain*, Moscow, 1953

Erickson, C., *British Industrialists: Steel and Hosiery, 1850–1950*, Cambridge, 1959

Erikson, R. and Goldthorpe, J.H., *The Constant Flux: A Study of Class Mobility in Industrial Societies*, Oxford, 1992

Evans, E.J., *The Forging of the Modern State. Early Industrial Britain 1783–1870*, London, 1983

Farrar, H., *The Book of Hurst: the Story of Hurst and the Surrounding Villages of Twyford, Ruscombe, Woodley, Winnersh, Newland and Sandlesham and Sandford*, Buckingham, 1984

Featherman, D.L., Jones, F.L., Hauser, R.M., 'Assumptions of Social Mobility Research in the US: The Case of Occupational Status', *Social Science Research*, Vol. 4, 1975

Featherman, D. and Selbee, K., 'Class Formation and Class Mobility. A New Approach with Counts from Life History Data', in M. Riley and B. Huber (eds.), *Social Structure and Human Lives*, Newbury Park, 1988

Finch, J., *Married to the Job: Wives' Incorporation in Men's Work*, London, 1983

Fogel, R.W., *Railways and American Growth. Essays in Econometric History*, Baltimore, 1964

Foster, J., *Class Structure and the Industrial Revolution. Early Industrial Capitalism in Three English Towns*, London, 1974

Fraser, D., *Power and Authority in the Victorian City*, Oxford, 1979

Fraser, D., *The Evolution of the British Welfare State*, London, 1973

Gair, Arthur, *Copt Hill to Ryhope. A Colliery Engineer's Life*, with a foreword by Frank Atkinson, Chester-le-Street, 1982

Gamble, A., *Britain in Decline. Economic Policy, Political Strategy and the British State*, Basingstoke, 1990

Ganzeboom, H.B.G., Luijkx, R. and Treiman, D.J., 'Intergenerational Class Mobility in Comparative Perspective', in Arne L. Kalleberg (ed.), *Research in Social Stratification and Mobility*, Vol. 8, 1989

Gardner, P., ' "Our schools":"their schools". The Case of Eliza Duckworth and John Stevenson', *History of Education*, 20, 3, 1991

Giddens, A., *The Class Structure of the Advanced Societies*, London, 1973

Gilbert, G.N., *Modelling Society: An Introduction to Loglinear Analysis for Social Researchers*, London, 1981

Gittins, D., *Fair Sex. Family Size and Structure 1900–39*, London, 1982

Glass, D.V. (ed.), *Social Mobility in Britain*, London, 1954

Glass, D.V. and Hall, J.R., 'A Description of a Sample Enquiry into Social Mobility in Great Britain', in D.V. Glass (ed.), *Social Mobility in Britain*

Glass, D.V. and Hall, J.R., 'Social Mobility in Britain: a Study of Inter-Generational Change in Status', in D.V. Glass (ed.), *Social Mobility in Britain*

Glenn, N.D., Ross, A. and Tully, J., 'Patterns of Intergenerational Mobility of Females through Marriage', *American Sociological Review*, 39, 1974

Goldthorpe, J.H., 'Women and Class Analysis: In Defence of the Conventional View', *Sociology*, 17, 1983

Goldthorpe, J.H., 'Women and Class Analysis: a Reply to the Replies', *Sociology*, 18, 1984

Goldthorpe, J.H., 'On Economic Development and Social Mobility', *British Journal of Sociology*, Vol. 36, 1985

Goldthorpe, J.H. with Llewellyn, C. and Payne, C., *Social Mobility and Class Structure in Modern Britain*, Oxford, 1980, 1987

Gray, R.Q., *The Labour Aristocracy in Victorian Edinburgh*, Oxford, 1976

Griffin, A.R., *The British Coalmining Industry*, Buxton, 1977

Grusky, D.B. and Fukomoto, I.K., 'Social History Update: A Sociological Approach to Historical Social Mobility', *Journal of Social History*, Vol. 23, No. 1, 1989

Grusky, D.B. and Fukomoto, I.K., 'Social Mobility and Class Structure in Early Industrial France' in A. Miles and D. Vincent (eds.) *Building European Society*

Guest, A.M., Langdale, N.S. and McCann J.C., 'Intergenerational Occupational Mobility in the Late 19th-Century United States', *Social Forces*, 68, 1989

Hagger, R.G., 'Pottery', in M.W. Greenslade and J.G. Jenkins (eds.), *A History of the County of Stafford* Vol. II, *The Victoria History of the Counties of England*, Oxford, 1967

Hammond, N.K., *Rural Life in the Vale of the White Horse, 1780–1914*, Reading, 1974

Harrison, J.F.C., 'The Victorian Gospel of Success', *Victorian Studies*, December 1957

Harrison, R., *Independent Collier. The Coal Miner as Archetypal Proletarian Reconsidered*, Hassocks, 1978

Hart, William, 'The Autobiography of William Hart, Cooper, 1776: A Respectable Artisan in the Industrial Revolution', edited with an introduction and notes by P. Hudson and L. Hunter, *London Journal*, Vol. 7, No. 2, Winter 1981 and Vol. 8, No. 1, Summer 1982 (2 parts)

Hartwell, R.M., *The Industrial Revolution in England*, Historical Association Pamphlet, No. 58, 1965

Hay, J.R., *The Origins of the Liberal Welfare Reforms 1906–1914*, London, 1975

Heath, A., *Social Mobility*, London, 1981

Heath, A., and Britten, N., 'Women's Jobs Do Make a Difference: A Reply to Goldthorpe', *Sociology*, 18, 1984

Hershberg, T., 'The New Urban History' in T. Hershberg (ed.), *Philadelphia. Work, Family and Group Experience in the Nineteenth Century*, New York, 1981

Hinton, J., *Labour and Socialism. A History of the British Labour Movement, 1867–1974*, Brighton, 1983

Hobsbawm, E.J., *Labouring Men*, London, 1964

Hobsbawm, E.J., *Worlds of Labour*, London, 1984

Hobsbawm, E.J., *Industry and Empire*, Harmondsworth, 1984

Hodge, John, *Workman's Cottage to Windsor Castle*, London, 1931

Holbrook-Jones, M., *Supremacy and Subordination of Labour*, London, 1982

Hollingworth, T.H., 'The Demography of the British Peerage', *Population Studies*, supplement to 18, 2, 1964

Holt, J.A., *Looking Backwards*, Bolton, 1949

Hope, K., 'Trends in the Openness of British Society in the Present Century', in D.J. Treiman and R.V. Robinson (eds.), *Research in Social Stratification and Mobility*, 1981

Hout, M., *Following in Father's Footsteps*, Cambridge, Mass., 1989

Howkins, A., 'In the Sweat of Thy Face: The Labourer and Work', in G.E. Mingay (ed.), *The Victorian Countryside*, Volume 2, London, 1981

Hunt, E.H., *British Labour History, 1815–1914*, London, 1981

Hurt, J.S., *Elementary Schooling and the Working Classes 1860–1918*, London, 1979

James, Thomas, *Some Experiences in My Life, by Thomas James, Plaindealings, Narberth*, Cardiff, c. 1930

Jeffreys, J.B., *Retail Trading in Britain 1850–1914*, Cambridge, 1954

Jenkins, A.E., *Titterstone Clee Hills. Everyday Life, Industrial History and Dialect*, self-published, 1982

Johnson, P., 'The Employment and Retirement of Older Men in England and Wales, 1881–1981', *Economic History Review*, 47, 1994

Jones, G. Stedman, *Outcast London. A Study in the Relationship between Classes in Victorian Society*, Oxford, 1971

Jones, G. Stedman, 'Rethinking Chartism' in his *Languages of Class*, Cambridge, 1983

Joyce, P., *Work, Society and Politics. The Culture of the Factory in Later Victorian England*, London, 1982

Joyce, P., 'Work', in F.M.L. Thompson (ed.), *The Cambridge Social History of Britain*, Vol. 2

Joyce, P., *Visions of the People*, Cambridge, 1990

Kaelble, H., *Social Mobility in the 19th and 20th Centuries. Europe and America in Comparative Perspective*, Leamington Spa, 1985

Kanter, R., 'Careers and the Wealth of Nations: a Macro-Perspective on the Structure and Implications of Career Forms', in M.B. Arthur, D.T. Hall and B.S. Lawrence (eds.), *Handbook of Career Theory*, Cambridge, 1989

Kelley, J., 'The Failure of a Paradigm: Log-Linear Models of Social Mobility', in J. Clark *et al.* (eds.), *John H. Goldthorpe.*

Kingsford, P.W., *Victorian Railwaymen*, London, 1970

Kocka, J., 'The Study of Social Mobility and the Formation of the Working Class in the Nineteenth Century', *Le Mouvement Social*, 111, 1980

Kocka, J., 'Family and Class Formation: Intergenerational Mobility and Marriage Patterns in Nineteenth-Century Westphalian Towns', *Journal of Social History*, 17, 1983–4

Lampard, R., 'Research Note. Parents' Occupations and their Children's Occupational Attainment: A Contribution to the Debate on the Class Assignment of Families', *Sociology*, 29, 4, 1995

Landes, D., *The Unbound Prometheus. Technological Change and Industrial Development in Western Europe From 1750 to the Present*, Cambridge, 1969

Langton, J. and Morris, R.J. (eds.), *Atlas of Industrialising Britain 1780–1914*, London, 1986

Laqueur, T., 'Literacy and Social Mobility in the Industrial Revolution in England', *Past and Present*, 64, 1974

Lash, S. and Urry, J., *The End of Organised Capitalism*, Oxford, 1987

Laslett, P., *Household and Family in Past time*, Cambridge, 1972

Lawson, J. and Silver, H., *A Social History of Education in England*, London, 1973

Lee, C.H., *Regional Economic Growth in the United Kingdom Since the 1880s*, Maidenhead, 1971

Lenin, V. I., 'Imperialism: The Highest Stage of Capitalism', in *Selected Works*, Peking, 1975

Liddington, J. and Norris, J., *One Hand Tied Behind Us: the Rise of the Women's Suffrage Movement*, London, 1978

Little, A. and Westergaard, J., 'The Trend of Class Differentials in Educational Opportunity in England and Wales', *British Journal of Sociology*, 15, 1964

Lipset, S.M. and Bendix, R., *Social Mobility in Industrial Society*, London, 1959

Lipset, S.M. and Zetterberg, H., 'A Theory of Social Mobility', in S.M. Lipset and R. Bendix, *Social Mobility in Industrial Society*, London, 1959

Lockwood, D., 'Sources of Variation in Working Class Images of Society', *Sociological Review*, 14, 1966

McAdam, John, 'Autobiography' in *Autobiography of John McAdam (1806–1883) with Selected Letters*, edited with an introduction by Dr Janet Fyfe, Edinburgh, 1980

McClelland, P.D., *Causal Explanation and Model Building in History, Economics and the New Economic History*, Ithaca, 1975

McKenna, F., 'Victorian Railway Workers', *History Workshop Journal*, 1, Spring 1976

McKenna, F., *The Railway Workers 1840–1870*, London, 1980

McKibbin, R., *The Ideologies of Class. Social Relations in Britain 1880–1950*, Oxford, 1990

McLauchlan, Thomas, *The Life of an Ordinary Man*, privately printed, 1979

McRae, S., 'Women and Class Analysis', in J. Clark *et al.* (eds.), *John H. Goldthorpe*

Makowski, K., 'Social Mobility in Nineteenth-Century Poznań', in A. Miles and D. Vincent (eds.), *Building European Society*

Malmgreen, G., *Silktown: Industry and Culture in Macclesfield 1750–1835*, Hull, 1985

Mann, M., *The Sources of Social Power*, Vol. ii, *The Rise of Classes and Nation-States, 1760–1914*, Cambridge, 1993

Mantoux, P., *The Industrial Revolution in the Eighteenth Century: an Outline of the Beginnings of the Modern Factory System in England*, London, 1955

Marsh, C., 'Social Class and Occupation' in R.G. Burgess (ed.), *Key Variables in Social Investigation*, London, 1986

Marshall, A., *Principles of Economics*, ninth edition, 1967

250		*Bibliography*

Marshall, G., Rose, D., Newby, H. and Vogler, C., *Social Class in Modern Britain*, London, 1989

Marshall, Samuel, *The Life of a Successful Farmer in Surrey*, Farnham, 1942

Marx, K., *Capital*, Vol. III, Moscow, 1959

Marx, K., 'The Eighteenth Brumaire of Louis Bonaparte' in K. Marx and F. Engels, *Selected Works*, Vol. 1, Moscow, 1962

Marx, K., 'Wages, Prices and Profit', in K. Marx and F. Engels, *Selected Works*, Vol. 1, Moscow, 1962

Marx, K. and Engels, F., *Collected Works*, Vol. 39, London, 1963

Mathias, P., *The First Industrial Nation*, London, 1969

May, T.E., *The Constitutional History of England Since the Accession of George the Third, 1760–1860*, Vol. II, London, 1963

Meacham, S., 'English Working-Class Unrest before the First World War', *American Historical Review*, LXXVII, 1972

Miles, A., 'Lower Middle Class Mobility in England 1839–1914', *Bulletin de Centre Pierre Leon*, 4, 1993

Miles, A. and Vincent, D. (eds.), *Building European Society. Occupational Change and Social Mobility in Europe, 1840–1940*, Manchester, 1992

Miles, William, *An Autobiography. From Pit Bank to Balliol College. A Mineworker became a Labour Election Agent for 20 years*, with a foreword by Christopher Hill, privately published, 1972

Mills, C., 'Who Dominates Whom? Social Class, Conjugal Household and Political Identification', *Sociological Review*, 42, 1994

Mingay, G.E., *Rural Life in Victorian England*, London, 1977

Mitch, D.F., '"Inequalities Which Every One May Remove": Occupational Recruitment, Endogamy, and the Homogeneity of Social Origins in Victorian England', in A. Miles and D. Vincent (eds.), *Building European Society*

Mitch, D.F., *The Rise of Popular Literacy in Victorian England: The Influence of Private Choice and Public Policy*, Philidelphia, 1992

Mitchell, B.R., *Economic Development of the British Coal Industry 1800–1914*, Cambridge, 1984

Mitchell, B.R. and Deane, P., *Abstract of British Historical Statistics*, Cambridge, 1962

More, C., *Skill and the English Working Class, 1870–1914*, London, 1980

More, C., *The Industrial Age. Economy and Society in Britain, 1750–1985*, London, 1989

Morris, R.J., *Class, Sect and Party, The Making of the British Middle Class: Leeds 1820–32*, Manchester 1990

Morris, R.J., 'Fuller Values, Questions and Contexts: Occupational Coding and the Historian', in K. Schurer, and H. Diederiks, *The Use of Occupations in Historical Analysis*, St Katherine, 1993

Mosteller, F., 'Association and Estimation in Contingency Tables', *Journal of the American Historical Association*, 63, 1968

Müller, W., 'Social Mobility in Industrial Nations', in J. Clark *et al.* (eds.), *John H. Goldthorpe.*

Mumford, L., *The City in History*, London, 1961

Musgrove, F., *School and the Social Order*, Chichester, 1979

Musson, A.E., *The Growth of British Industry*, London, 1978

Newby, H., *Country Life. A Social History of Rural England*, London, 1987

Olson, M., *The Rise and Decline of Nations. Economic Growth, Stagflation, and Social Rigidities*, New Haven, 1982

Pahl, R., 'Is the Emperor Naked? Some Questions on the Adequacy of Sociological Theory in Urban and Regional Research', *International journal of Urban and Regional Research*, 12, 1988

Parkin, F., *Class, Inequality and Political Order*, London, 1971

Payne, G., *Mobility and Change in Modern Society*, Basingstoke, 1987

Payne, G., 'Social Mobility in Britain: a Contrary View', in Clark *et. al.* (eds.), *John H. Goldthorpe*

Payne, P.L., *British Entrepreneurship in the 19th Century*, London, 1974

Pelling, H., 'The Concept of the Labour Aristocracy', in H. Pelling, *Popular Politics and Society in Late Victorian Britain*, London, 1968

Penn, R., 'Trade Union Organisation and Skill in the Cotton and Engineering Industries in Britain, 1850–1960', *Social History*, 8, 1983

Penn, R., *Skilled Workers in the Class Structure*, Cambridge, 1985

Penn, R.D. and Dawkins, D.C., 'Structural Transformations in the British Class Structure: A Log Linear Analysis of Marital Endogamy in Rochdale 1856–1964', *Sociology*, vol. 17, 1983

Perkin, H., 'The Recruitment of Elites in British Society since 1880', *Journal of Social History*, Winter 1980

Perkin, H., *Origins of Modern English Society*, London, 1985

Perkin, H., *The Rise of Professional Society. England Since 1880*, London, 1989

Perkins, A., *The Book of Sonning: the Story of an English Village*, Chesham, 1977

Pinol, J.L., 'Occupational and Social Mobility in Lyon from the Late Nineteenth to the Early Twentieth Century', in A. Miles and D. Vincent (eds.), *Building European Society*

Pollard, S., 'Wages and Earnings in the Sheffield Trades 1851–1914', *Yorkshire Bulletin of Economic and Social Research*, 6, 1, 1954

Pollard, S, *A History of Labour in Sheffield*, Liverpool, 1959

Pollard, S., *Britain's Prime and Britain's Decline: The British Economy 1870–1914*, London, 1989

Pooley, C.G. and Doherty, J.C., 'The Longitudinal Study of Welsh Migration to English Towns in the Nineteenth Century', in C.G. Pooley and I.D. White (eds.), *Migrants, Emigrants and Immigrants. A Social History of Migration*, London, 1991

Portocarero, L., 'Social Mobility in France and Sweden: Women, Marriage and Work', *Acta Sociologica*, XXVIII, 1985

Preston, B., *Occupations of Father and Son in Mid-Victorian England*, Reading, 1977

Price, R., *Labour in British Society. An Interpretive History*, London, 1986

Pugh, M., *The Making of Modern British Politics 1867–1939*, Oxford, 1982

Purkiss, Edward, *Memories of a London Orphan Boy*, with a foreword by Rev. A.E. Ramsbottom, Bexley, 1957

Razzel, P.E., 'Social Origins of Officers in the Indian and British Home Army', *British Journal of Sociology*, 14, 1953

Razzel, P.E., 'Statistics and English Historical Sociology', in R.M. Hartwell (ed.), *Industrial Revolution*, Oxford, 1970

Reddy, W., *Money and Liberty in Western Europe*, Cambridge, 1987

Reeder, D., 'The Reconstruction of Secondary Education in England', in D.K. Müller, F. Ringer and B. Simon (eds.), *The Rise of the Modern Educational System*, Cambridge, 1989

Reid, A., 'Intelligent Artisans and Aristocrats of Labour: the Essays of Thomas Wright', in Jay Winter (ed.), *The Working Class in Modern British History*, Cambridge, 1983

Reid, A., 'The Division of Labour and Politics' in H. Husung and H. Mommsem (eds.), *The Development of Trade Unionism and Politics in Great Britain and Germany*, Brighton, 1988

Richards, E., 'Women in the British Economy since about 1700: an Interpretation', *History*, 59, 1974

Ridge, J., (ed.), *Mobility in Britain Reconsidered*, Oxford, 1974

Roberts, E., *A Woman's Place. An Oral History of Working Class Women 1890–1940*, Oxford, 1984

Roberts, R., *The Classic Slum. Salford Life in the First Quarter of the Century*, Harmondsworth, 1973

Roberts, T. Lloyd, *Life Was Like That*, with a foreword by Sidney Walton, Bala, no date of publication

Rooney, Ralph, *The Story of My Life*, with a preface by J.H., Bury, 1947

Rose, D., 'Review of The Constant Flux', in *ESRC Data Archive Bulletin*, 54, 1993

Ross, E., 'Survival Networks. Women's Neighbourhood Sharing in London Before World War 1', *History Workshop*, 15, 1983

Royle, E., *Modern Britain. A Social History, 1750–1985*, London, 1987

Rubinstein, W.D., *Men of Property*, London, 1981

Rubinstein, W.D., *Elites and the Wealthy in Modern British History. Essays in Social and Economic History*, Brighton, 1987

Runciman, W.G., *Relative Deprivation and Social Justice*, London, 1965

Samuel, R., 'The Workshop of the World: Steam Power and Hand Technology in mid-Victorian Britain', *History Workshop Journal*, 3, Spring 1977

Sanderson, M., 'Literacy and Social Mobility in the Industrial Revolution in England', *Past and Present*, 56, 1972

Sanderson, M., 'A Rejoinder', *Past and Present*, 64, 1974

Savage, M., Barlow, J., Dickens, P., and Fielding, T., *Property, Bureaucracy and Culture: Middle Class Formation in Contemporary Britain*, London, 1992

Savage, M., 'Social Mobility and Class Analysis: a New Agenda for Social History', *Social History*, 19, 1994

Savage, M. and Miles, A., *The Remaking of the British Working Class, 1840–1940*, London, 1994

Sayer, A., 'The Difference that Space Makes', in D. Gregory and J. Urry (eds.), *Social Relations and Spatial Structures*, London, 1985

Schofield, R.S., 'English Marriage Patterns Revisited', *Journal of Family History*, 19, 1985

Schüren, R., 'Intergenerational Occupational and Marital Mobility in German Cities in the Nineteenth and Early Twentieth Centuries', in A. Miles and D. Vincent (eds.), *Building European Society*

Sewell Jr., W.H., *Structure and Mobility. The Men and Women of Marseille, 1820–1870*, Cambridge, 1985

Shaw, G., 'Retail Patterns', in J. Langton and R.J. Morris (eds.), *Atlas of Industrialising Britain*

Shotton, Ernest Richard, *The Personal History and Memoirs of Ernest Richard Shotton*, privately printed, 1978

Smith, F.B., *The People's Health 1830–1910*, London, 1979

Smith, W. and Beddoes, K., *The Cleobury Mortimer and Ditton Priors Light Railway*, Oxford, 1980

Smith, William, 'The Memoir of William Smith', edited by Barry S. Trinder, *Transactions of the Shropshire Archaeological Society*, LVIII, part 2, 1965–8

Snell, K.D.M., *Annals of the Labouring Poor: Social Change and Agrarian England, 1600–1900*, Cambridge, 1987

Sørensen, A.B., 'Theory and Methodology in Social Stratification', in U. Himmelstrand (ed.), *The Sociology of Structure and Action*, Vol. 1, *Sociology: From Crisis to Science*, London, 1986

Sorokin, P.A., *Social and Cultural Mobility*, Glencoe, 1927

Southall, H.R., 'The Tramping Artisan Revisits: Labour Mobility and Economic Distress in Early Victorian England', *Economic History Review*, 44, 1991

Southall, H.R., 'Mobility, the Artisan Community, and Popular Politics in Early Nineteenth Century England', in G. Kearns and C.W. Withers (eds.), *Urbanising Britain: Class and Community in the Nineteenth Century*, Cambridge, 1991

Spurgeon, R., 'Wokingham' in *Berkshire. Old and New*, Berkshire Local History Association, 1985

Spurr, Robert, 'The Autobiography of Robert Spurr. A Social Study of Nineteenth-century Baptist Working Class Fortitude', edited by R.J. Owen, *Baptist Quarterly*, vol. 26, April 1976

Stanworth, M., 'Women and Class Analysis: A Reply to John Goldthorpe', *Sociology*, 18, 1984

Steedman, C., *Policing the Victorian Community. The Formation of the English Provincial Police Forces 1865–80*, London, 1984

Steedman, H., 'Defining Institutions: the endowed grammar schools and the systematisation of English secondary education', in D.K. Müller, F. Ringer and B. Simon (eds.), *The Rise of the Modern Educational System*, Cambridge, 1989

Stone, L., *The Crisis of the Aristocracy, 1558–1640*, Oxford 1965

Stone, L., *Family, Sex and Marriage in England 1500–1800*, London, 1977

Stovel, Katherine W., Savage, Michael, and Bearman, Peter, 'Ascription into Achievement: Models of Career Systems at Lloyds Bank, 1890–1970', *American Journal of Sociology*, 102, 2, 1996

Sutton, William, *Multum in Parvo; or the Ups and Downs of a Village Gardener*, Kenilworth, 1903

Szreter, R.S., 'The Genesis of the Registrar-General's Social Classification of Occupations', *British Journal of Sociology*, 35, 1984

Szreter, S. *Fertility, Class and Gender in Britain: 1860–1940*, Cambridge, 1996

Tawney, R.H., *Equality*, London, 1938

Taylor, A.J., 'Coal' in M.W. Greenslade and J.G. Jenkins (eds.), *A History of the County of Stafford*. Vol. II, *The Victorian History of the County of Stafford*, Oxford, 1967

Thernstrom, S. *Poverty and Progress: Social Mobility in a Nineteenth-Century City*, Cambridge, Mass., 1964

Thernstrom, S., *The Other Bostonians: Poverty and Progress in the American Metropolis, 1880–1970*, Cambridge, Mass., 1973

Thomas, D., 'The Social Origins of Marriage Partners of the British Peerage in the Eighteenth and Nineteenth Centuries', *Population Studies*, 26, 1972

Thompson, F., *Lark Rise to Candleford*, London, 1984

Thompson, F.M.L., *Victorian England: The Horse-drawn Society*, London, 1970

Thompson, F.M.L. (ed.), *The Cambridge Social History of Britain, 1750–1985*, 3 Volumes, London, 1990

Thompson, F.M.L., *The Rise of Respectable Society. A Social History of Victorian Britain, 1830–1900*, London, 1988

Thompson, P, *The Edwardians*, London, 1975

Trainor, R., *Black Country Elites. The Exercise of Authority in an Industrialized Area*, Oxford, 1993

Tressell, R., *The Ragged Trousered Philanthropists*, London, 1955

Trinder, B.S., *A History of Shropshire*, Chichester, 1987

Tringham, N.J., 'Economic History' in M.W. Greenslade (ed.), *A History of the County of Stafford*, Vol. 14, *Lichfield, The Victoria History of the Counties of England*, Oxford, 1990

Tropp, A., *The School-Teachers*, London, 1957

Turner, H.E., *Trade Union Growth, Structure and Policy. A Comparative Study of the Cotton Unions*, London, 1962

Vale, E., *Shropshire*, London, 1949

Van Dijk, H., Visser, J., and Wolst, E., 'Regional Differences in Social Mobility Patterns in the Netherlands Between 1830 and 1940', *Journal of Social History*, 17, 1983–4

Van Leeuwen, M.H.D. and Maas, I., 'Log-linear Analysis of Changes in Mobility Patterns', *Historical Methods*, 24, 1991

Vincent, D., *Bread, Knowledge and Freedom. A Study of Nineteenth-Century Working Class Autobiography*, London, 1981

Vincent, D., *Literacy and Popular Culture. England 1750–1914*, Cambridge, 1989

Vincent, D., *Poor Citizens. The State and the Poor in Twentieth-Century Britain*, London, 1991

Vincent, D., 'Mobility, Bureaucracy and Careers in Early Twentieth-Century Britain', in A. Miles and D. Vincent (eds.), *Building European Society*

Vincent, D., 'Shadow and Reality in Occupational History. Britain in the First Half of the Twentieth Century', in D. Bertaux and P. Thompson (eds.), *Pathways to Social Class. A Qualitative Approach to Social Mobility*, Oxford, 1997

Walby, S., 'Gender, Class and Stratification. A New Approach', in R. Crompton and M. Mann (eds.), *Gender and Stratification*, Cambridge, 1996

Waller, P.J., *Town, City and Nation. England 1850–1914*, Oxford, 1983

Wardle, D., *English Popular Education 1780–1970*, Cambridge, 1970

Wardle, James, *The Story of My Life*, with a foreword by W. Gregory Harris, London, 1924

Warner, F., *The Silk Industry of Great Britain*, London, 1920

Watts, W.W., *Shropshire. A Geography of the County*, Shrewsbury, 1919

Westergaard, J. and Resler, H., *Class in a Capitalist Society: A Study of Contemporary Britain*, London, 1975

Whipp, R., *Patterns of Labour. Work and Social Change in the Pottery Industry*, London, 1990

Widdowson, F., *Going Up into the Next Class. Women and Elementary Teacher Training 1840–1914*, London, 1980

Winstanley, M., *The Shopkeeper's World, 1830–1914*, Manchester, 1983

Witz, A. 'Gender and Service-class Formation', in T. Butler and M. Savage (eds.), *Social Change and the Middle Classes*, London, 1995

Wokingham. A Chronology, compiled by the Wokingham Society, 1978

Yeo, S., *Religious and Voluntary Organisations in Crisis*, London, 1976

DISSERTATIONS

Dupree, M.W., 'Family Structure in the Staffordshire Potteries', Oxford University D.Phil, 1981

Howe, L., 'The Social and Economic Development of the North Staffordshire Coalfield, 1790–1918', Keele University M.A. thesis, 1972

Jackson, E.A., 'Nuneaton – a Study in Urban Development', B.A. Dissertation, Victoria University of Manchester, 1955

Jackson, J.N., 'The Population and Industrial Structure of Macclesfield', Manchester University Ph.D thesis, 1959

Miles, A. 'Occupational and Social Mobility in England 1839–1914', University of Keele Ph.D thesis, 1992

Moseley, H.A., 'The Potteries Coalfield', Leeds University M.Sc thesis, 1950

Norris, J., 'Gender and Class in Industry and Home. Women Silk Workers in Macclesfield 1919–39', Keele University M.A. thesis, 1985

Rowley, R.T., 'The History of the South Shropshire Landscape', Oxford University B.Litt Dissertation, 1967

Index

Abbott, A., 77
academics, 112, 141, 151
accountants, 236
Acts of Parliament
  Beer (1830), 216
  Dissenters' Marriage (1836), 204
  Education (1870), 62, 118, 142 (1902), 62
  Hardwicke's (1753), 204
  Registration of Births, Deaths and Marriages (1836), 15, 203
Adams, A., 143, 150, 152
agriculture, agricultural workers, 11, 32, 33, 37, 38, 40, 42, 44, 52–3, 54, 63, 68, 70, 71, 72, 80, 86, 90, 94, 111, 117, 121, 123, 127, 132, 156, 159, 177–8, 192, 205, 211, 237
Ambrose, E., 23, 89
America, 2, 5, 9, 13, 14, 17, 19, 48, 49, 60, 106, 208
Anderson, G., 78
Anderson, I., 140
Anderson, M., 11, 77, 148
Anderson, P., 27
architects, 112, 191
aristocracy, see elites
artisans, see handicraft
apprenticeship, training, 67, 77, 90, 93, 96, 121, 129, 148, 152, 191, 192
Armstrong, C., 91
Ashley, J., 25, 139, 141
Ashton, 8
Associated Shipwrights' Society, 113
autobiography, autobiographers, 3, 4, 18, 62, 63, 76, 86, 98, 105, 106–15, 116–44, 149–52, 162, 169, 179, 189, 190, 205

Bacon, C., 122, 125, 150, 151
Bagehot, W., 9, 49
bakery industry, bakers, 25, 40, 150, 193
Balne, E., 125, 134, 136, 137
Bankhead, 121
Barnsley, 129
Barr, D., 78, 120, 121, 123, 125, 128–9, 132, 142
Bechhofer, F., 79
Benson, J., 84

Bethnal Green, 15, 35, 37, 38, 39, 43, 208, 211
Birmingham, 111, 124
Black Country, 77, 84
Booth, C., 78, 94, 97, 98, 111, 114, 115, 180
bourgeoisie, see middle class
Bowd, J., 24
Bowyer, W., 122, 123, 126
brewery industry, workers, 37, 73, 90, 194
Brierley, B., 119, 131, 151, 152, 222
Bromley, 134
Brown, E., 127, 129, 140, 141, 142
Brown, J., 121, 133, 138, 139, 149, 162
building and construction workers, 37, 52, 93, 193
  see also masons
bureaucracy, bureaucratisation, 2, 51, 67, 69, 77, 80, 89, 92, 94, 96, 98, 110–15, 122, 125, 128, 129–30, 134, 135, 136, 141, 144, 178, 183, 184, 185, 186, 187, 188, 189, 212
Burnett, J., 18, 86, 98
Burslem, 8
Burstow, H., 22
businessmen, 71, 72, 73, 79–80, 99, 105, 126, 127, 128, 130–4, 138, 141–2, 150, 152, 156, 162, 164, 170, 177, 179, 191, 195
  see also petty bourgeoisie, small masters
Buxton, 121

cabmen, 90, 94, 135
Cadburys, 184, 185, 222
Cain, E., 126
Cambridge, 149
Campion, S., 118, 223
Cannock Chase, 84
capitalism, 2, 9, 13, 14, 34, 51, 56, 114, 185, 187
Cardiff, 151
careers, 4, 17, 18, 76, 78, 79–81, 97, 98, 99, 103, 105–15, 116, 122–30, 142, 147, 148–9, 150, 160, 161, 162–3, 175, 182, 183, 184–5, 186, 188, 189–90
  impact of gender upon, 149–52, 184–5, 186